Searchin'
for Toothpick Sam

ALSO BY JAMIE SELKO
AND FROM MCFARLAND

*Minor League All-Star Teams, 1922–1962:
Rosters, Statistics and Commentary* (2007)

Searchin' for Toothpick Sam

A Baseball Card Odyssey

Jamie Selko

Foreword by Mark Armour

McFarland & Company, Inc., Publishers
Jefferson, North Carolina

ISBN (print) 978-1-4766-9249-4
ISBN (ebook) 978-1-4766-4965-8

LIBRARY OF CONGRESS AND BRITISH LIBRARY
CATALOGUING DATA ARE AVAILABLE

Library of Congress Control Number 2023058727

© 2024 Jamie Selko. All rights reserved

No part of this book may be reproduced or transmitted in any form or by any means, electronic or mechanical, including photocopying or recording, or by any information storage and retrieval system, without permission in writing from the publisher.

Front cover image: 1961 Topps card for Toothpick Sam Jones (Topps® trading cards used courtesy of The Topps Company, Inc.)

Printed in the United States of America

*McFarland & Company, Inc., Publishers
Box 611, Jefferson, North Carolina 28640
www.mcfarlandpub.com*

With love to the former "Moosie,"
still the Q.O.M.H.

Acknowledgments

Thanks to Baseball-Reference.com and Project Scoresheet/Retrosheet and the folks who formed both the groundwork and framework of that project, Bill James and David Smith. Without Retrosheet, the "Best Games" for each player would not have existed at all.

Thanks also to Topps for allowing me to use the cards scattered throughout the text, with special thanks to Ms. Kit Vogelsong who shepherded me on my way through the (to me) labyrinthian channels to get said permission and to Mr. Rob Steines, SVP of Topps Legal Affairs, who granted same.

And, of course, thanks to the hundreds of players who so willingly signed my cards and answered my questions. They made my day many times over.

Table of Contents

Acknowledgments — vi
Foreword by Mark Armour — 1
Preface — 3
Introduction: How a Whim Became a Quest Which Became an Obsession — 5

1. The Back Story — 13
2. The Quest for Fire — 24
3. Bringing It All Back Home — 169
4. Just the Facts, Ma'am: Or the Devil Is in the Details — 172

A Final Point: A Note on Pre-Investigatory Prejudice — 179
Appendices — 183
Chapter Notes — 187
Index — 197

Root and I talked it over and decided that we would give the Professor an Enatsu* baseball card at the party. So, while he was napping in the kitchen, we crept into the study and I showed Root the cookie tin. He was immediately fascinated and seemed to forget we were keeping a secret from the Professor. Sitting on the floor, he began to examine each card, reverently admiring their every detail.

"Be careful with them," I fussed nervously. "They're important to the Professor." But Root hardly seemed to hear me.

It was the first time he had really had a chance to look at baseball cards. He knew that people collected them—his friends had shown him theirs—but it was as if he had avoided developing an interest in them. He was not the sort of boy who would ask his mother for something frivolous.

But once he had seen the Professor's collection, there was no going back. Another part of the world of baseball had opened up before him, and it held a very different appeal from that of the real game. Each card was a talisman of an imaginary game that was separate from the one he saw played out on the field or heard on the radio. A photograph capturing a crucial moment, an inspiring story, and the historical record inscribed on the back—all captured on a rectangular card in a clean plastic case you could hold in the palm of your hand. Everything about the cards fascinated Root....—Yoko Ogawa, *The Housekeeper and the Professor* (2003), 2009 American edition

To possess their cards was to know them a little. That illusion of interaction was fortified by the tangible qualities of the cards, how gratifying they were to hold, the surface roughened with a scrim of gum dust.—Nicholas Dawidoff, *The Crowd Seems Happy* (2008)

---

* Yutaka Enatsu was the best pitcher in Hanshin Tigers history. He won 159 games in nine seasons, winning at least 20 games four times and leading the league in strikeouts six consecutive seasons from the start of his career, striking out 1,728 batters in 1,688 innings those six years, including 340 in 1970 and 401 as a 20-year-old in 1968. The Japanese John Smoltz, he then became a reliever for the Nankai Hawks, Hiroshima Carp, Nippon Ham Fighters, and Seibu Lions, leading his league in saves five times.

Foreword

Mark Armour

Collectors are an odd breed, admits this collector, with habits that are difficult to explain to the satisfaction of non-collectors. This is not specific to baseball cards—people who collect things that are not otherwise functional have to put up with the occasional side-eye as they wander through life. We have all seen this look, but we carry on. After all, there are worse things.

In my 50 years of collecting baseball cards, I have met all manner of collectors. Many of us start off as completists, wanting to own an example of every baseball card that ever existed, until we realize how bloody many baseball cards there have been and how much some of them cost. Assuming this realization doesn't put you off completely, the next step is generally to determine how best to narrow it down, how you might find enjoyment in this world with a small subset of *everything*.

You might decide to collect only Hall of Famers. This takes up far less space than collecting *everything*, but it's going to cost a lot of money—for many card sets, the Hall of Famers are 5 percent of the cards but 98 percent of the cost. You could collect cards from your favorite team, like the Giants or the Brewers—that's a lot of cards, especially if you include the 21st century. Or you might just want a handful of favorite players. Maybe Willie Mays is one of them, who will cost money, but maybe you also love Chris Speier, who will not. I once read a story about a guy who was trying to corner the market on the 1964 Curt Flood card, perhaps to make an Andy Warhol–inspired wall hanging?

Foreword by Mark Amour

Many of us end up focusing on our childhoods, when we fell in love with baseball and its cards. For me, this would be the late 1960s and early 1970s, and in fact that is where my collection is focused. I have cards outside of that window, but if the proverbial fire were raging through my house, I would be grabbing those cards as soon as the people and animals were safe. I owned more cards 25 years ago, but I have a better collection today.

I had known Jamie Selko for a few years when I heard first about his 1961 cards. Here's another thing about baseball card collectors: when we run across someone with a collection completely different than our own, it makes us happy. Ha, you thought *I* was crazy? I don't have autographed cards, but I am filled with admiration for people who find a passion (obsession?) and just keep at it.

Jamie's baseball card story is quite honestly one of the more amazing tales I have ever heard in my decades in this hobby. I don't want to give away the story, but I admire that he started with a quixotic quest and that just as he saw the finish line in sight, he decided to both expand the goal and to start over at the beginning. I tip my hat, honestly.

Jamie is a good dude with a fun story, and he's a fine writer. After you read his book, I expect your own hat will be tipped.

—Mark Armour

Mark Armour is a noted baseball author (six books [so far] including Paths to Glory *and* In Pursuit of Pennants)*, president of SABR's board of directors, founder of SABR's Baseball Biography Project, and one of the two revivifiers of SABR's Baseball Cards Committee.*

Preface

"One begins to read between the pages of a book/the shape of sleepy music, and suddenly you're hooked."[1]

Things sneak up on you.

Some come like a thunderclap, surprising and unexpected. Perhaps you've been avoiding watching film noir ever since you first heard someone raving about *Touch of Evil* back when you were in college, and then one day, bored out of your skull five months into Covid, you figure, "Oh, what the heck" and give noir a shot, select *Out of the Past* from your Netflix menu, and "suddenly you're hooked." Maybe any time someone suggested, "Let's go get some sushi!" you went "Yuck! I'm not eatin' raw fish!" and then one day you were finally talked into it (by cajolery or promise of a reward) and now you go to your favorite sushi place at least once a week. Or it could be a girl you've known for years—perhaps she lived across the street from you, perhaps you knew her in high school, perhaps you have been work pals—and then, one day, it's as if the scales have fallen from your eyes and all of a sudden she's someone you've never seen before and you realize that she's what you've been looking for all your life.

Other times, it's like moss growing on a rock in your garden. You see it every day, and then one morning when you're drinking your coffee, you look out your window and you realize that the hard gray has been replaced by a blanket of soft green. Your daughter changes through the years from chubby little tickle pot to a stunning young lady, but you only notice it when the transformation is complete, and you wonder how the years slipped by without you seeing the change that took place right before your eyes.

Thus it was with my search for the perfect autographed baseball

Preface

card set, going from an offhand, first-time, one-off decision to get some information from Steve Bilko (and, as an afterthought, putting one of his baseball cards in the envelope to see if he'd sign it) to selling off all my other cards to get some (not quite) disposable income to throw into the coffers on board the *Pequod*.

I went from once having complete sets of Topps, Leaf and Fleer cards from 1957 to 1986 (and almost complete sets of Topps and Bowman cards from 1953 to 1956 [and yes, I do know that Bowman stopped making cards in 1955]) and thousands of signed cards and other autographed items to now having nothing but the 1961 sets I was trying to get signed. The rest, signed and unsigned, were gone, all gone.

And then I started selling off my third and second '61 (both *almost* completely) signed sets to try and find the one object that still stands, even as I am writing these words, between me and Glory.

A signed 1961 Topps #555 Sam Jones.

Introduction

*How a Whim Became a Quest
Which Became an Obsession*

In 1976, in a mimeographed "magazine" about collecting baseball cards the name of which I cannot recall, I read (I was going to say "happened to read," but when the item is a five-by-eight, eight-page quasi-periodical, one doesn't just skim the headlines) a piece about Steve Bilko which included his address. On a whim, I wrote to Mr. Bilko.

After writing that little note, I was thrilled when a little over a week later (yep, from Oregon to Pennsylvania and back in fewer than 10 days. In those myth-enshrouded days of yore, it cost 13 cents to mail a first-class letter, the equivalent of 60 cents in today's debased coinage), I received his reply and thought, "Wow! This is pretty cool—I wonder if more players answer their mail" and set out to discover if there was indeed a source of baseball players' addresses. It didn't take long to find out that, by jingo, there was, for by happy circumstance, Jack Smalling published a book which had the address of every living Major League player. Heaven in a book (and not for the first time). In the event, it turned out that around 98 percent of the addresses in the book *were* correct, and it also turned out (though it took several years to find this out) that about 95 percent of the 1961 players were willing to sign and return cards sent to them. In that one quick step (buying the address book), the whim had turned into a quest. In the beginning, I was mailing out cards to five or so players a week and eagerly checking the mail for returned cards. Then I started mailing out 10 a week, then 20 (these numbers are, of course, approximations), and then as many as 50 or so.

Searchin' for Toothpick Sam

(It should be noted here that the first autograph I ever got was Joe DiMaggio's. It was in 1961, when DiMaggio was on a tour of military bases in Germany, and one of his stops was at the Coleman Barracks in Mannheim. I heard that he was having lunch at the Officer's Club, so I took my latest copy of *Baseball Digest* and went down to said club. The guard at the door graciously let me in [even though my dad was a lowly E-8], and I went to DiMaggio's table and asked him if he would please sign the cover. I still remember the smiles on his and the assorted generals' and colonels' faces when he obliged me.)

Now, by this time, in addition to the '61, I had added the '60, '62, '63 Fleers and '60 Leafs to my "get signed" roster as well as cards from oddball sets such as the old Cramer *Baseball Legends* cards, the Fleer *World Series* cards, and even illustrated three-by-fives I constructed myself with a photo of the player I was writing to cut from a baseball magazine and glued to the card. The next escalation was when I decided—well, first let me say that by this time, I had determined to get six complete 1961 sets to leave to my kids, an idea which quickly changed to nine sets (one complete nine-pocket sheet of every card, for purposes of symmetry)—that I was going to get three complete signed sets of 1961s. I was not so far gone as to think that I would ever be able to accumulate six complete signed sets, but I did want to have three of each signed so that the top entire row of all of my nine-pocket sheets would have a signed card in it (again, symmetry).

As the alert reader may foresee, things soon got out of hand. Believe it or not (but both my wife and the ledger I kept with the sendee's name, date mailed out, and date received back will verify this), the most cards I ever sent out in one day was 115 (remember, this was before the days of self-sticking stamps and envelopes, so I had a glue taste in my mouth the rest of the day, and there were so many notes to the players to sign that my very signature changed from its former minuscule but legible form to the rapid and sharp-pointed scrawl which it has remained to this day) and the most I ever received back in a single day was 38. Can anyone other than an autograph collector specializing in baseball cards imagine what a joy that was?

Here's a photo of a couple of pages in my card send-out log. The first column is the date I mailed the card to the player (in this case,

Introduction

both pages are from January 17, 1999), the second is the player, and the third is the date the card came back in the mail and any remarks appurtenant thereunto. As you can see, 45 of the 54 cards came back signed, and four were sent to an incorrect address. You can also note that one came back in May and another (Bill Mazeroski) showed up a whole year later (but show up it did).

At about this time, I still needed approximately 20 of the 1961 Topps set to have every individual player's card signed. My attempt at getting signatures on the 1962 T set was lagging as I still needed around 40–50 signed cards, in part due to my increased concentration on the '61s and in part because there were almost 20 players in the set who didn't sign the cards I sent. With the '62s, this was a problem because, unlike the '61s, I had only had one card per player, which meant that every time a card wasn't returned, I had to purchase a replacement to keep my set complete, and then if *that* card was not returned, repeat the process.

By this time my #1 1961 set was missing only individual signed cards of Sam Jones, Leon Wagner, Willie Jones, Winston Brown, Hal Bevan, Ken R. Hunt (see below), Bob Cerv (see below) and the All-Star cards of Danny Murtaugh and Nellie Fox to be complete (more on what "complete" means below). I needed only the Roberto Clemente card for a completely signed Fleer set, my Leaf set was only missing four players (Sam Jones, Willie Jones, Marshall Renfroe, and Stover McIlwain), and I had signed cards from all of the living players in the Cramer set.

As fate would have it, Bill Corcoran, the man famed for finding and setting up opportunities to acquire signatures of many hard-to-find players, including many in Latin America, was going to do a Wagner signing. However, as I was stationed in Berlin at the time, I found out too late to get my Wagners to him in time for the signing (and as a result I wasn't able to get an autographed '61 Wagner for another 20 or more years).

Next, I found out that Willie Jones was going to do a signing, so I got my three Willie J. cards together and sent them to the promoter who was doing the signing. Unfortunately for me (and far more so for Mr. Jones), Willie died a couple of days before the signing was to

#	Date mailed	Player	Card type	Date returned	Reason
1	2 Mar 99	Paul Pettit		9 Mar	
2	"	Billy Pierce		13 Mar	
3	"	Jack Pierce		13 May	
4	"	Don Pisker	SPD?		gone
5	"	Dick Radatz		25 Mar	
6	"	Curt Raydon	bot		gone
7	"	Ron Reynolds		WA	
8	"	Bobby Richardson		19 Mar	
9	"	Phil Rizzuto		16 Mar	
10	"	Robin Roberts		11 Mar	
11	"	Frank Robinson		19 Mar	
12	"	Humberto Robinson		8 Apr	
13	"	Tony Roig		7 Mar	
14	"	John Romonosky		12 Mar	
15	"	Phil Roof		15 Mar	
16	"	Dick Rozek		NDV	
17	"	Red Schoendienst		WA	
18	"	Joe Scott		WA	
19	"	Hal R. Smith		11 Mar	
20	"	Hal W. Smith		11 Mar	
21	"	Al Spangler		13 Mar	
22	"	Jerry Staley		10 Mar	
23	"	Wally Stohlard		9 Mar	
24	"	George Strickland		10 Mar	
25	"	Jake Striker		12 Mar	
26	"	Tom Sturdivant		Apr 15	
	"	Haywood Sullivan		17 Mar	

Above and opposite: My card send-out log. First column: date mailed out; second column: player's name; third column: if not returned, what type card was sent; fourth column: date returned; fifth column: reason not returned (WA=wrong address, gone=not returned, player's decision).

Introduction

#	Date	Name	Notes
1	2 Mar 99	Ron Teasley	13 May / No sign
2	"	Ralph Terry	16 June
3	"	Gus Triandos	11 Mar
4	"	Hal Trosky	10 May
5	"	Bob Turley	15 May
6	"	Jerry Walker	7 June
7	"	Ray Webster	7 Mar
8	"	Billy Werber	15 May
9	"	Wes Westrum	22 Mar
10	"	Steve Whitaker	? gone
11	"	Ted Wieand	15 Mar
12	"	Hoyt Wilhelm	9 May
13	"	Matt Williams	31 May
14	"	Jim Willoughby	16 Mar
15	"	Dave Wissman	14w ?
16	"	Curly Wardow	13 Ma
17	"	Jim Wohlford	12 May
18	"	Wilbur Wood	61-Rosch / gone
19	"	Gene Woodling	10 May - Stroke
20	"	Jim Woods	11 Mar
21	"	Clyde Wright	76 5Pc / gone
22	"	Early Wynn	No longer signs
23	"	Jimmy Wynn	16 May
24	"	Steve Yeager	76 55Pc / gone
25	"	Richie Zisk	WA
26	"	George Altman	12 May
	"	Ernie Broglio	7 Mar

9

Searchin' for Toothpick Sam

take place. I got my cards back, but it took me almost 15 years to get a signed W. Jones card.

Meanwhile, two new sets had come out, the stunningly beautiful (to me) Diamond Classics sets and the very cool (to me) Fritsch *One Year Wonder* sets. Knowing I was *never* going to get a signed '60 Leaf McIlwaine and that I was *almost certainly* not going to find a signed '63F Clemente, I lost interest in those two sets and let them go. I also lost interest in getting the '60 and '62 Topps sets signed and let them go as well, because my mania was a jealous mania and would brook no rivals. In their places, I started concentrating on the two new sets that had caught my fancy as well as on my 1976 SSPC set.

In the event, I eventually got cards signed by all of the players who were still living when the Diamond Classics sets came out with the exception of five gentlemen, one of whom may have died before the set was in fact actually issued. But over two decades of trying to find signed cards of those five players, the only one I was ever able to acquire was Stan Coveleski. The few chases I was still on were exciting, but as I needed to get fewer and fewer cards signed, they of course became harder and harder to find until it got to the point where I was lucky to add one card a year, and the thrill of the chase had been replaced by a very occasional explosion of cardboard-based endorphins. I was stuck in the doldrums, doldrums in which an island of unexpected joy was rarely sighted.

Of the 117 cards in the *One Year Wonders* sets (sadly not continued after three nonidentically designed sets had been printed), six featured players who had predeceased[1] the issuance of the cards and were therefore impossible to get signed. Of the remaining 111, there were six living players from whom I never got a returned, signed card. One, Glen Clark, whose address neither I nor apparently anyone else ever found, died in 2018. Another, Chet Boak, died within months of the set being issued, and I hadn't sent a card out to him before it was too late. Three players, Ron Henry, Roy Heiser (both of whom, over the years, I sent out *at least* five cards to) and Pidge Browne (to whom I sent three cards before his death), never responded. The final player, Jorge Rubio, I was never able at any time to even get an address to send cards to. (As it so happens, it turns out that both Glenn and

Introduction

Rubio died within the last two years [as I am writing this].) That means 40 years of searching in a strictly figurative autograph wilderness (I hate to break it to the grammar apostates in the audience, but "figurative" literally does not mean "literal")[2] with nary a positive result.

I might as well have been looking for Nazi gold buried by aliens using sasquatch labor on Oak Island.

And so I aged out of my youthful hopes[3] into the reality of my (so-called) "golden years"[4] with the realization that my unfinished sets were in reality never-to-be-finished sets. In fact, it was my attempt to get my SSPC cards signed that showed me that things (specifically ballplayer signing habits) had changed a lot since the late 1950s and early 1960s. Whereas, as stated above, I was getting a 95 percent–plus return rate on the '61s, the players active in the 1976 SSPC set were only signing between 75 and 85 percent of the time. After about three years of working on the SSPCs, I gave up on the set, which went into the sell-'em-and-see-what-you-can-get-for-'em hopper to help fill my '61T jones,[5] and I disposed of my non–'61 autographed cards.

All of which leads us to…

1

The Back Story

I was 13 in 1961, the year of Mantle, Maris, and Ruth, the year of the Great Chase and the mythical Asterisk. I was living in military housing (words which should bring back many pleasant memories to any "military brats" in the reading audience), and baseball was a one-dimensional word to me, without a breath of history to give it life. My dad, though born in Brooklyn, had not only never taken me to Ebbets Field, but he also had, in fact, never even mentioned the word baseball to me. We had never played catch, never talked about the legends of the game, never bonded as fans. Yet slowly, as spring turned to summer and despite complete radio silence from my father about it, I became aware of a focus in the background hum of AFN radio, the married-housing street talk, and the newspaper I read (then *The Stars and Stripes*, now simply *Stars and Stripes* and soon to be nothing at all). The talk was of "The Chase," and I began to listen with a will to understand what all the fuss was about.

In the beginning, all I picked up on was the excitement, an excitement of which I did not feel a part, but in which I wanted to share. I bought my very first *Sport* magazine (25 cents, which I still have [the one with Joe DiMaggio and Mickey Mantle on the cover]) and my first *Sporting News*, also 25 cents and all baseball—page after page on every team, three or more press photos to every page, at least two (and often more) columns from every Big League city by dozens of the country's most famous sports writers, box scores from AAA leagues, loads of coverage of the lower classifications, and stats, stats, stats. Boy, what a paper that was. And then…

And then I bought my first pack of baseball cards.

If ever there was an instance of love at first sight, this was it. I

Searchin' for Toothpick Sam

can't say exactly what it was, whether it was all those great color pictures of the players I was learning about or the fact that, on the back, there were numbers, records, a past, micro-histories, and cartoons (by famous *Mad* artist Jack Davis, I came to discover) catered specifically to the player on the front. They were wonderful, they were incredible, and it was love at five cents a pack.[1] The first series had come and gone (not, of course, that I had any idea that cards came in series back in the day), so my collection started with card #110.[2] Boy howdy and I hope to shout, if I got a quarter, I headed right down to the P.X. (the post exchange), plunked it down, and walked out the proud owner of 25 more baseball cards.

In the storied days of yore, baseball cards came out in series throughout the season at the rate of around one a month from either March to September or April to October. In the '61 set, there were 88 cards in each series (unlike nowadays, where the basic 2024 card sets will be coming out from December 2023 until mid-spring), so I didn't know that I had missed the first series already. At any rate, I soon had six or more of every card from 110 to 176, and that meant six or more Willie Mays cards and an equal number of Billy Williams rookie cards (although back in those more innocent days, there was no special cachet attached to "rookie cards").

My burning goal, because I had no idea how many cards were in a set, was to have 200 different cards, and I would have traded my stamp collection (incredible as it may seem today, from a third to half of all the boys I knew collected stamps, another former youthful hobby that has gone the way of the buggy whip) for 10 cards I didn't already have. Then, for a moment, new cards! Enough new cards for me to fly past 200 on up to 264, but they were in short supply in Mannheim (where my dad was stationed), and after about a week, the well began to run dry.[3]

The summer dragged on, and no new cards. July and August came and went, but again, no new cards (apparently, not every P.X. got every new series when they came out). One day in early September, I saw the top half of a card that had been torn in half lying on the ground, the card of a player I had not seen before. I searched around and after a minute found the bottom half—#489, big Walt

1. The Back Story

Dropo, the pride of Moosup, Connecticut. Obviously, the card had been destroyed by someone who already had five Walt Dropos and, enraged, had rent it asunder, but I didn't care, because I knew what the torn Walt Dropo in my hand meant—new cards were in town! After not receiving any Series Four cards, Series Five and Six were both in at the same time, and soon I had multiple multiples of every card from 353 to 522: hordes of Berras, Clementes, Marichals, Kalines, Sniders, the MVP subset, the Baseball Thrills subset.... Not having any idea of how many cards came in a set, and still not having caught on to the idea of series, I kept buying, hoping for new cards.

In late September, they came. For the first time in my life and the only time until I was a senior in high school, I was in possession of a five-dollar bill (my dad, a child of the Depression, was not free with his money), and I bought an entire box, 100 packs at a nickel a pack, of what was to become known as the "61 Highs." And yes, once again I had multiple multiples of Mays, Aaron and Mantle All-Star cards. But what good were they? Why would anyone need more than two—one to keep and one to use as trade? In fact, I couldn't even trade them for cards I needed from Series One or Series Three, because everyone else had the Series Seven cards and no one had any Series Three cards.

I collected cards (A) because I now liked baseball and (B) because I loved baseball cards. They were not an investment[4] like hog futures or land in Florida. Cards were my friends and a joy. Always the mark, in 1993 I traded a really nice 1961 Mantle (#300) for a '61 Bob Davis (#246) and a '61 Rudy Hernandez (#229) because I had never been able to find those cards from the elusive third series to complete my set. The "trader" saw me coming and is probably still chuckling about putting one over on the rube. Why did I do that? Because I had several Mantles and none of Hernandez or Davis. I traded '61 Mantle All-Star cards for '62 "commons" because I needed the '62s and had a superfluity of the '61 Mantle All-Stars.

I was what most collectors used to be, a baseball fan. I no longer collect cards, because there are eight (18?) different companies which issue four or more sets each, many of which seem to be only available in boxed sets from the various companies themselves, and the sets may include one-of-a-kind cards.

I gave up collecting when the rookie card sickness swept the hobby and an Ankiel rookie card became "worth" more than a 60-year-old Musial card (and I can't even begin to speculate how many '61T Berra cards an Ohtani rookie card would bring on the open market). I gave up collecting because companies say, "We make exactly the same number of every card," but when you buy a box of cards, you get 28 Travis Jankowskis, 19 Greyson Greiners, one Kelly Jansen, and no Mike Trouts.

But hey, that was then, this is now. I miss Woodstock too, but that's not coming back either. Besides, I've digressed....

Aside #1: The Inner Life of My Cards as It Relates to the Inner Life of the Me

I know that this may sound odd to some readers, but each card assumed a personality for me. I have always had a deep affinity for inanimate objects of all types, from trees to books. I assigned feelings and longings to them, even though I knew full well that they, in fact, had none.

There is no artifice in the comments about the cards which will follow below for, ever since I was naught but a mere stripling, I did such things as make sure to get every single bit of cereal out of a box—even tearing out the waxed paper bag-like container which held the cereal (which, in those by-gone days, was glued to the bottom of the box) to insure that each grain of cereal would fulfill its destiny (I didn't want any piece of cereal to feel sad because it hadn't realized its mission in life). If I was eating a bag of Peanut M&Ms, I wondered if the last pieces were yelling, "Take me next!" or trying desperately to avoid their dismal fate of being masticated into a sludge and then swallowed by trying to hide in the dim recesses of the tiny baglet in which they found themselves.

I still think that way (my wife used to think it was strange but now thinks it's funny). Whenever we're driving out in the country and we see an abandoned house, I wonder if it recalls the joys and dramas which took place within the

1. The Back Story

confines of its four walls. In the part of the country where we live, a lot of the farms used to use old school buses for the transport of crews of braceros to and from the fields and orchards that abound in the region we call home, buses that are now rusting out and enveloped in berry vines, and I wonder if the bus misses being part of a bustling and lively community, and when the last time it was that anyone stepped through its door. I taught my kids and grandkids that, when they see a sidewalk that has become overgrown with moss (for we do get moss here west of the Cascades) that they should walk on it, even if it takes them a bit out of their way, so that the sidewalk can know the joy of use. I tip a spoonful of chocolate into a glass of milk softly to watch it slowly dissolve into the milk and imagine Atlantis sinking into the sea. I put milk into my coffee a drop at a time without stirring so as to watch the swirls as the color of the wondrous brew slowly changes. A single erratic[5] in a field captures me. Looking down on the fog in a river valley from a hillside calms me. I have been charged and changed by a tree of diamonds, when the rising sun appeared behind a pair of bare, ice-encrusted trees standing on a ridgeline in early morning, and the tree takes on the form of a natural chandelier,[6] far surpassing the works of man. If you take the time to look, the world sparkles.

My quest for the completing of a fully signed set of the '61s, what I came to call a "Perfect Set," led me down some strange, obsessive paths. How far into the weeds alongside those paths did my search for the perfect set go? Well, for one thing, it was a "preexisting condition" for what evolved into a far deeper dive into the 1961 season than I could possibly have foreseen or even imagined back in 1976.

It crept upon me unawares, and it probably (stupidly?) wasn't until around the mid–'80s when I started sending team cards out for coaches to sign that the first hints of my Poe-like obsession began to manifest itself (and oh, how that dread unsigned Sam Jones thrums in my ears, unceasing and inexorable). By turn of the century, I had begun to send out team cards for non-carded players to

Searchin' for Toothpick Sam

sign, and in the early teens (oh, frabjous when!), I found a gentleman (Brooklyn's own Robert Wong) who could make facsimile '61T cards of those uncarded players for me so I could try to get them signed. Around the same time, I began to attempt to accrue signatures of all the umps who had worked a game in the '61 season, and within a few years I (naturally) decided that I needed cards of the umps also. Cutting to the chase, I eventually wound up having Mr. Wong make well over 400[7] different cards for me. In addition to the ones named above, I had cards made of all the parks, stadiums and fields used by a Major League team. I had cards made of the team owners, the team presidents (if they differed from the owner), the GMs, coaches, broadcasters, league officials, and even some trainers, announcers, and a couple of BP pitchers.

I had cards made of players who had been traded during the season in the uniforms of their new teams. I had dozens of cards made for prospects, some of whom became All-Stars like Ray Culp and some, like the legendary Steve Dalkowski, who never appeared in a Major League game. I had a 10-card set of Babe Ruth cards (first homer, 100th homer, career-record breaking homer, 200th, 300th, 400th, 500th, 600th, 700th, and last homer) made in the style of the Baseball Thrills subset, along with six other cards for that same subset. I had at least two, usually three and sometimes even four multi-player cards made for each team. I had a Mantle/Mays card made, an Early Wynn/Warren Spahn card, and a Ted Williams/Stan Musial card. I had a card celebrating the two Bahamians in the Majors that year as well as one for the two Virgin Islanders. Satchel Paige in his '61 Portland Beavers uni? Check. Al Pinkston, the Mexican League Ty Cobb (he had started playing in the Mexican League when he was 41 and played until he was 47, winning four consecutive batting titles and averaging .382 for those seven years), and Hector Espino, the Mexican League Babe Ruth (he hit a then-record 453 home runs in Mexico)? Check. Rising young Japanese star Sadaharu Oh and his Yomiuri Giants teammate, slugging superstar Shigeo Nagashima? Check.

Oh, but it went even further than that. I had cards of *The Sporting News* publisher J.G. Taylor Spink and minor league executives

1. The Back Story

George Trautman and Frank "Shag" Shaughnessy made. I had cards made for Allan Roth, baseball's first paid sabermetrician, long, long before that was even a word, and for Bill Weiss, godfather of Minor League stats. I had one made for Lee Allen, historian at the Hall of Fame, and another for Fred Lieb, dean of the baseball writers. I even had one made for Goodwin Goldfadden, the Obi Wan of sports books—if he didn't have it, it wasn't.

Then I spiraled even deeper down the rabbit hole. As mentioned above, I was now determined to get the signature of every single player who played a game in the Majors in 1961. One might think that that would not be that difficult (with the exceptions of the players who passed away in the 1960s, more specifically Ken Hubbell and Jim Umbricht, who both died in 1964), but one would be wrong. There was Freddy "Chi-Chi" Olivo, who had died in 1977, and had apparently not been a signer. Al Kenders was a *very* hard get, and he kept at least three '61T Phillies team cards I sent him before he passed in 2013 (all three were already signed by some of his teammates). His backstopping comrade, Ron Henry,[8] never responded any of the many, many times over the 20 years I tried to get his OYW card signed (and also lost many a '61T High Number Twins team card). Roy Heiser didn't seem to have ever signed anything, and George Brunet, who pitched in OB for 30 years up until he was 50 (the last 12 in Mexico, where he won 101 games after his 40th birthday), also apparently signed almost nothing while he lived in the States and signed even less when he moved to Mexico permanently. Chet Boak (see above) was a non-signer, and Sammy Drake was extraordinarily difficult, as were Bobby Prescott and some half a dozen others.

(I am happy to be able to report that, as noted previously, in 2020, I did finally get the last two players I needed for a full signed roster of 1961 players and, indeed, now have an item signed by every single 1961-er once I was able to acquire both a Heiser and a Boak. What is odd about this search is the fact that I was able to get items signed by both Ken Hubbs and Jim Umbricht [see above] years before I was able to find ones signed by Henry [D: 2016] and Heiser [still alive as of this writing]).

Searchin' for Toothpick Sam

Now, I am not completely divorced from reality, and I know that baseball cards and autographs (and autographed baseball cards) have absolutely no intrinsic value whatsoever and that none of these last dozen autographs came cheaply, but to me they were worth every widow's mite and every single lepton.

However, although getting every '61 player's signature was the most successful (and logical) of my various sorties into the mirky (and unfortunately scoundrel-infested) signed '61 netherworld, the tale does not end here at its seeming Mount Doom conclusion.[9] For example, while I had started off-handedly getting umpires in a scattershot manner, I now went at it in earnest. I attempted to purchase press photos of each umpire in a real game action shot, but even at this late date, I still need five of those. (Of course, I already had headshots of all the umps.) As for my umpire autograph pursuit, one ump, Joe Linsalata, left baseball on bad terms, and even though I sent him five requests while he yet lived, I never got a response before he passed away. Finally, however, in 2019, a contact I know informed me that he had a check with Mr. Linsalata's signature on it for sale, and at long last, Joe was mine. Another ump, Vinnie Smith, I finally got from the same source in (early) 2020. Unfortunately (for me alone and most probably not another soul on the face of the earth) I am still two signatures shy of umpire completion, having been unsuccessful in my many attempts to locate anything signed by either Harry Schwarts (D: February 1963) or Frank Walsh (D: 1985).

By now the alert reader will surmise that the descent into the grim maw of obsession[10] did not stop at mere fulfillment of the Great 1961 Every Autograph Quest and that the near-completion of the umpire saga is not the end of the tale either, not by a long shot. Having had the "cards" of the team owners made, I wanted their signatures as well. Having the "cards" of the GMs made, I wanted their signatures as well. Having "cards" of prospects who *never* reached The Show made, I needed to find their addresses and get them to sign the cards as well. I tried over the course of a couple of years to get items signed by team broadcasters (both radio and television if the team had different fellows handling the task), but that proved to

1. The Back Story

be quite difficult, if not impossible. (The less well known and popular they were, the harder they were to find, and I suppose that makes an odd sort of sense in some way. I mean, with getting signed cards, in general, the less well-known a player is, the less his signed cards go for, unless, like Herman Hill or Harry Agganis, they die young and unexpectedly early in their careers.)

Not as difficult, however, as my almost totally futile attempts to get autographed material from the various sports writers from the newspapers that covered the teams in their hometowns and whose columns were featured every week in the late, great *Sporting News*, a doomed effort if ever there was one. I did get John Kuenster's (*Baseball Digest*) signature as well as Jerome ("The Save") Holtzman's and a few authors who had at least tenuous ties to the 1961 season, but mostly my attempts at garnering signatures from the Squires of the Fourth Estate proved fruitless. Without rechecking, I think Shirley Povich might be the only one I was ever able to find (and it cost way more than what one would think an autograph of a newspaper sports columnist's signature would go for).

In its late stages, as my '61 mania worsened, it spread from autographs and '61-style cards to printed ephemera. I already had my 1961 and 1962 *Sporting News Official Baseball Guide,* 1961 and 1962 *Sporting News Baseball Register,* 1961 and 1962 *Sporting News Dope Book,* 1961 and 1962 *Who's Who in Baseball,* 1961 and 1962 *Hillerich and Bradsby Famous Slugger Yearbook*s, 1961 *Baseball Stars of 1960,* 1962 *Baseball Stars of 1961,* and *Best Sports Stories of 1961,* so I was set on the book front. Since I still had all of the '61 *Baseball Digest* issues, I went all-in at getting the (at the time) numerous baseball pre-season magazines that used to accompany the coming of spring in America. Sure, I still had my '61 *Street and Smith*, undoubtedly recalled with great affection by all the readers of a certain age and era,[11] my *Sports Illustrated 1961 Baseball Issue,* and my *Sports All Stars Baseball, True Baseball Yearbook* and *NBC Baseball,* but there were many lesser mags that needed purchasing as well (such as *Inside Baseball, Complete Baseball, Baseball Thrills,* and *Baseball 1961*). Then, there were the monthlies and quarterlies that came out during the season to reacquire such as *Dell Sports, Great Moments in Sports,*

Searchin' for Toothpick Sam

A sample of the printed ephemera attesting to my '61 madness.

A Treasury of Sports Stars in Action, Who's Best in Sports.... And don't forget the the one-off magazine specials such as the praiseworthy *Baseball Photo Album of Major League Stars* and the 1961 edition of *Old Timer's Baseball Photo Album*. Plus, there were even "special edition" magazines devoted to The Chase itself to find and purchase.... Then all I would need was to just resurrect and reconstruct a complete run of the '61 *Sporting News*, and then...

... And then what?

And then what indeed.

So here we are, with me writing about my heroic (used here in its ironic-sarcastic sense) attempt to get the entire 1961 Topps Baseball set signed and endeavoring, no doubt in vain, to explain the hold that set had on me and what it meant then and means to

1. The Back Story

me to this day. Written from the point of view of my dotage, it is the story of my (undoubtedly) mostly misspent yet glorious and evergreen-in-my-memory youth.

To paraphrase (and hideously misuse) Judge Dan Haywood's (played by Spencer Tracy in *Judgment at Nuremberg*) response to Dr. Ernst Janning's (played by Burt Lancaster) weak attempt at justifying the horror he was a part of ("I never knew it would come to that"), it "came to that" the first time I sent a card away to Mr. Bilko to get signed.[12]

2

The Quest for Fire[1]

A card-by-card record with remarks on each player's willingness to sign and willingness to go the proverbial "extra mile" as well as the impression gotten from each card's photo either in a classification (i.e., avuncular, Little Leaguer, etc.) or what the author's fervid brain imagined the player was saying or thinking at the moment the photo was taken.

(Before getting into the individual cards, I must note that on any card with mentions of inscriptions or notations, all such were specifically requested by me.)

And now, let us proceed....

Card #1, Dick Groat, headshot in Forbes Field. His was the first of many avuncular impressions that the '61s made on me. His wry smile seemed to say that he was glad that you got the off-kilter joke he just told you (think Steven Wright or Emo Phillips). Mr. Groat not only always signed every item I ever sent him (including two hand-fashioned three-by-fives with magazine photos of him as a Duke basketball player[2] and later as an NBA-er), but he answered all the questions I asked him—highest-scoring game in college (48 against North Carolina), highest-scoring game in the NBA (25 against the Knicks), whether the Pirates' front office put pressure on him to quit playing basketball (yes).... Up until his passing at age 92, his SR (Signing Rating) was A+. His card bears the inscription "1960—N.L. MVP."

Best games in the 1961 season: On August 29, he went 4–6 against the Cubs, and on September 18 he went 3–4 with three doubles and three RBI against the Cardinals. Mr. Groat started the 1961 season with an 11-game hitting streak and was hitting .362 on April 24.

2 . The Quest for Fire

Card #2, Roger Maris, headshot in Yankee Stadium. (His surname was Maras and was of Croatian derivation, and it appears thusly in the 1954 and 1955 *Sporting News Baseball Guide*. The family anglicized it to Maris in 1955.) He looks just like what he was, the most popular kid in his class and the #1 jock at his high school. He starred in football, basketball, and track for Shanley High School, and in fact still holds the *national* all-time single-game record for most touchdowns on returns with four: two on kickoffs, one on a punt return, and one on an interception. He signed everything I ever sent to him, and he passed away too soon at only 51 years of age in 1985. SR: A.

Best games in the 1961 season: In the second game of a July 25 doubleheader against the White Sox, he went 3–5 with two home runs and five RBI. On June 22, against the Athletics, he went 4–5 with four RBI. Oh, and on October 1, he hit his 61st home run off Boston's Tracy Stallard, still the non-juiced record for a single season. He hit his record-tying 60th home run on September 26. It was one of only three home runs he hit against the Orioles that year.

Card #3: Johnny Buzhardt, follow-through of a "pitch," photo taken in Connie Mack Stadium. To me, he appears a trepidatious young man, eager and yet somehow aware of what

Dick Groat was the third pick in the 1952 NBA Draft after having been a two-time first-team All-American at Duke. Interestingly (and a good trivia question), by the time he graduated, he broke the all-time scoring record which had been held by his Pirates teammate Johnny O'Brien.

was awaiting him on the ill-favored 1961 Phillies. He was the winning pitcher when the Phillies broke their 23-game 1961 losing streak (July 29–August 20), the longest such streak since 1900, and his six wins that year were the second-most on the team. Mr. Buzhardt was always willing to sign the items I sent, and he passed at 71 in 2008. SR: A.

Best game in the 1961 season: On August 20, he broke the Phillies' 23-game losing streak by beating the Braves, 7–4. He went the distance and added an RBI double.

Card #4, Lenny Green, headshot in what appears to be the batting cage in Pompano Beach Municipal Park. Lenny looked as if he was surprised by something, as if a mouse just popped up from under a fielder's glove or a baseball just sprouted legs and ran away. He was coming off his best year in the majors and heading into what would be his two most productive seasons. Reportedly a fine fellow, he quickly returned all the items I sent with his signature affixed to them. Mr. Green died on his 86th birthday in 2019. SR: A.

Best game in the 1961 season: On July 16, he went 5–6 with three runs scored in the second game of a doubleheader against Cleveland.

Card #5, Johnny Romano, batting stance[3] in Hi Corbett Field, Tucson. The message I get from this card: Johnny is trying to figure out what pitch is coming next. He looks really determined; in fact, it even appears as if he's biting his lower lip! Johnny is wearing a batting glove on his left hand, and this was the only appearance that this now omnipresent appurtenance made in this entire set. I could *almost* identify the makes of the cars parked behind Johnny (I think the one to the left *might* be a 1956 Caddy, and the other car has the general appearance of an indeterminant 1954 model. A gearhead would know), but the card's background was just too fuzzy for positive identification. Another note about this particular card is that it almost always appears to be a skosh out of focus and have a slight pinkish hue. Mr. Romano always signed and returned my cards. An SR: A man, Mr. Romano was 84 when he passed away in 2019.

Best game in the 1961 season: On June 6, Johnny went 4–5 against the Senators with two homers, three runs scored, and four RBI.

2. The Quest for Fire

Card #6, Ed Roebuck, throwing in the bullpen of Holman Stadium in Vero Beach. It looks as if he's in the early stages of warming up and hasn't started to throw hard yet. He certainly seems focused on the job at hand, though, I must say. He returned every card I sent to him. Mr. Roebuck was 84 when he died in 2019. SR: A.

Best game in the 1961 season: Mr. Roebuck missed almost all of the '61 season with an arm injury, pitching in only five September games. On the 18th, he pitched two scoreless innings against the Cubs with two strikeouts.

Card #7, Chicago White Sox team[4] card. Mine is signed by coaches Ray Berres, John Cooney, Tony Cuccinello, and Don Gutteridge. I also have a team card signed by non-carded players Dean Look, Mike Degerick, Mike Hershberger, Alan Brice, and Warren Hacker, and another signed by Joel Horlen.

Card #8, Dick Williams, follow-through on a swing in Municipal Stadium in Kansas City. His eyes look laser-focused on the task at hand, I tell you what. The dude looks seriously serious. Not only did Mr. Williams return everything I sent him before he died at 82 in 2011, he often included a signed postcard also. SR: A+. His card bears the inscription "'67 Miracle/Red Sox."

Best game in the 1961 season: He appeared as a pinch-hitter for the Orioles against the Red Sox on July 14 and hit a three-run homer.

Card #9, Bob Purkey, follow-through on a "pitch" in Crosley Field. Well, his card lives up to his name, because he certainly appears perky in his photo. He also happens to look like a 12-year-old, not a bad trick for a 31-year-old gent (and he also has a 12-year-old's smirk). Mr. Purkey signed and returned every item I sent him and passed at 78 in 2008. SR: A. On Mr. Purkey's card is the notation "N.L. all star/1958–61–62."

Best game in the 1961 season: On the 16th of August, Bob threw a four-hit shutout against the Dodgers with seven strikeouts, matching his season high, putting the Reds one game up on the Dodgers in the pennant race.

Card #10, Brooks Robinson, apparently waiting for a pitch which is either being thrown in a cave or in some no-longer-in-use underground factory. Truth be told, he doesn't look very confident about his chances of success. He is one of the nicest Hall of Famers, both by reputation and by the fact that, although he was probably swamped with requests, he took the time to sign all the cards I ever sent him (at least 12 in all from the sets I was trying to get signed). An SR: A+, he passed away September 26, 2023, at the age of 86.

Best game in the 1961 season: Mr. Robinson went 4–5 against the White Sox on September 22 with a triple and three RBI.

Card #11, Curt Simmons, headshot taken in Forbes Field. He looks like a guy who's just glad to be on a card, just back from a stint in the minors in 1959 after being in the big leagues since 1947. Making it back as a 30-year-old is a feat not often accomplished in the cut-throat and heartless game of baseball. Mr. Simmons signed everything I ever sent him and was an SR: A before his death at age 93 in 2022..

Best game in the 1961 season: On August 5, Curt shut out the Phils, 7–0, and also went 2–3 at the plate with two RBI.

Card #12, Moe Thacker, the squatting half of the last all-Moe battery (the other half being Moe Drabowsky), headshot in Rendezvous Park in Mesa. I'm sorry, but to me he seems like someone has just told him that his dog died. Before being sent to the Cubs, he had been stuck in the Yankees' farm system for six years behind Yogi Berra, Elston Howard and Johnny Blanchard (among others who also wound up being traded). I'd've thought that he'd look happier. Mr. Thacker signed all the cards I ever sent him, SR: A, and was 63 when he died in 1997.

Best game in the 1961 season: Moe went 2–3 against the Reds on June 4 with an RBI single.

Card #13,[5] Chuck Cottier, waiting for a "pitch" in County Stadium. First of all, he is not in a Tigers uniform and is instead wearing a Braves one. The Braves' insignia has been replaced by a superimposed Tigers one, and Chief Wahoo has been excised (if only it were that easy to get rid of all the racist and demeaning relics of our past [and by past, I mean pre–2022]) from his sleeve. Chuck is another teeny-looking lad, and in this photo he looks like he's standing in against one of his old high school opponents, that is, kinda cocky. He is SR: A. In addition to his autograph, his card has the notation

2. The Quest for Fire

"All Star Western Lg. 1957/All Star Southern League 1958" written on it.

Best game in the 1961 season: Chuck went 3–3 with three RBI against the Athletics on July 15.

Card #14, Don Mossi, following through on a "pitch" in Briggs Stadium. I am not going to add to the frequent descriptions of Mr. Mossi other than to say that, on this particular card, his eyes look sorta spooky. One thing I will say is that he signed everything I sent him and occasionally added an item on his own volition. Mr. Mossi passed in 2019 at ninety, having been an SR: A+.

Best game in the 1961 season: Don threw a two-hit shutout against the Senators on May 4. (Also, on June 28, he had three RBI against the White Sox.)

Card #15, Willie Kirkland, headshot, possibly in Candlestick Park (he's wearing a Giants uniform). Unfortunately, and it may be because of my personal (non)experiences with Mr. Kirkland, but it appears as if he's saying, "Whatchu want?" I probably, over the years, sent a dozen cards to him, and I never got a single one returned. SR: F.

Best game in the 1961 season: He went 3–3 with three homers against the White Sox on July 9.

Card #16, Billy Muffett, in his wind-up in Yankee Stadium. Billy has the look of a high school coach who teaches shop (because in those days, coaches had to teach *something*). In addition to always signing and returning everything I sent him, he always enclosed a signed postcard. Mr. Muffett died in 2008 at age 77, an SR:A+ man.

Best game in the 1961 season: He threw 5⅔ scoreless innings against Baltimore on September 16.

Card #17, TOPPS BASEBALL CHECK LIST, 1st Series. In an in-game photo taken in Wrigley Field, Dick Stuart has just sent a shot to left field, and because Cubs catcher El Tappe has leapt to his feet, one can assume that there might be a play at the plate. Mine is signed by both (and I'm thinking that it may be unique).[6]

Card #18, Jim Grant, taken in Yankee Stadium, and I'm not sure what it is that he's doing, but more than anything else, it looks like he's playing catch with a four-year-old child. His pose is not a follow-through, nor is it either a return throw from the catcher or a fielding pose. Whatever it is, however, he looks pretty satisfied doing it. He was, of course, known to one and all as "Mudcat." Mr. Grant always returns all of the items I send to him, and he frequently added a postcard in the SASE (plus, you gotta check out his return address if you send an item to him—it's worth the $1.18 you'd spend to get it. SR: A+. His card is annotated "Cy Young 1965/AL All Star 63/65").

Best game in the 1961 season: He threw a three-hitter with nine strikeouts against the Yankees on August 18.

Card #19, Clete Boyer, waiting for a "pitch," taken in Yankee Stadium. On this card, Clete looks calm and confident, as if he not only knows exactly what pitch is coming but its speed and location as well. Sometimes he signed and sometimes he didn't, signing less frequently as time went on. He was seventy when he died in 2007. SR: C.

Best game in the 1961 season: On July 25, he torched the White Sox with two home runs and four RBI.

Card #20, Robin Roberts in Connie Mack Stadium. He, like Mudcat Grant above, appears to be playing catch with a youth, except Robin, because of his more upright stance, looks as if his partner might be five or six years old. The look on his face, however, tells us a completely different story. At best, it appears to be apprehensive. At worst, as if he felt gripped by a sudden sense of impending doom. If that indeed is what it was, then he was correct, for he was destined to go a horrendous 1–10 with an equally horrid 5.81 ERA in 1961. Even though he was a Hall of Famer, Robin signed and returned everything I sent him. An SR: A+, he died in 2010 at 83.

Best game in the 1961 season: On June 5, Robin won his only game of the season by holding the Giants to two runs on six hits in a 3–2 thriller.

Card #21, Zorro[7] Versalles, headshot in what appears to be Griffith Stadium. Zoilo was a mere lad of 20 when the season started, but he doesn't appear to be much worried about being overmatched. Despite the sad circumstances that surrounded him later in his life, Mr. Versalles signed every card I sent to him. An SR: A man, he died when he was only 55 in 1995.

2. The Quest for Fire

Best game in the 1961 season: On May 27, Zoilo went 5–5 against the Senators. On May 10, after 19 games, he was hitting .349.

Card #22, Clem Labine, headshot, member of the Crewcut Company, taken in what appears to be Wrigley Field. In this image, he looks like a farm implement salesman in Iowa trying to convince a farmer that he *really* needs a new International Harvester Farmall tractor. Before passing away at 80 in 2007, he was a solid SR: A.

Best game in the 1961 season: On May 13, he threw 4⅓ scoreless innings against the Reds, allowing only two hits.

Card #23, Don Demeter (batting stance [?], menacing pose [?], artist's model for a sculpture [?]) taken in Wrigley Field. Actually, it looks like he's daydreaming while waiting for the ice cream truck to show up. Don not only signed everything I sent, he is another former player who also stuck a signed postcard in the SASE. SR: A+. His card bears the inscription "Texas League All-Star/1956/A.A. All Star/1957."

Best game in the 1961 season: On September 12, he got his revenge on the team that had traded him earlier in the season by going 4–5 with five runs, seven RBI, and three home runs against the Dodgers in a 19–10 slugfest. Nine home runs were hit in that contest, one of Sandy Koufax's worst starts ever: 1⅓ innings in which he gave up six earned runs.

Card #24, Ken Johnson, headshot, apparently taken in Griffith Stadium. To be honest, he looks like the guy Clem Labine (see above) is trying to sell the tractor to. Another SR: A 100 percent signer, Mr. Johnson passed away in 2015 at 82.

Best game in the 1961 season: Ken threw a shutout for the pennant-bound Reds on September 4 at Philadelphia.

Card #25, *Reds' Heavy Artillery*, featuring Vada Pinson, Gus Bell and Frank Robinson. They look as if they're trying to figure out what these strange sticks they're holding could possibly be used for.

Card #26, Wes Stock headshot, looks like it was shot in an adit. Not meaning to cast any aspersion on Mr. Stock, but in this particular photo, Wes looks like the kind of guy who thought that Junior Samples was America's funniest comic and is also trying to remember how to laugh. A fine signer, though. SR: A. Wes had two seasons with at least five wins and no defeats, going 5–0 in 1961 and 7–0 in

Searchin' for Toothpick Sam

1963, which is noted on his card. I think that he is the only pitcher to have had two such seasons. Wes was 19–4 (.826) as an Oriole.

Best game in the 1961 season: Wes threw 6⅔ innings of two-hit ball against the Athletics on June 28 and had five strikeouts without walking a batter.

Card #27, Jerry Kindall, fixin' to "throw a runner out," taken in Wrigley Field. The look on his face says, "Here comes a game-winning double play, I betcha." Noted NCAA coach and another fine signer (SR: A), he passed in 2017 at 82.

Best game in the 1961 season: On August 16, he went 3–4 with two runs and three RBI against the Phillies.

Card #28, Hector Lopez, headshot taken in Yankee Stadium. Insouciance. Total and complete insouciance. He signed everything I ever sent him. He passed away at 93 in 2022. SR: A.

Best game in the 1961 season: Hector went 3–6 with two runs against the Tigers on April 26.

Card #29, Don Nottebart, headshot apparently taken in his dad's newly repaneled basement. Gee, he looks happy. In fact, it looks like (although I realize full well that it wasn't) the first photo ever taken of him in a Braves uniform, right after he signed straight out of high school but before they sent him to Wellsville. An SR: A man, he died at 71 in 2007.

Best game in the 1961 season: On June 7, he went the distance in a 3–1 win against the Reds. He gave up only four hits, and the run scored against him was unearned.

Card #30, Nellie Fox, headshot taken in Yankee Stadium. First carded member of the Plug Platoon (also known [to me at least] as the Chew Crew [or the less well-known Shnooze Who]). In this photo he looks like a cartoon portrayal of a guy with a bad toothache. Because I started collecting autographs too late to have personally found out how good a signer Mr. Fox was, no rating given (although it is not too hard to find commons signed by him).

Best game in the 1961 season: Nellie went 4–4 with four runs scored against the Athletics on April 27.

Card #31, Bob Schmidt, headshot taken in what may be Candlestick Park. Bob looks like a guy sitting alone in a bar mourning the

2. The Quest for Fire

loss of Ol' Sniffy, his best treeing hound. Terrific signer, though (SR: A). He died in 2015 at 82. His card has "All Star/Tex. Lg. 1956/AA 1957/N.L 1958" noted on it.

Best game in the 1961 season: On June 17, he went 1–4 against the Phils with a two-run home run.

Card #32, Ray Sadecki, headshot taken at Al Lang Field in St. Petersburg, Florida. He looks five years younger than he really was, and he was only 20. He also looks as if the girl he asked to the junior prom just said yes. He also looks like he just found out his mom is making his favorite pie for dessert. He also looks like he just got his learner's permit. He also looks like he was separated at birth from Wally Cox. I could go on, but I think you catch my drift. As a signer, he was an SR: A. Mr. Sadecki passed away in 2014 at 73.

Best game in the 1961 season: Ray went 10 innings and struck out 10 in a 3–3 tie with the Cubs on June 6. He also went 2–4 with an RBI in that game.

Card #33, Gary Geiger, headshot in Fenway Park. Another happy fellow, on this card he looks like he just drew to an inside straight and got lucky. Or he just met his (future) wife for the first time and already knows that she's just that (his future wife, that is). An SR: A, Mr. Geiger passed at 59 in 1996.

Best game in the 1961 season: Against the Indians on July 18, Gary went 3–4 with two home runs and four RBI.

Card #34, Wynn Hawkins,[8] headshot taken in Hi Corbett Field in Tucson. He looks like the featured guest speaker at a junior high graduation, earnestly telling the kids how much fun they're gonna have in high school (without adding "now that the living hell that is junior high is over"). SR: A.

Best game in the 1961 season: On May 21, Mr. Hawkins threw his only career shutout, a two-hitter against the Twins.

Card #35, Ron Santo, batting stance, picture taken in Wrigley Field. A mere two years removed from high school, he looks as if he could still sneak into a sock hop at the gym without anyone asking him what he's doing there. A beloved Cubs television color man for many years, he signed everything I sent, SR: A+. (Editorial aside: The baseball writers did him and his family a grave injustice by not voting him into the Hall of Fame before his passing at 70 in 2010.)

Best game in the 1961 season: Ron punished the Reds on June 28, going 4–6 with four runs, two homers and seven RBI.

Card #36, Jack Kralick, headshot taken in Griffith Stadium. He looks like what the British used to (still do?) call an "earnest young man," ready to start his exciting new life as a chartered public accountant. He was hard to pin down, and I think that he may have signed two or three of the cards I sent before

disappearing into Mexico, where he died at 77 in 2012. SR: C-/D+.

Best game in the 1961 season: Jack shut out the Senators on four hits on April 23 and singled in the only run in a 1–0 win.

Card #37, Charlie Maxwell, headshot taken in Yankee Stadium. He looks like a satisfied middle-management businessman, ready to settle down in front of his color (!) TV[9] with a martini and watch some *Have Gun—Will Travel*. "Paw Paw" (so named because he, already a native Michigander playing for the Tigers, bought himself a home in beautiful Paw Paw) was also called "Sunday" Charlie (for a while anyway) after hitting four home runs in four successive at-bats against the Yankees during a double-header in Briggs Stadium on May 3, 1959. Still hanging in at 93, he signed everything I sent him. SR: A.

Best game in the 1961 season: Charlie slammed a three-run, pinch-hit, game-winning homer against the Senators on August 2.

2. The Quest for Fire

Above and opposite: **Although Ray Sadecki and his (non-carded) teammate Tim McCarver appeared in the same game on August 17, 1960, they missed the rare chance of forming a teenage battery, as Tim entered the game as a pinch-hitter. They did form a slightly less rare 20-year-old battery on June 15, 1961.**

Card #38, Bob Lillis, faking a fielding play in Holman Stadium, Vero Beach. I tell ya what, he's not keeping his eye on the ball—instead, he's looking straight at the camera. That is not the Dodger way, Bob! Another postcard adder, SR: A+.

Best game in the 1961 season: Bob thrilled the home fans by going 3–4 against the Cubs on July 25.

Card #39, Leo Posada, batting stance, photo taken in Connie Mack Field in West Palm Beach. All I can say is that Leo certainly looks serious about sticking with the A's in 1961. Oh, and that very early on, he was for some reason supposed to be Jorge's pop. He always signed everything I sent him. SR: A (Mr. Posada passed away in 2022).

Best game in the 1961 season: Leo went 4–5 against the Angels on August 31, hitting a triple, a home run, and two singles, scoring twice and driving in four teammates.

Card #40, Bob Turley, follow-through, near the batting cage in Yankee Stadium. Boy, he looks confident, loose, relaxed, and ready to go on this card. A good signer, he passed at 82 in 2013. SR: A.

Best game in the 1961 season: Bob did not have a good season in '61, and his best effort took place in the second game of a doubleheader against the Angels when he went seven and two third innings and struck out eight batters while giving up two runs. He also walked nine batters.

Searchin' for Toothpick Sam

Card #41, NL Batting Leaders. Mine is signed by all four (Dick Groat, Norm Larker, Willie Mays, and Roberto Clemente).

Card #42, AL Batting Leaders. Mine is signed by all four (Pete Runnels, Al Smith, Minnie Miñoso, and Bill Skowron).

Card #43, NL Home Run Leaders. Mine is signed by all four (Ernie Banks, Ed Mathews, Hank Aaron, and Ken Boyer).

Card #44, AL Home Run Leaders. I do not have one signed by all four players. I do have one signed by Mickey Mantle, Rocky Colavito, and Jim Lemon, and one signed by Roger Maris, Lemon, and Colavito.

Card #45, NL ERA Leaders. Mine is signed by all five players (Mike McCormick, Ernie Broglio, Don Drysdale, Bob Friend, and Stan Williams).

Card #46, AL ERA Leaders. Mine is signed by all four players (Frank Baumann, Jim Bunning, Art Ditmar, and Hal Brown).

Card #47, NL Win Leaders. Mine is signed by all four players (Ernie Broglio, Warren Spahn, Vern Law, and Lew Burdette).

Card #48, AL Win Leaders. Mine is signed by all five players (Chuck Estrada, Jim Perry, Buddy Daley, Art Ditmar, and Milt Pappas).

Card #49, NL Strikeout Leaders. Mine is signed by all four players (Don Drysdale, Sandy Koufax, Sam Jones, and Ernie Broglio).

Card #50, AL Strikeout Leaders. Mine is signed by all four players (Jim Bunning, Pedro Ramos, Early Wynn, and Frank Lary).

Card #51, Detroit Tigers Team card. Mine is signed by coaches Phil Cavarretta, Tom Ferrick, and Don Heffner. I also have a team card signed by non-carded players Joe Grzenda, Howie Koplitz, and Frank House, and another signed by Bill Freehan.

Card #52, George Crowe, batting stance in Sportsman's Park. Just as with Leo Posada above, Big George does not look like he's playing games. A terrific basketball player and a better man, he passed at 89 in 2011. SR: A.

Best game in the 1961 season: He was successful in his first pinch-hitting appearance on April 18 against the Dodgers, his only hit of the season and the final hit of his career.

Card #53, Russ Nixon, headshot, member of the Crewcut

2. The Quest for Fire

Company, taken in Yankee Stadium. Russ looks like he's eyeing the Harley his wife won't let him buy. Russ hit .348 in his 439-game Minor League career, including .387 in the Florida State League in 1954 (slash line .461/.555/1.106) and .385 the next year in the old Three-I League (slash line .462/.520/.981). He had a twin brother, Roy, who played five years of pro ball and hit .299. (There is a really good photo of Russ and Roy on the Twins Trivia website along with a photo showing his underhanded free throw shooting style.) Russ held (and as far as I know, still holds) the Major League record for most games played by a non-pitcher without ever stealing a base (he did try seven times). Mr. Nixon was 81 when he died in 2016. SR: A.

Best game in the 1961 season: On May 7, he went 2–4 with three RBI against the Twins.

Card #54, Earl Francis, delivery follow-through, taken during Spring Training in McKechnie Field. By the look on his face, it seems he just unleashed a real hummer. An SR: A fellow, he died in 2002 at 66.

Best game in the 1961 season: On June 29, he pitched eight innings against Los Angeles and gave up two earned runs while striking out 10 Dodgers, beating Sandy Koufax.

Card #55, Jim Davenport, headshot on the dugout steps in a UI park (I can't tell if he is wearing home whites or traveling grays). Jim looks like he just saw someone being bullied and is trying to decide if he wants to get involved or not. An SR: A, Mr. Davenport was 82 when he died in 2016.

Best game in the 1961 season: Jim went 4–5 against the Pirates on September 11 with two doubles.

Card #56, Russ Kemmerer, headshot in Comiskey Park. Russ looks like he's envisioning his retirement, picturing himself sitting on a beach somewhere savoring a rum punch, watching the girls go by. A good signer (SR: A), Mr. Kemmerer died at 82 in 2014.

Best game in the 1961 season: On April 10, he gave up two hits and no runs in four innings against Washington.

Card #57, Marv Throneberry, getting ready to catch the ball in Yankee Stadium. He was Faye's brother (card #282), and in this photo he looks very trepidatious, as if he's playing burnout with Steve Dalkowski.[10] SR: A, he was only 60 when he died in 1994.

Searchin' for Toothpick Sam

Best games in the 1961 season: On April 29, he drove in five runs for the Athletics while going 3–4 against the White Sox, including a grand slam off Herb Score. Traded to Baltimore, he went 3–4 against his former club with two home runs and three RBI.

Card #58, Joe Schaffernoth, headshot in Wrigley Field. To me, it looks like he's thinking, "Hmmm … do I want the butter brickle or the rum raisin?" Mr. Schaffernoth, who was 78 at the time of his demise in 2016, was a dependable signer. SR: A. I have one card of him which has "Western Lg All Star 1956" written on it and another which has "Sent to Indians/July 7 1961."

Best game in the 1961 season: On April 29, he struck out five in 3⅓ innings for the Cubs against L.A.

Card #59, Jim Woods, headshot in Jack Russell Memorial Stadium in Clearwater. A stunned Jim looks like someone just asked him to explain the difference between "farther" and "further." SR: A. His card has "Western League / All Star 1959" inscribed on it.

Best game in the 1961 season: He had two hits and four RBI in one inning against the Pirates on May 21.

Card #60, Woodie Held, fielding pose in Municipal Stadium. Woodie looks like the ball is either a cobra that has hypnotized him or he's doing one of his patented "human statue" poses. Either way, he was a fine signer, SR: A. He passed away in 2009 at age 77.

Best game in the 1961 season: On September 28, he drove in five runs while hitting two homers for Cleveland and going 3–5 with three runs against the Twins.

Card #61, Ron Piche, headshot taken at McKechnie Field in Bradenton. By the look of the photo, Stephen Hawking is explaining the Singularity Theorem to him.[11] A little trivia for you: he was a member of the '61 Braves staff, the only (I think) staff with three Canadians on it. He was good signer (SR: A). He passed away at 75 in 2011.

Best game in the 1961 season: On October 1, in his only start of the season, he went 10 innings to defeat the Giants, 3–2. He struck out seven batters.

Card #62, Al Pilarcik, batting stance in Memorial Stadium. He looks like the pitcher he's facing insulted his mother. Or perhaps like

2. The Quest for Fire

a member of a beer league softball team who's determined to show the other fellows that he's "still got it!" An SR: A, he died at 80 in 2010.

Best game in the 1961 season: On September 4, after being traded to the White Sox, he went 2–4 with a three-run home run against the Senators.

Card #63, Jim Kaat, headshot in Griffith Stadium (almost all of the '61 Topps Kaat cards I've seen have a washed-out quality to them). Yet another of the angry young man crowd, he looks like someone just dissed the pinstripes on his '56 Chevy. Jim was used as a pinch runner 85 times, including 10 times in 1961, scoring three runs. A good signer, gets an SR grade of A. Jim's card has the notation "Jim won 16 Gold Gloves."

Best game in the 1961 season: He pitched a five-hit shutout against the White Sox on August 24, tripling and scoring the first run. He had five two-hit games at the plate in 1961, and the best was his 2–3, two-double day against the Senators on May 26.

Card #64, Alex Grammas, headshot, taken in Sportsman's Park. He looks like he's just been greeted by someone whose name he really *should* remember (we all know that feeling). A good signer and a postcard sender, SR: A+. Mr. Grammas died at 93 in 2019. His card has "A.A. All Star 1953" written on it.

Best game in the 1961 season: Alex went 2–3 with five RBI against the Dodgers on August 24.

Card #65, Ted Kluszewski, headshot in Comiskey Park. He's the father of a girl that you're taking out on a date that you *really* do not want to get on the wrong side of. An SR: A+, he passed at only 63 in 1988.

Best game in the 1961 season: Big Klu went 2–4 with two home runs and five RBI on Opening Day at Baltimore.

Card #66, Bill Henry, follow-through, taken in Al Lopez Field in Tampa. It took him a *lot* of effort, but the ball reached the catcher on the fly (by the way, check out his 1964 ERA). Mr. Henry passed at 86 in 2014. He had been an SR: A.

Best game in the 1961 season: On April 14, he pitched two scoreless innings and struck out three Cardinals to earn the win.

Searchin' for Toothpick Sam

Card #67, Ozzie Virgil, taken in Briggs Stadium. Sometime catcher, father of future All-Star catcher Ozzie Virgil, here picturing a fungo fly over the distant fence in his mind and wondering if he should do a bat flip. Ozzie was the first Major Leaguer from the Dominican Republic. The player in the background is Bob Bruce, who also signed the card. Decades ago, Virgil was an occasional signer, but then he stopped altogether. SR: D.

Best game in the 1961 season: On May 11 he got his year's only RBI with a pinch-hit home run for Detroit against the Senators.

Card #68, Deron Johnson, batting stance, taken during Spring Training in Al Lang Field. He's got that "think I'm not good enough, eh? Well, I'll show you!" look. In his six years in the minors, Deron never had fewer than 24 home runs, leading his league three times. A good signer (SR: A) before he passed at only 53 in 1992.

Best game in the 1961 season: On August 16 for the Athletics, he went 3–4 with two runs scored, a homer, and three RBI against the Twins.

Card #69, Earl Wilson, former catcher (à la Kenley Jansen), engaged in some soft warm-up tosses, taken in Yankee Stadium. He hit .195 in the Bigs with power: 35 home runs, including two as a pinch-hitter. I had heard that he was a tough sign, but I (mostly) didn't experience that. SR: B+. Mr. Wilson died in 2005 at age 70.

Best game in the 1961 season: Well, he didn't play Major League ball in '61, but he did pitch a shutout for Seattle in the Pacific Coast League.

Card #70, Bill Virdon, batting stance in Forbes Field. He looks like he's still smiling about that World Series win. A signed postcard sender, he rates an SR: A+. His card has the inscription "N.L. R.O.Y. 1955."

Best game in the 1961 season: On May 13 against the Reds, he went 3–3 with three runs, a triple, and a home run.

Card #71, Jerry Adair, "fielding" a grounder, in what appears to be Kansas City's Municipal Stadium, thinking, "This one is *not* getting past me!" He was SR: A before his untimely passing at 50 in 1987.

Best game in the 1961 season: Against Minnesota on May 10, he went 3–4 with two home runs and four RBI.

2. The Quest for Fire

Card #72, Stu Miller, wind-up in either Candlestick or Scottsdale Stadium—there just isn't enough of the park showing to tell which it is. The player in the background is Jim Marshall. Stu is shown here wondering, "Should I surprise him with my 81 MPH fastball?" (He was famous for the three speeds he threw while pitching: slow, slower and slowest.) He was an SR: A man before his death in 2015, aged 87. The inscription on his card reads "907 G O/B."

Best game in the 1961 season: Pitching in relief against the Dodgers on September 10, he gave up one hit in five scoreless innings of work.

Card #73, Al Spangler, headshot in County Stadium. Al looks like he got caught in class with a spitball wad in his mouth and now he's trying to decide if he should swallow it or just let it fly. He is an SR: A.

Best game in the 1961 season: He went 2–4 with three runs scored on July 5 against the Phillies.

Card #74, Joe Pignatano, batting stance, but I am ashamed to say that I cannot identify the park.[12] Joe was one of the last two Brooklyn-born players to play for the Brooklyn Dodgers, and in this photo he looks homesick. An SR: A, he was almost 93 when he died in 2022.

Best game in the 1961 season: He went 4–4 with two runs, a homer, and three RBI against Detroit on May 31.

Card #75, *Lindy Shows Larry,* featuring Lindy McDaniel and Larry Jackson in Sportsman's Park. Lindy is asking Larry to help him identify the object in Lindy's hand.

Card #76, Harry Anderson, headshot, taken in Crosley Field. My first impression: The first time his wife asked him if he wanted almond "milk" or soy "milk" in his coffee, Harry's thought processes derailed for a moment. He now drinks his coffee black. SR: A, he died at 66 in 1998.

Best game in the 1961 season: He only played in four games, and his last appearance in the Majors (against the Braves), he got a pinch-hit single.

Card #77, Dick Stigman, follow-through, taken in Yankee Stadium. He looks sad that he had to part with the ball and hopes to see it again sometime soon. SP: A. The notation on Mr. Stigman's card reads "A.L. all star 1960."

Best game in the 1961 season: In his first appearance of the season on June 11, he shut down the Athletics for four innings, allowing only one hit and striking out six batters.

Card #78, Lee Walls, follow-through on a swing, Connie Mack Stadium. Even though it hasn't been recorded (or even written) yet, Lee is thinking about the Tom Jones cover of "Curly" Putman Jr.'s song "The Green, Green Grass of Home" and is struggling to hold back the tears. SR: A, Mr. Walls was only 60 when he passed in 1993.

Best game in the 1961 season: Against the Dodgers on July 14, he entered the game in the eighth inning as a pinch-hitter and remained in the game, taking over at third base. He went 2–2 with two triples, two runs scored, and two RBI.

Card #79, Joe Ginsberg, batting stance in Comiskey Park. He's glancing over at Lee (see immediately above) and wondering how a grown man can be so affected by a mere song. A good signer, SR: A, Joe Inked "Original Met" on his card.

Best game in the 1961 season: He went 2–4 for Boston against the Athletics on June 5.

Card #80, Harmon Killebrew, headshot in Griffith Stadium. I see a man proudly unashamed of going bald. He was an SR: A signer (for free for many years, charged a small fee that went to charity after his apotheosis) before his passing in 2011 at 74.

Best games in the 1961 season: On June 21, he hit a pair of two-run home runs against the Orioles. He also had a 5–6 day against Boston on June 12 with a home run and four RBI.

Card #81, Tracy Stallard, headshot (and I do mean *headshot*. I am pretty sure that he had the largest head in baseball, at least until Bruce "The Head" Howard arrived on the scene in 1963). Tracy looks like he's contemplating his navel, or, rather, someone else's navel. A good signer, SR: A, Mr. Stallard was 80 when he died in 2017. He wrote "Maris 61st HR/10/1/61" on the card for me.

Best game in the 1961 season: Against the Senators on July 3, he pitched five scoreless innings and fanned eight.

Card #82, Joe Christopher passed away in 2023, headshot, taken

2. The Quest for Fire

in McKechnie Field during Spring Training. The look on Joe's face reminds me of myself looking at any of my kids when they were but wee. Always a good signer, he's an SR: A man.

Best game in the 1961 season: On July 22, he went 4–4 against the Braves.

Card #83, Bob Bruce, follow-through, Briggs Stadium. Here he is pictured showing off to his high school girlfriend ("Yeah, I'm all that"). He was an SR: A man before his demise at 83 in 2017.

Best game in the 1961 season: In his first game of the season (April 23 against the Angels), he started and went 8⅓ innings and allowed one run on six hits.

Card #84, Lee Maye, headshot. He looks like what he was before, during and after he was in the Majors, that is, soulful Arthur Lee Maye, front man for Arthur Lee Maye and the Crowns, who sang doo-wop and soul. They were pretty darned good at it, I might add.[13] SR: A, he died at 67 in 2002.

Best game in the 1961 season: On July 17, he went 3–4 against the Reds with two doubles, a home run, four runs, and three RBI.

Card #85, Jerry Walker, headshot in Miami Stadium. He looks like an affable young man with a pleasant (and non-fake) smile. Career high points: he pitched in an All-Star Game at 20 and saved Early Wynn's 300th win. SR: A, he wrote "Won 1st ML game at 18" and "Saved Early Wynn's 300th victory" on the card at my request.

Best game in the 1961 season: He gave up only an unearned run in his complete-game, 2–1 win over his old Orioles team on August 9.

Card #86, Los Angeles Dodgers Team card. Mine is signed by coaches Leo Durocher, Carrol Beringer, Clay Bryant, and Art Becker. I also have a team card signed by non-carded players Maury Wills, Gordy Windhorn, Ed Palmquist, Doug Camilli, and Charlie Smith, and another signed by Minor League managers "Spider" Jorgensen and Danny Ozark.

Card #87, Joey Amalfitano, waiting in the field between pitches in Scottsdale Stadium. "Determined to show that he was worth his $40,000 bonus,[14] Joey plans on which base he should throw to should the ball be hit his way." Another post card kinda guy, he gets an SR: A+.

Searchin' for Toothpick Sam

Best game in the 1961 season: On June 30, he went 3–4 with a triple against the Pirates.

Card #88, Richie Ashburn, headshot in Rendezvous Park in Mesa. He looks like exactly what he was, a calm, easy-to-get-along-with fellow. Long a beloved Phillies broadcaster, he was SR: A, before passing away in 1997 at 70 years of age.

Best game in the 1961 season: He hit .304 over his last 47 games to lift his average from .225 to .257. On May 2, he went 3–4 against the Giants and scored twice.

Card #89, Billy Martin, pre-nose job headshot, taken in Crosley Field. "Say that again to my face!" (to a 55-year-old, overweight marshmallow salesman). In all fairness, I have to say that Mr. Martin signed everything I sent to him before he passed, even while engaging in a Godzilla-Rodan-type struggle with "The Boss." SR: A, he was only 61 when he died in 1989.

Best games in the 1961 season: He went 3–5 on September 23 with three runs against the Senators, and on the 29th, he went 3–5 with a home run and a triple against the Tigers.

Card #90, Gerry Staley, headshot in Payne Park in Sarasota. He looks like a semi-successful door-to-door salesman who still harbors hopes of reaching the Big Leagues (of sales, that is). An SR: A, he was 87 when he died in 2008. His card notes "N.L. all star 52–53"/"A.L. all star 1960."

Best game in the 1961 season: he pitched for three teams in 1961 (White Sox, Athletics and Tigers), with his best stint coming for the A's: three hitless innings on July 27 against the Indians. His best game for the Chisox was two hitless innings against the Yankees on June 4, and his best outing for the Tigers was two scoreless innings against Baltimore with three strikeouts on August 17.

Card #91, Walt Moryn, follow-through of a swing, taken in Crosley Field. Moose, who spent eight years in the Dodgers organization waiting for Duke Snider or Carl Furillo to grow old and who then made an All-Star team at age 32 for the Cubs after showing that he could, indeed, hit Major League pitching (and who in this shot appears to have an absolutely *enormous* head), has this year's biggest smile. SR: A. Mr. Moryn, who had served on an ammunition ship in

2. The Quest for Fire

the South Pacific in World War II, passed away when he was 70 in 1996.

Best game in the 1961 season: On July 9, he went 2–4 against the Braves with two home runs and four RBI.

Card #92, Hal Naragon, headshot. He looks like he's telling a wait person for the third time that no, he does not want to look at the dessert menu, thank you very much. An SP: A, Mr. Naragon was 90 when he passed in 2019.

Best game in the 1961 season: On July 26, he went 3–4 against the Senators and scored twice. Over his last 40 games he hit .324 to raise his BA from .243 to .302.

Card #93, Tony Gonzalez, headshot taken in Connie Mack Stadium. The look says, "Don't even *think* about calling me 'boy.'" SR: A.

Best games in the 1961 season: On April 13 against the Dodgers, he went 3–4 with two runs, a homer, and three RBI. On August 25, against the Braves, he went 3–5 with two triples, scoring thrice. On July 27, he was hitting .329. From there until season's end, 53 games, he hit only .210, finishing the season at .277.

Card #94, Johnny Kucks, looking in for the "sign," taken in Griffith Stadium. Actually, he's *supposed* to be looking for the sign, but instead his eyes are looking at a woman 13 rows up behind home plate. A good signer (SR: A), he passed away in 2013 when he was 81. He noted "AL All-Star 1956" on the card.

Best game in the 1961 season: Johnny didn't pitch in the Majors in 1961, or indeed, ever again. He did throw two shutouts for Rochester of the International League that year.

Cards #95, Norm Cash, on-deck pose in Yankee Stadium. It looks like he's glancing back at the dugout to make sure no one is pinching his mitt. Oddly, despite leading the Majors in 1961 with a .361 BA, he had but 56 multi-hit games and only 11 games with at least three hits. On May 3, he was hitting .302 but hit .364 the rest of the season, including going 8–13 in his last three games with three homers, five RBI and six runs. A good but not great signer before his early demise (he was just 52 when he died in 1986), he was an SR: B.

Best game in the 1961 season: In a fantabulous season, his best

Searchin' for Toothpick Sam

game was against the Athletics on July 23, when he went 4–5 with four runs and five RBI.

Card #96, Billy O'Dell, after "delivering" a pitch in Scottsdale Stadium. Here shown calling his Corgi, Brumose. An SR: A, he was 85 when he died in 2018.

Best game in the 1961 season: On the Fourth of July at Wrigley Field versus the Cubs, he took over for Eddie Fisher after Eddie started the game by giving up three straight hits, including two doubles. Billy allowed only two hits while striking out a career-high 13 Cubs during his nine innings of "relief."

Card #97, Jerry Lynch, fixin' to throw the old pellet in Crosley Field. "Okay, fellas, I found it. Now what do I do with it?" (He was used as a pinch-hitter 524 times during his career, hit 18 homers, and drove in 90 runs in that role.) Another postcard sender (SR: A+), Mr. Lynch was 81 when he died in 2012. His then-record "18 pinch hit HRs" is noted on his card.

Best game in the 1961 season: In '61, Jerry appeared as a pinch-hitter 59 time for the pennant-bound Reds. In that capacity, he hit .404 with five home runs and 25 RBI. He had a .525 OBP and slugged .851 (OPS 1.376). Picking out one game that is more important than any other is beyond my powers of discernment.

Card #98, TOPPS BASEBALL CHECK LIST 2nd Series. Featured are Joe Adcock, Ernie Banks and Don Zimmer, photo shot during a game in Wrigley Field. There are three varieties.[15] My variety A is signed by Joe Adcock and Ernie Banks, my variety B is signed by all three, and my variety C is signed by Joe Adcock and Don Zimmer.

Card #99, Don Buddin, getting ready to "field" a grounder in Yankee Stadium. Looking like the eager beaver type, his face seems to say, "Okay, this time I bet I catch it for sure!" SR: A, before his passing at 77 in 2011.

Best games in the 1961 season: Don had two games in which he went 3–4 and scored three times: June 15 against the Tigers and three days later against the Senators. Over 10 games from June 10 to 18, he hit .500 and raised his average from .196 to .270.

Card #100: Harvey Haddix, headshot in Wrigley Field. He looks like he's watching a grandchild take his or her first steps. Harvey, a

2. The Quest for Fire

good hitter, hit nine triples, three more than Mark McGwire hit in 5,389 more at-bats. Always a good signer, he earned an SR: A rating. In 1994, Mr. Haddix passed away at age 68.

Best game in the 1961 season: On August 3 against the Cardinals, he threw a four-hit shutout in which he allowed only one runner to reach second base.

Card #101, Bubba Phillips, headshot taken in Municipal Stadium. He looks like a guy who was into a shark for five large and whose long-shot trifecta he put his last two Franklins on at the track just paid off. Always a good signer. SR: A, he was 65 when he died in 1993.

Best game in the 1961 season: On July 6, Bubba went 4–4 against Boston, scoring three runs and driving in three more. He doubled and hit two home runs.

Card #102, Gene Stephens, headshot in Memorial Stadium. Shown here as a handsome young man with his feet set firmly on the ground and his eyes looking toward a bright future. A willing signer (SR: A), Mr. Stephens passed at 86 in 2019. Gene inscribed "3 hits in 7th inning/vs Detroit June 18, 1953" for me.

Best game in the 1961 season: He played for Kansas City and Baltimore, with his best game coming as an Athletic against the Angels on the Fourth of July when he had a 3–4 day and scored twice with two RBI.

Card #103, Ruben Amaro, father of Ruben Amaro, Jr., follow-through on swing in Connie Mack Stadium. One of those fortunate, young-looking fellows, he appears to be proud that his hit made it all the way to the outfield grass on the fly. By the way, he is in the *Salon de la Fama del Beisbol,* and his father is in both the Mexican and Cuban Halls of Fame. Before his passing in 2017 when he was 81, he was an SR: A man.

Best games in the 1961 season: Against the Cardinals on April 28, Ruben went 4–6. On September 12, he went 3–4 with three runs scored, a home run, and a triple.

Card #104, John Blanchard, headshot taken in Al Lang Field. Picture this: take off the baseball cap, replace it with a cowboy hat, give him some Wild Bill Hickok facial hair and tresses, and change the Yankees uniform to a buckskin jacket. Yeah, I can see that.... A former SR: A, Mr. Blanchard died at 76 in 2009.

Best games in the 1961 season: On June 18, he went 3–5 against the Tigers with two home runs, and on September 6 he went 2–4 with two homers and four RBI against the Senators.

Card #105, Carl Willey, starting his wind-up in County Stadium. He looks like he is seriously thinking about shaking off the catcher but knows well that one doesn't shake off Del Crandall with impunity. Ranked SR: A, he was 78 when he passed in 2009.

Best game in the 1961 season: On August 15, Carl threw a five-hitter against the Pirates, winning 4–1.

Card #106, Whitey Herzog, headshot in Yankee Stadium. To me, he looks like he's trying to get up the nerve to go over to the Yankees dugout and ask the Mick for an autograph. SR: A.

Best game in the 1961 season: On August 17, he went 3–4 against the Tigers with a home run and three RBI.

Card #107, Seth Morehead, headshot in Wrigley Field. He looks like what he was, a good ol' boy from Louisiana. I can picture him around the smoker with a beer in his hand, tellin' the boys (for the 30th time) about beating the Dodgers in the last game they played as the *Brooklyn* Dodgers. A solid SR: A, he always returned my items before passing at 71 in 2006. Mr. Morehead, at my request, wrote "733 Ks in in 727 IP," referencing his Minor League totals.

Best game in the 1961 season: On May 4, Seth threw a scoreless inning against the Dodgers, striking out Tommy Davis and Wally Moon.

Card #108, Dan Dobbek, headshot. He has the most modern-looking hair of any player in this set, that goofy not-a-crew-cut, front-half-of-a-mullet look (but without the mullet, way too soon for the mullet). Cleaned up nicely after a week in the mine, he shows up scrubbed and scented at Magda's house to ask her father if he can take her to polka night at the lodge. SR: A. He wrote "SW LG All Star/1956" on the card.

Best game in the 1961 season: Dan hit two home runs and had five RBI against the Athletics on May 19.

Card #109, Johnny Podres, headshot. Round-headed and pudgy,

2. The Quest for Fire

he looks like the plump kid in movies like *Goonies* and *The Sandlot*. But did they beat the Yankees in 1955? I think not. He always signed my items. SR: A, Mr. Podres passed away at 75 in 2008.

Best game in the 1961 season: On May 10, Johnny shut out the Phils and had two hits.

Card #110, Vada Pinson, getting loose in the on-deck circle in Crosley Field. All I can say is that the man looks sharp. Unfortunately, he was not a very good signer, and I lost at least two *Reds Heavy Artillery* cards (#25), signed by both Gus Bell and Frank Robinson, to him. He did sign one '61 for me and the '63 Fleer, so I can't give him a flat-out F, but an SR of D- is the best I can do. He was only 57 when he died in 1995.

Best games in the 1961 season: Vada had 23 games with at least three hits in 1961. On July 9, he went 3–4 and scored five runs against the Dodgers. On August 12, he went 4–4 with four RBI against the Giants. In May, he hit .406 to raise his average from .143 to .315.

Card #111, Jack Meyer,[16] following through on a pitch in Connie Mack Stadium. He passed away in 1967 before I started collecting signed cards, but items signed by him are hard to come by, so…

Best game in the 1961 season: Coming back from injuries in '61, he pitched in a single game in 1961 on April 30, giving up two runs in two innings against the Cards and, seeing that his arm hadn't recovered, retired.

Card #112, "Chico" Fernandez, "fielding" a grounder at Henley Field in Lakeland. The first Tigers shortstop to hit at least 20 home runs in one season, he seems to be smiling in every picture I see of him. On this card, he seems tickled plum to death while waiting for the horsehide spheroid to find a comfortable, though ephemeral, home in his mitt. Mr. Fernandez was an SR: A+ and signed everything I ever sent him before his death at 84 in 2016.

Best games in the 1961 season: Humberto had two four-hit games in '61. On April 26, he went 4–5 against the Yankees with three RBI, and on August 12 he went 4–6 against the Twins with five RBI.

Card #113, Mike Fornieles, headshot in Yankee Stadium. That look just screams, "Yeah, that's right—I'm the guy who set the A.L.

record for most games pitched in a season with 70. You wanna make something of it?" He was only the third player of the modern era to pitch in at least 70 games, the first two being the Giants' Ace Adams in 1943 and the Phils' Jim Konstanty in 1950. A dependable signer (SR: A), Mike passed at 66 in 1998.

Best game in the 1961 season: He made two starts in 1961. On June 5, he pitched a complete game against the Athletics, winning 6–2, and on June 15, he pitched six scoreless innings in defeating the Senators.

Card #114, Hobie Landrith, "catching," perhaps in Connie Mack Stadium. Probably most famous for being the Mets' first pick in the dispersal draft, Hobie looks like the guy everybody invites to their parties, the guy who cracks jokes, talks to wallflowers, makes sure everybody gets home okay, and stays to help clean up when the party's over. He had been an SR: A+, until his death a age 93 in 2023. His son David played in the minors for two years. Of course, I had to have him write "1st draft choice/N.Y. Mets, 1962" on the card.

Best game in the 1961 season: On August 22, against the Giants, Hobie went 4–5 with three runs, two RBI, and two doubles.

Card #115, Johnny Antonelli, headshot, still in his Giants uniform in Candlestick Park. He appears to be wondering if the trade the Giants made with the Indians is a good opportunity for him to resurrect his career. (It wasn't. He made only two scoreless appearances [totaling 1⅓ innings] the entire 1961 season and only pitched in four games after July (just once in September.) Started out as a good signer but went downhill as the years passed. SR: B-/C+. Mr. Antonelli passed away, aged 89, in 2020.

Best game in the 1961 season: 1961 was not a good year for the former Giants ace. He was unscored-on in only five of his 20 appearances (which averaged about three innings each), 11 of which were two innings or fewer. He had one good game: on May 22, he pitched nine innings in relief against the Athletics and allowed only seven hits and one run in a game the Indians lost in 12 innings.

Card #116, Joe DeMaestri, headshot, member of the Crewcut Company, taken at Al Lang Field during Spring Training. He looks like any player who got traded from the Athletics to the Yankees

2. The Quest for Fire

looked in the 10 years between 1955 and 1964—as pleased as punch. An SR: A, he died in 2016 at 87.

Best game in the 1961 season: Joe went 3–5 against the Tigers on June 18. He got half of his season total of hits, half of his RBI, and scored his only run of the season in that game.

Card #117, Dale Long, headshot, member of the Crewcut Company, in a Giants uniform in Connie Mack Stadium. My, what a happy face—but is it hiding a dark secret? Did he just sell a used car to a rube without mentioning that there's sawdust in the transmission? Did he just trade a 1962 Rudy Hernandez to some mark for a 1961 Mantle? Does he know where the assistant principal was last Thursday night? We'll never know, 'cause he ain't sayin'. A good signer, though (SR: A), before passing away at 87 in 2016.

Best games in the 1961 season: On May 27 against the Twins, Mr. Long went 4–4 with three runs, and on June 2 he went 2–4 with a homer and five RBI against the Athletics.

Card #118, Chris Cannizzaro, batting stance, taken in Sportsman's Park. Confident, as anybody with those eyebrows would be,[17] this young fellow *knows* he belongs in Cardinals togs. (His son Chris Cannizzaro, Jr., would play seven seasons in the minors, the last four at the Triple-A level.) An SR: A grade replier, he died in 2016 at 78.

Best game in the 1961 season: He pinch-hit against the Phils on August 5 and got his only hit of the season.

Card #119, *A's Big Armor*, featuring former Yankees Norm Siebern, Hank Bauer, and Jerry Lumpe. The trio is standing around the batting cage in Municipal Stadium, engaged in a contest of wills to see who can keep their bats on their shoulders the longest. All three were SR: A.

Card #120, Ed Mathews, headshot, taken in Connie Mack Stadium. This is the look of a young man secure in his place in baseball history (after nine years as a star in the majors, he was still only 29 years old, the second-fastest player to reach 200 home runs as well as the second-fastest to reach 300). What he didn't know was that he would never again be the player after 30 that he was before it. Despite his Jimmie Foxx–like early and rapid decline, he is still rated the second-best third baseman of all time, and rightfully so. I

Searchin' for Toothpick Sam

honestly do not remember how many cards I sent to Mr. Mathews to sign before, because of bad luck with other major stars that started in the early 1980s, I started getting all my Hall of Famers' cards signed either at shows or through their own sites. I'm pretty sure, however, that he was an SR: A before I switched tactics on general principles. Mr. Mathews was 69 at the time of his demise in 2001.

Best games in the 1961 season: Eddie had a slew of big games in '61. On September 23 he went 3–3 with three runs against the Cubs with two homers and four RBI, and 3–3 again on August 13 with one homer and three RBI. On June 8, he went 4–4 against the Reds with two homers, and on July 23 , he went 4–5 against the Pirates. There were other big games, but you get the picture.

Card #121, Eli Grba, Crewcut Company member, photo taken in Yankee Stadium when he was still a Yankee. He looks as if he's taking an eye exam with his glasses on. An SR: A, Eli passed at 84 in 2019.

Best game in the 1961 season: On August 8, he threw a complete game to beat the White Sox, 5–2, with the runs unearned. He also struck out a career-high 10 batters. At bat against the Senators on July 22, he went 2–3 with a two-run homer (Eli batted .241 with 11 homers in the minors and .216 with three homers in the majors.)

Card #122, Chicago Cubs Team card. Mine is signed by coaches El Tappe, Vedie Himsl, Harry Craft, and Goldie Holt. I also have a team card signed by non-carded players George Freese, Jim McAnany, Dick Burwell, and Moe Morhardt, another signed by George Freese, Cuno Barragon, Dick Burwell, and Moe Morhardt, and a third signed by minor league managers Gene Handley and Joe Macko.

Card #123, Billy Gardner, headshot, a longtime member of the Chew Crew, photographed in Yankee Stadium. Have you ever watched the FX series *Justified*? Fine returner, he's an SR: A.

Best game in the 1961 season: He went 4–4 and scored twice against the Twins on May 19.

Card #124, J.C. Martin, in the act of "fielding," shot in Yankee Stadium. He looks like he just picked up something he found on the ground and is about ready to ask the closest person, "Pardon me, did

2. The Quest for Fire

you just drop this?" A fine signer, he's SR: A. I could not let him go without inscribing "Miracle Mets 1969" on the card.

Best game in the 1961 season: J.C. went 3–4 against the Senators on September 3.

Card #125, Steve Barber, headshot: 1960s heartthrob, the look is one of two things: either he is saying, "You think I'm bluffing? Well, why dontchya call me?" or an attractive woman was eyeing him and he is giving her his "I'll call your bluff. Now what are ya gonna do?" look. An SR: A before his passing at 68 in 2007.

Best game in the 1961 season: On May 6, Steve shut out the Athletics while striking out 10 batters.

Card #126, Dick Stuart, showing batting stance in either Crosley Field or Connie Mack Stadium. Shown here telling a teammate, "You don't think I can put one in the street? Well, let's just see about that." For me, SR: A, but I've heard otherwise. In the DH era, he would have been a superstar (easy 400 homer guy, possibly 500). He was 70 when he died in 2002.

Best game in the 1961 season: Dr. Strangeglove (he led his league in errors seven consecutive years) went 3–4 with two home runs and five RBI versus the Cardinals on September 2.

Card #127, Ron Kline, headshot: "Whaddya mean I can't drive home? Gimme them keys." He signed and returned everything I ever sent him. An SR: A, in 1952, Ron was one of the 10 youngest players in the NL—in fact, *seven* of the top 10 were Ron's teammates on the woeful 42–112 Pirates team, and in further fact, four were still teenagers. In his last three years in the Bigs, he was among the 10 oldest. He died in 2002.

Best game in the 1961 season: Traded from the Angels to the Tigers in midseason, "Moose" tossed a four-hit shutout against Boston on August 18. His best game as an Angel was on July 3 when, in seven innings of work, he allowed no earned runs against the Athletics.

Card #128. Rip Repulski, follow-through on a swing in Yankee Stadium. "Oops! There goes another car windshield." A good returner (SR: A), he died in 2001 at 69 years of age.

Best game in the 1961 season: Accruing only 25 at-bats, he got a pinch-hit against Minnesota on April 18 and subsequently scored.

Searchin' for Toothpick Sam

Card #129, Ed Hobaugh, headshot, member of the Crewcut Company, at Pompano Beach Municipal Park. Able to bravely overcome a congenital case of Kirk Douglas Chin, he is shown here telling a doubter of his pitching skills, "I scoff at your baseless braggadocio, mock you for your transparent prevarications, your transpicuous tergiversations, and your uncouth and baseless unconfidence in my abilities. I bid you good day, sirrah!" He is ranked SR: A.

Best game in the 1961 season: He beat the Angels on May 30, striking out a career-high eight batters.

Card #130, Norm Larker, headshot, taken in Holman Stadium. Looks as if he might be telling a reporter, "Of course I'll hit .320 again this year!" An SR: A+ returner, he died when he was 76 in 2007.

Best games in the 1961 season: Norm had two 3–3 days, one against the Reds on July 19 and the other against the Cardinals on July 22.

Card #131, Orioles manager Paul Richards, headshot. Shown here wishing that Steve Dalkowski could throw two strikes in a row. SR: A, he died in 1986 at 77.

Card #132, White Sox manager Al Lopez, on the dugout steps. Shown here giving the kibosh sign on his long-time nemesis, Casey Stengel. An SR: A man, he was 97 when he died in 2005.

Card #133: Yankees manager Ralph Houk, capo di tutti capi of the Chew Crew, headshot. The Major earned a Silver Star, a Bronze Star, and a Purple Heart in World War II. SR: A, he died in 2010, aged 90.

Card #134: Senators manager Mickey Vernon, headshot. Shown here wondering what he's got himself into. SR: A, he died at 90 in 2008.

Card #135, Reds manager Fred Hutchinson, headshot. Shown here reacting to someone challenging him to a fight. Since he was deceased before I started collecting, I had a *very* hard time finding three signed copies of his card. He was only 45 when he passed away in 1964.

Card #136, Dodgers manager Walt Alston, headshot. Shown here reacting to a reporter's question about how it felt to have all four of his starters ranked among the top eight in strikeouts in the league.

2. The Quest for Fire

SR: A, and even his daughter was kind enough to return a card which arrived after his demise, describing his one at-bat in the Bigs.[18] He passed at 72 in 1984.

Card #137, Braves manager Chuck Dressen, headshot. He died in 1966, long before the idea of getting cards signed popped into my head. Nineteen sixty-one cards signed by him are quite hard to find, and some of those that do show up are forgeries. He is shown here asking if anyone else hears "that noise."

Card #138, Pirates manager Danny Murtaugh, headshot. Shown here thinking about his father's poteen, he died the same year I started collecting, 1976. He did sign the few cards I sent him before he passed, so, for me at least, SR: A.

Card #139, Cardinals manager Solly Hemus, headshot. SR: A, Solly was one of only nine player-managers in the 1950s, and he was the last until Hank Bauer (see below) in 1961. He was 94 when he passed away in 2017.

Card #140, Gus Triandos, follow-through after a "swing," probably taken in Yankee Stadium. I remember that the first time I saw this card, I thought he looked a bit like Babe Ruth. In this photo, it really looks like he held a personal grudge against the ball he just "hit" and was taking immense satisfaction from having done so. (By the way, Gus had a brother named George who played in the minors for eight years and hit .295.)[19] He was an SR: A man before passing at 82 in 2013.

Best game in the 1961 season: On the Fourth of July, Gus hit two homers and drove in four runs against Cleveland.

Card #141, Billy Williams, batting stance, taken in Wrigley Field. That is a photo of a confident young man, I tell you what. He signed everything I sent to him, so, for me, he is an SR: A.

Best game in the 1961 season: Billy punished the Giants on May 2, going 4–4 with a grand slam and driving in five runs.

Card #142, Luis Arroyo, headshot, part of the Chew Crew in Yankee Stadium. He appears to be thinking, "You think your weak stuff can match what I'm throwing? I don't think so." An SR: A man, Mr. Arroyo died at 88 in 2016.

Best game in the 1961 season: Here's a relief appearance you won't see again: In the second game of a double-header on July 30, Luis pitched 6⅔ innings without giving up a run and struck out six Orioles in the bargain.

Card #143, Russ Snyder, follow-through on a swing in Yankee Stadium. With that cheesy half-grin, he appears to be letting the photographer know that he's in on the joke. SR: A

Best game in the 1961 season: On September 21, Russ went 4–4 with two runs and two RBI against the Yankees.

Card #144, Jim Coker, squatting, with coach Andy Cohen in background. Oh my gosh, Jim looks so very sad. He died when he was only 55 in 1991, and had been SR: A.

Best game in the 1961 season: On July 5, Jim went 3–3 against the Braves.

Card #145, Bob Buhl, headshot. Outlined against a pale blue sky, our hero tries, through the sheer force of his will, to stare a circling gull down out of the sky. Mr. Buhl holds the record for the most ABs in a season without getting a single hit, set in 1962, when he went 0–70. A good signer, SR: A.

Best game in the 1961 season: On May 30, Bob had a complete-game, 3–1 win over the Phils, allowing just four hits.

Interesting side note: Bob had as many extra base hits in his 17-year career as he had steals, two each.

Card #146: Marty Keough, headshot, member of the Crewcut Company, taken in Griffith Stadium. I can't tell if he has a look of mild displeasure or of intense cogitation on his face. Brother and father of Major Leaguers. SR: A, either way.

Best games in the 1961 season: He went 3–4 on Opening Day against the White Sox. He also went 4–7 in a 15-inning game against the White Sox on June 10, hitting a walk-off home run in the 15th.

Card #147: Ed Rakow, shot from waist up, must have been in Holman Stadium. Ed, fresh off a 12–6 season at Spokane, looks forward toward a long career as a Dodger, not knowing that, by the time his card came out, he'd be toiling in the spice mines of Kansas City.[20] He was SR: A before he passed away at 65 in 2000.

Best game in the 1961 season: On August 10, Ed struck out six Twins in a scoreless 3⅔-inning stint.

2. The Quest for Fire

Card #148: Julian Javier, getting ready to "field" a ball in Sportsman's Park. Julio, the father of outfielder Stan Javier, appears to be calling a puppy in this photo. He and his son, Stan, combined for 2,827 hits, 1,503 runs and 381 steals in the majors. Early on, he was a good signer, but his reply percentage dropped as the years went by. SR: B.

Best game in the 1961 season: Julio went 5–5 against the Pirates on May 27. He had three four-hit games in which he collected seven runs and seven RBI.

Card #149, Bob Oldis, headshot, loyal Chew Crew member, photo taken in Connie Mack Stadium. He looks like he just heard the judge sentence him to three years hard time for conspiring to commit flagrant and deliberate mopery, the judge telling him that his lawyer's writ of replevin had no standing in his case.[21] SR: A. His card bears the notation "All Star/1956/SA/1957—9/AA/World Champions/Pirates/1960."

Best game in the 1961 season: Alas, Bob only played in five games in 1961 and went 0–5.

Card #150, Willie Mays, headshot: If this is not the worst Willie Mays card, then I don't want to see a worse one (compare this to his 1954 card). He looks just plain aggravated in this shot, like the photographer interrupted him on his way to an important meeting. He signed the first few cards I sent, but then stopped signing except at shows. (Of course, I didn't know that and kept sending cards that came back signed by a secretary, thereby rendering some of my signed multi-player cards worthless, along with MVP and All-Star cards.) SR: F-. (See card #490.)

Best game in the 1961 season: Well, let's see.... Was it the May 13 game against the Braves when he went 2–4 and drove in six runs? Ummm … nope. Was it the June 29 game against the Phillies when he went 4–5 with three homers and five RBI? Nope, nope, nope. Well, then, how about his April 30 game against the Braves when he went 4–4 with four home runs and eight RBI? I think we have a winner!

Card #151, Jim Donohue, headshot. "Hey, guys, guess what! My dad just gave me the keys to the Catalina!" An SR: A, Mr. Donohue died at 79 in 2017.

Searchin' for Toothpick Sam

Best game in the 1961 season: Traded from Detroit to L.A. in early June, his best game was as an Angel. On July 19, Jim started and went 8⅓ innings to beat the Twins, 2–1. He gave up five hits and struck out seven.

Card #152, Earl Torgeson, headshot in Sarasota's Payne Park. Don't be fooled by the glasses—you didn't want to mess with Torgy.[22] A bit of trivia for you: In the second episode of the *Dick Van Dyke Show*, "My Blonde-Haired Brunette," Rob Petrie (Dick Van Dyke) gives his son Richie (Larry Mathews) a few packs of baseball cards, and later Richie goes over to talk to his dad. In his hand he is holding the cards, and the bottom (and therefore visible) card is a '61 Topps Earl Torgeson. He passed away at age 66 in 1990 and was an SR: A replier.

Best game in the 1961 season: After going 1–15 as a pinch-hitter for the White Sox, Torgy was traded in June to the Yankees, for whom he went 2–18. He did play both games of a doubleheader at first base for the Yankees on July 9, and, although he went 0–4, he did draw five walks that day.

Card #153, Don Lee, headshot, first sergeant of the Crewcut Company, son of Thornton Lee. Now we know where the idea for Spock's ears came from. His father, Thornton, won 117 games in the majors. Don was an SR: A. He wrote "1962 Miracle Angels" on his card. (In only their second year of existence, the Angels were in first place on July 4. On the 13th, they were a half-game out of first, and they were in second place as late as September 12.)

Best game in the 1961 season: On July 21, Don beat the Twins, 4–3, throwing a complete game and striking out seven.

Card #154, Bobbly Del Greco, batting stance in Connie Mack Stadium. A most decidedly hawkish looking fellow. One of 10 children, he had eight of his own.[23] An SR: A type, he passed at 86 in 2019.

Best games in the 1961 season: He was traded from Philadelphia to Kansas City in early July. His best game as a Phillie was against the Giants on June 29 (3–5, two runs), and for the A's it was September 5, when he went 3–5 with three runs and four RBI against the Angels.

Card #155, Johnny Temple, headshot. It looks as if he is making

2. The Quest for Fire

that motorboat noise that babies like. You know (to bastardize Lauren Bacall's incredibly sultry line from *To Have and Have Not*), the one where you put your lips together, let them go all flaccid, and blow.

Oddly, I have no clear memory of how Mr. Temple responded to my autograph requests. I do, however, have a quite clear recollection that, for several years, for some unknown reason I thought that he was deceased and didn't even bother write to him, so...

Best game in the 1961 season: Johnny had 11 games with at least three hits, among them an April 23 game against the A's when he went 3–3 with four runs and three walks and a May 21 one against the Twins in which he was 4–6 with three runs.

Aside #2: The Life My Cards Led

Back when I first started collecting, I, like many of the older readers of this educational and (hopefully) entertaining tome, kept my collection rubberbanded in the proverbial shoebox. I even, oh wretched child that I was, fastened a few of them to my bike frame with clothespins so that when the spokes hit 'em, the bike would sound like I was riding a motorcycle. Alas, now that I am an aged and wretched recluse, I realize that even eight flapping baseball cards, while indeed somewhat louder than a non-carded bike (though not anywhere near as loud as a bike armed with fresh playing cards, which kept their integrity much longer) is far (to the eighth order of magnitude) from the real thing (and, if you are riding a Harley, at least two orders of magnitude farther).

Also, like many readers, I was not content to let my cards linger in dark, boxy solitude, oh no. I felt a strange compulsion to arrange them into more orderly sets than the seemingly haphazard way they appeared when I opened a nickel pack of these rectangular beauties, and arrange them I did. Or, rather, rearrange them. I mean, sure, you *could* be content with the staunchly traditional and conservative yet quotidian "numerical order." Or you *could* put them in a much more reasonable, cosmically systematic order based not on a mere, random number, but rather on more rational and compelling qualities, qualities with a more real-world justification.

Searchin' for Toothpick Sam

So, back when my entire collection amounted to a little more than 200 cards, I set out to make sense of my new microverse. First, of course, I stacked the cards in teams, the most natural of all rearrangements. Next, also of course, I reorganized them by position, the second-most natural of assignments. Then, if I remember correctly, I arranged them by age, by height, position by height, position by weight, then circled back to position by age. I would do this each time I got a new pack of cards. (Of course, the constant reshuffling of my cards meant that they drifted farther and farther away from today's Holy Grail–like "mint," but I didn't [and wouldn't have, even if I knew what was coming]) give two hoots about that. Rearranging the cards (and the very cards themselves) filled me with a strange sense of joy and wonder. The joy remained until cards stopped being issued in series (although by then I was a certified *baseball* nut) but I kept on collecting them, basically because I thought it was somewhat more than a wonder that a 2.5 × 3.5 rectangle could not only tell us a person's life story in a nutshell, but it also had a photo of the person in question and cartoons to boot. How cool was that?

My own life was becoming more and more filled with errata, miscues, faux pas, false starts, dead ends, disappointments, passionate but unrequited crushes, insults, injuries, and worse, but the cards never let me down. The first crinkle when I opened a fresh pack, the quick punch of the vaguely sarcophagal yet redolent bouquet of that pink bubble-gumly slab, the piquant, almost stinging taste of the way-too-sweet yet pleasantly biting first explosive release of the compound sugars on my tongue (unsullied by the later evils of high fructose corn syrup and aspartame), followed by the almost as rapid disappearance of any flavor at all and then the minutes spent working a quickly congealing gob with a consistency somewhere between Silly Putty and sinusatic mucilage until your jaws got tired.... Man, kids of today just don't know what they're missin'.

Card #156, Ken [L.] Hunt, headshot taken in Yankee Stadium, still in a Yankees uniform, a member of the Crewcut Company (but just one more missed haircut away from being unceremoniously

2. The Quest for Fire

drummed out). He looks like a proud father watching one of his kids get a ribbon for winning the elementary school talent contest, tap dancing division. The stepfather of Butch Patrick (he played Eddie Munster on *The Munsters*), he is buried close to his lifelong friend (and one-time roomie) Roger Maris (see above).[24] Mr. Hunt signed everything I ever sent him before passing away in 1997. SR: A.

Best game in the 1961 season: On May 27, Ken went 4–5 with two doubles and a home run against the Tigers.

Card #157, Cal McLish, headshot in Al Lopez Field. He looks like he's playing hide-and-go-seek and it's his turn to be the counter (the "seeker"). As can be clearly seen, Calvin Coolidge Julius Cæsar Tuskahoma McLish was of Native American heritage. There was a strange dichotomy in Cal's 15-year Major League career. During his 10 years in the National League, he was a poor 36–52 (.409) with a 4.50 ERA,[25] while during his five years in the American League he went 56–40 (.583) with a 3.55 ERA. Even though he would never sign his full name for me (and yes, I did ask him to), he was an SR: A. Mr. McLish was 84 when he died in 2010. In 1946, Cal was one of the 10 youngest players in the league. In his last two years, he was one of the 10 oldest. He signed his card and noted "Pitched in Majors at 18/A.L All Star 1959."

Best games in the 1961 season: On June 13, against the Angels, C. C. J. C. T. McLish beat the Angels, 2–1, with seven Ks. On July 16, unbelievable by today's standards, he went 12 innings before losing to Boston, 5–3.

Card #158, Pete Daley, headshot, and even though the photo looks like it was taken in a small fishing village on the Outer Banks, it is actually Connie Mack Field in West Palm Beach. Pete looks like he just caught a grocer with his thumb on the scale. A dependable returner, SR: A. He noted "All Star A.A. 1954" at the top of the card and "All Star Piedmont 1949" on the bottom.

Best game in the 1961 season: Pete went 3–5 with two runs and two RBI in a 13–12 loss against Boston on June 18.

Card #159, Baltimore Orioles Team card. Mine is signed by coaches Jimmy Adair and Harry Brecheen. I also have a team card signed by non-carded players Barry Shetrone, Frank Zupo, Jim

Searchin' for Toothpick Sam

Lehew, and John Papa, one signed by Boog Powell and Jim Lehew, and a third signed by Dick Hyde, John Papa, and Frank Zupo.

Card #160, the incomparable Whitey Ford, headshot taken in Yankee Stadium. He's still thinking, "Why didn't Casey start me in Game One?" A fine signer back in the day, SR: A, before I decided that it was probably better to get his cards signed at a signing event. Mr. Ford passed away 12 days from his 92nd birthday in 2020 while this book was being written.

Best game in the 1961 season: In a season full of good games (he was 25–4), his best was his June 18 win over the Tigers when he gave up three hits and no runs and struck out 12 batters in eight innings.

Card #161, Sherman Jones, "pitching" follow-through in Wrigley Field. While it is stated on various card sites that the photo is that of Eddie Fisher (the fellow Giants hurler, not the crooner formerly married to Betty Lin, Debbie Reynolds, Connie Stevens, former Miss Louisiana Terry Richard, and Marylin Monroe[26]), in reality it is indeed none other than "Roadblock" himself depicted on the card. (If you look at pictures of them side to side, you can easily see how they might be confused, but not so much alike that a little research wouldn't have sufficed to disabuse a clear-thinking and independent investigator of this particular commonly held misapprehension.) Anyhow, misidentification on the part of the lazy aside, what I see when I look at this card is Sherm saying, "That's right, I'm the guy who just went 10–0. Bring it." He was SR: A when he died at 72 in 2007.

Best game in the 1961 season: "Roadblock" started one game in 1961. On July 5, pitching against his former Giants teammates (he had been traded to Cincinnati on April 27 without pitching for the Giants, who had sent him back to the minors at the start of the season) he pitched $8\frac{1}{3}$ innings and gave up four hits and two runs, claiming the win.

Card #162, Jay Hook, headshot at Crosley Field. Jay appears to be already thinking about his future as an auto designer for Chrysler. SR: A. The card has an "Original Met" inscription.

Best game in the 1961 season: Rocked in his first three starts ($10\frac{2}{3}$ innings, 10.97 ERA), he was banished to the bullpen, where his

2. The Quest for Fire

most effective effort was against the Giants on August 22, allowing one run in four innings.

Card #163, Ed Sadowski, headshot, possibly in Fenway Park. Uniform number two in the 1961 version of the *League of Avuncular-Looking Big Leaguers*, this "uncle" looked like the one who would watch the game on his basement den with a six-pack and his kids and would yell at the umpires in Polish. Was SR: A (D: 1993). He was Ted Sadowski's (card #254) brother and their brother Bob also played in the Majors.

Best games in the 1961 season: On July 15, he went 3–5 with a double and a home run against the Indians, and on August 5 against the Orioles, he had a second 3–5 day with a home run.

Card #164, Felix Mantilla, head and shoulders shot, location unidentifiable (but if he's wearing whites [I can't tell for sure], he's in County Stadium). He looks like he's looking for his wife in the stands, hoping that she saw the nifty play he just made. SR: A.

Best game in the 1961 season: In the second game of a July 5 doubleheader in Philadelphia, Felix went 2–3 with a home run and two RBI and also scored twice.

Card #165, Gino Cimoli, batting stance, McKechnie Field. He is exuding confidence, as befitting a strikingly good-looking only child and high school super-star athlete.[27] A good signer, he was an SR: A before passing at 81 in 2011. I also have a card signed by him which states "Traded to Braves 1961."

Best games in the 1961 season: Gino played for two teams in 1961. On April 24, for the Pirates, he went 3–5 versus the Braves, and on June 24, he went 3–6 for the Braves against the Cubs with three runs scored.

Card #166, Danny Kravitz, headshot, C.O. of the Crewcut Company. Your high school football coach redux. An SR: A, he was 82 when he passed away in 2013.

Best game in the 1961 season: Mr. Kravitz did not appear in a Major League game after 1960.

Card #167, San Francisco Giants Team card. Mine is signed by coaches Larry Jansen, Wes Westrum, "Whitey" Lockman, and "Salty" Parker. I also have a team card signed by non-carded players Bill Haller, Dom Zanni, Johnny Orsino, Dick LeMay, and Bob Farley.

Searchin' for Toothpick Sam

Card #168, Tommy Davis, head and shoulders shot, taken during Spring Training in Vero Beach. This high school phenom (he had offers to play D-1 basketball) is depicted standing tall and facing a future full of promise. In this writer's opinion, a severe ankle injury in 1965 kept him from a Hall of Fame career. He kept his average up [.304 and climbing pre-injury, .288 post-], but he lost a lot of speed and a great deal of his power thereafter (.451 SA pre- vs. a very pedestrian .379 post-). A Boys High teammate of basketball Hall of Famer Lenny Wilkens, he was SR: A before passing away in 2022. Mr. Davis was kind enough to write "From Boys High to Batting Champ 62 63" for me.

Best game in the 1961 season: On July 1, Tommy went 4–4 against the Phillies.

Card #169, Don Elston, headshot. If Huck Finn ever wore a baseball cap, this is what he would have looked like. The first really good reliever for the Cubs, he pitched in at least 50 games six seasons in a row for them, a total that seems less than pedestrian nowadays but which ranked him in the top 10 from 1958 to 1962. SR: A, he died at 65 in 1995.

Best games in the 1961 season: On April 22, Don threw four innings of scoreless, two-hit ball, striking out five Phillies. On May 14 against the Dodgers, Don threw four innings of scoreless, one-hit ball. By the way, Mr. Elston's ERA for April was 0.00. From then on, it was 6.58 over 51 more appearances.

Card #170, Al Smith, headshot, taken in Comiskey Park. I can totally picture this dude, big stogie in hand, sitting at a table and listening to some Howlin' Wolf–style wailer in a down and dirty blues club with sawdust on the floor like Big Duke's Blue Flame or the Checkerboard Lounge. Mr. Smith passed away at 73 in 2002, having been SR: A.

Best game in the 1961 season: On June 6 against the Tigers, Al went 4–4 off future Hall of Famer Jim Bunning with a homer and three RBI.

Card #171, Paul Foytack, following through on a "pitch," Frank House in the background in Briggs Stadium. Paul looks s-o-o-o tired in this photo, so very, very tired. Good signer, though, SR: A. Mr. House signed the card also.

2. The Quest for Fire

Best game in the 1961 season: On August 22 against the Indians, he won, 8–1, allowing five hits in a complete game.

Card #172, Don Dillard, follow-through of a "swing" in Municipal Stadium. He appears to be reminiscing about something (perhaps his 1956 season in the Florida State League, where he terrified opposing pitchers) rather than focusing on the task at hand. Don was an SR: A before his passing in 2022.

Best game in the 1961 season: Don went 3–6 against the Angels on July 15 with a home run.

Card #173, *Beantown Bombers* featuring Frank Malzone, Vic Wertz, and Jackie Jensen, photo taken in Yankee Stadium. (All three gentlemen were SR: A club members.)

Card #174, Ray Semproch, headshot, member of the Crewcut Company, taken in Briggs Stadium. My gosh, if he doesn't look like yet another proud Polish papa staring long and hard at the young man who just came to the door asking if he might please see his daughter. SR: A.

Best game in the 1961 season: He pitched only twice in 1961. In his first appearance, he allowed an unearned run in one inning against the Angels.

Card #175, Gene Freese, headshot taken in Comiskey Park. Another high school teacher, trying to explain photosynthesis to one of the students who is actually paying attention to his lecture. He was a good signer, and his brother George got into a few games for the Cubs in '61. SR: A, he passed away aged 79 in 2013.

Best game in the 1961 season: On September 19, Gene went 2–3 with three runs, four RBI, and two home runs against the Pirates.

Card #176, Ken Aspromonte, head and shoulders shot possibly taken in Comiskey Park. Brother of Bob (see #396, below), Brooklyn-born and bred and coming off his best season ever, Ken is staring into a bright, imagined future with an All-Star Game or two, perhaps a trip to Europe once in a while.[28] SR: A, Mr. Aspromonte added "Coastal Plain All Star 1950/PCL All Star 1959" to his signature.

Best game in the 1961 season: He played for the Indians and the Angels in '61. On June 9, for the Angels against Boston, he went 3–3.

Searchin' for Toothpick Sam

For the Indians on August 19, he went 3–5 with two doubles against the Yankees.

Card #177, Don Larsen, follow-through on a "pitch," taken in Yankee Stadium. He looked sad that was wearing Athletics gray instead of Yankees pinstripes, and his mind was wandering back to those glorious days of yore when his drinks were comped at Toots Shor's place, where the elite of the sporting world, the press, and Broadway came to dine, drink and debate the finer issues of the day's culture. Don was 45–24 (.652) as a Yankee and 36–67 (.350) for the other six teams he pitched for. He hit .242 in the majors and was used as a pinch-hitter 77 times. A good signer (SR: A) up until he passed away on New Year's Day, 2020, at 90.

Best game in the 1961 season: Don played for the Athletics and the White Sox. On September 2, Don, a good-hitting pitcher, went 3–4 against the Indians. On August 26, he pitched five one-hit innings for the White Sox versus the Senators and went 2–2 with a home run.

Card #178, Bob Nieman, head and shoulders shot, in what appears to be Sportsman's Park. Bob's card always left me in a quandary—uncle-type or teacher-type? The potential dilemma was solved by my deciding that he looked like an English teacher who took his nephews to ball games. He died young (he was 58) in 1985, but he had been a fine (SR: A) returner.

Best game in the 1961 season: On April 30, he went 3–4 against the Cardinals while playing for the Phillies. Playing for the Indians, he went 3–4 against the Twins on July 16.

Card #179, Joe Koppe, batting stance, taken in Wrigley Field, Bobby Malkmus in the background. For some reason, Koppe reminds me of a young, more athletic, and less creepy-looking Steve Buscemi. Joe (who committed 595 errors during his 16-year career in pro ball) had a brother, Lawrence, who played in the minors for several years. An SR: A guy, Mr. Koppe died at 75 in 2006.

Best game in the 1961 season: Joe started the season with the Phils and then went to the Angels. He had three 3–4 games, but his best game was against the Indians on August 13, when he went 3–5 with a grand slam.

Card #180, Bobby Richardson, batting stance, in Yankee

2. The Quest for Fire

Stadium. He looks like a choir boy, which, according to everything I've ever read or heard, matches him perfectly. Terrific signer, SR: A+.

Best game in the 1961 season: On August 24, he went 5–5 against the Angels with two RBI.

Card #181, Fred Green, follow-through in Forbes Field. A scarecrowy-looking sort of fellow, all lean and lank, even in this photo he looks like his body joints are lubricated by WD-40.[29] His son, Gary, was also a major leaguer. An SR: A, he died at 63 in 1996.

Best game in the 1961 season: Fred threw three innings of scoreless relief against the Cardinals on May 28.

Card #182, Dave Nicholson, headshot. Born in the wrong era, he is a sterling example of today's "Three Perfect Outcomes" school of baseball thought. Possessor of an odd batting stance and a crescent-shaped swing (today he would be praised for his "launch angle"), he was also the possessor of awesome power, once hitting a ball completely out of Comiskey Park. He had been an SR: A signer before his death in 2023.

Best game in the 1961 season: Mr. Nicholson did not play in the majors in '61. He did, however, lead all Southern Association batters by a wide margin with 149 strikeouts.

Card #183, Andre Rodgers, headshot. The first Major Leaguer from the Bahamas (joined in '61 by the second, Tony Curry [see below]), he appears to be casting a longing eye back to the gentle climes of Nassau. He had three brothers who played in the minors, and he was a charter member of the Bahamas Sports Hall of Fame. SR: A (D: 2004).

Best game in the 1961 season: He went 3–4 against the Giants on August 9 with two runs and a two-run home run.

Card #184, Steve Bilko, head and shoulders shot in Henley Field. An archetype of the "fun" Polish uncle, the one who takes his sons and nephews to ball games, chugs beers at one of the many local *polskie kluby towarzyskie* and *zakony braterskie* (Polish social clubs and fraternal orders) in his neighborhood, and dances with his maiden aunts at festivals. Some Steve Bilko trivia: He led the PCL in homers three consecutive years, 1954–1956, clubbing 148 home runs and driving in 408 runs over that span while winning three consecutive

Searchin' for Toothpick Sam

MVP Awards (and the Triple Crown in 1955). The most popular player in Los Angeles history until Sandy Koufax became "Sandy Koufax," he was being paid more to stay in the PCL than he would have been making in the majors. A dependable signer, he was SR: A. Big Steve was only 49 when he died in 1978.

Best game in the 1961 season: On July 16 against the Senators, he went 3–4 with three runs and and a three-run home run.

Card #185, Herb Score, follow-through on a "pitch" in Comiskey Park, Dick Donovan in the background (and I'd bet a Jackson that that large fellow to his right rear is Ted Kluszewski). "For all sad words of tongue or pen/ The saddest are these: 'It might have been!'" (from John Greenleaf Whittier's 1856 poem "Maud Muller"). After I had read many articles published about Herb Score (none of which I can specifically remember), I asked him if it was either a subconscious fear of being struck by another line drive or a "coach's decision" to change his motion that kept him from ever approaching the pitcher he was before he was hit by Gil McDougald's line drive on May 7,

Big Steve Bilko won four home run and four RBI championships in the minors, including three in a row in the PCL with 37, 55, and 56 from 1955 to 1957. In 1956, he won the Triple Crown with a .360 batting average and 164 RBI to go with his 55 home runs. He also scored 163 runs that year and had a .453/.687/1.140 line. Steve is in the Pacific Coast League Hall of Fame.

2. The Quest for Fire

1957. He took the entire onus on himself, blaming his lack of success on the fact that he rushed back too soon and hurt his arm while pitching on a damp night, and then when he came back, he changed his motion and hurt his arm permanently. (His pre-line drive stats: 38–20, .655/2.63 ERA/547 Ks in 513 IP, 9.6/9; his post-injury stats were 17–26, .393/4.43 ERA/290 Ks in 346 IP, 7.6/9.) Mr. Score was the first pitcher in MLB history to both pitch in enough innings to qualify for the ERA crown and strike out more than one man per inning. Herb spent 34 years calling games for the Indians, from 1964 to 1997. An SR: A, this beloved Cleveland citizen passed away at 75 in 2008.

Best game in the 1961 season: On May 9, this shoulda-been Hall of Famer allowed only two hits in a 4–2 win over the Indians. He did walk six batters in the game.

Card #186, Elmer Valo, head and shoulders shot, Yankee Stadium. Oh my gosh, my initial reaction to this photo was almost exactly like the one I had for Steve Bilko just two cards back, the difference being that this Slavic uncle (in this case Czech rather than Polish) reads books rather than watching bowling on the television and reads the editorials in the newspaper rather than just the sports and comics. He was the opposite of Big Steve in another, more baseball way: whereas Steve struck out 19.8 percent of the time (per PA), Elmer's K rate was a mere 4.7 percent. Elmer also walked 15.5 percent of the time compared to Steve's not-bad 11.7 percent. By the way, the long-held, Red Smith–inspired myth of him playing for the A's in the last game of the 1939 season (which would have made him a "four-decade player") has been pretty much dispelled.[30] Some Elmer Valo trivia: he is the only player to be on both sides of a team's relocation to another city three times: Philadelphia-Kansas City; Brooklyn-Los Angeles; and Washington-Minnesota. One of the most popular players in Philadelphia's long sports history, he had an SR of A. Among the 10 youngest players twice and the 10 oldest four times, he was 78 when he passed in 1998.

Best game in the 1961 season: Splitting his season between the Phillies and the Twins, he was used as a pinch-hitter in all 83 of his games. On August 25, against the Braves, Elmer hit a home run.

Card #187, Billy Klaus, headshot, in Comiskey Park, member of

Searchin' for Toothpick Sam

the Crewcut Company, brother of major leaguer Bobby. He was the crabby neighbor who kept any spaldeens (or later on, your frisbees) which unfortuitously ended up in his yard. Including his years in the minors, he collected over 2,000 hits in pro ball. Mr. Klaus passed away at 77 in 2006. He was an SR: A.

Best game in the 1961 season: He went 3–4 and hit a home run against the Indians on June 29.

Card #188, Jim Marshall, head and shoulders shot, Wrigley Field; the cap is a Cubs cap with the intertwined SF superimposed upon it, and the uniform is a Cubs home uniform. Stranded in the

Billy Klaus finished second (to Herb Score) in the 1955 American League Rookie of the Year ballot. Between Japan, the minors, and the majors, he collected 2,063 hits and scored 1,070 runs in pro ball.

dismal, petite bourgeoisie backwater Podunk outback of San Francisco, Jim reflects back on his years in the Athens of the Midwest, Chicago. Jim hit over 200 homers in the minors before he finally got a shot at the Bigs and would hit 79 more in his three post–MLB seasons in Japan. In all, he hit 309 home runs in pro ball back when 300 homers was a very big deal at any level. SR: A.

Best game in the 1961 season: On June 16 against the Cubs, he stroked a pinch-hit home run.

Card #189, TOPPS BASEBALL CHECK LIST, 3rd Series. The Reds have Cubs rookie Ron Santo caught in a rundown between second and third in Wrigley Field. Pictured in addition to Santo are

2. The Quest for Fire

Reds shortstop Leo Cardenas, third baseman Gene Freese and, running to cover third, pitcher Jay Hook. There are two varieties of this card, and I have two signed type A, one signed by Hook and Santo and another signed by Bob Skinner (who may be the runner on the little B&W photo on the back), and one type B signed by Santo.

Card #190, Stan Williams, headshot, member of the Crewcut Company, photo taken in Memorial Coliseum. Stan is scanning the skies, hoping to see a plane pulling an *Angelyne* banner, apparently unaware that none would appear until 1984. A good signer and question answerer, SR: A+. "N.L. All Star 1960" is also written on the card.

Best game in the 1961 season: Stan threw a shutout against the Braves on June 17, allowing five hits and fanning 12.

Card #191, Mike de la Hoz, head and shoulders shot taken during Spring Training at Hi Corbett Field in Tucson. At the time one of the few players with a three-part surname, this youngster is definitely a man on the go! SR: A.

Best game in the 1961 season: Miguel went 4–5 against the Angels on July 15.

Card #192, Dick Brown, headshot taken in Yankee Stadium. He's trying to figure out if the nice-looking young lady behind the first base dugout is waving to him or his teammate Rocky Colavito. His brother, Larry, was in the majors for 12 years. Mr. Brown was only 35 when passed away in 1970, so I cannot comment on his signing proclivities.

Best game in the 1961 season: On April 29, he hit a grand slam against the Red Sox.

Card #193, Gene Conley, head and shoulders shot. Having spent a few seasons trying to guard Wilt Chamberlain in the key,[31] Gene was looking forward to the far easier task of facing hitters in the batter's box. An SR: A, Mr. Conley was 86 when he passed in 2017. He wrote "18.9 Rebounds/48 mins. NBA" for me.

Best game in the 1961 season: On September 12, he went all the way to beat the Orioles, 3–2, in 10 innings.

Card #194, Gordy Coleman, head and shoulders shot, taken in Wrigley Field. A three-sport star in high school (he led his high school to the state finals his senior year and got a football-basketball scholarship to Duke), he is smiling in almost any photo you find of him

Searchin' for Toothpick Sam

(except, of course, if he is up to bat in a game). He looks like the sort of fellow who, in high school, would befriend anyone, jock or nerd, cheerleader or wallflower. His cousin, Larry Littleton, also played in the majors. He was only 59 when he passed in 1994 and was an SR: A.

Best games in the 1961 season: Three games stand out in Gordy's fine ' 61 season. On June 17, against the Phillies, he went 4–5 with two home runs and four RBI. On July 2, he went 5–6 against the Braves, winning the game with a 13th-inning home run off Warren Spahn. On September 23, he went 3–4 with two homers and five RBI against the Giants.

Card #195, Jerry Casale, headshot, Comiskey Park. Tan him up, make his hair longer (and plastered with more "product"), give him an earring, some tats and gold chains and voila—*Jersey Shore*! A good hitter, he batted .216 with four homers in the majors and .252 with 14 more home runs in the Minors. This Brooklyn boy owned a bar for many years after his baseball career was over and died at 85 in 2019. SR: A.

Best game in the 1961 season: His best effort as a pitcher was two innings of scoreless relief with three strikeouts against the Senators on June 11. His best game at bat was a 2–2 day with a double, a home run, two runs, and two walks against his former team, the Red Sox, on May 9.

Card #196, Ed Bouchee, Chew Crew member, batting stance in Wrigley Field, seen here daring the ball boy to show him his best stuff. I really dig his long-sleeved green undergarment. An SR: A fellow, Mr. Bouchee was 79 when he died in 2013. Ed wrote "Rookie of the Year 1957 NL" for me.

Best games in the 1961 season: On July 21 he went 3–5 against the Cardinals with a double, a home run and three RBI. On September 18, against the Dodgers, he was 3–4 with a homer and three RBI.

(Here, instead of at card 177 where Series 3 started, is one of the color shift changes about which you will read more later.)

Card #197 Dick Hall, head and shoulders shot, taken in Yankee Stadium. Put a long, whitish-gray beard on him and change his baseball cap for a pointy cap and you have one of the two unnamed (at least in the common tongue) wizards of Middle Earth. In college

2. The Quest for Fire

at Swarthmore, he played five sports and excelled in them all. He had fantastic control, throwing just one wild pitch in his 16-year, 1,259⅔-inning major league career. In his nine seasons in Baltimore, he issued only 80 non-intentional walks in 770 innings, 0.94 per nine IP, and he gave up no earned runs in 8⅔ innings of post-season ball. He started his career in the majors as an outfielder, and he once hit 13 home runs in the old Western League. Before his death at age 92 in 2023, he had been an SR: A+.

Best games in the 1961 season: On April 27, he pitched a two-hit shutout against the Senators. On July 5, he tossed a four-hit, no-walk, nine-strikeout shutout against those same Senators. Overall in '61, Dick was 4–0 with an ERA of 0.29 in 30⅔ innings of work against Washington, allowing just 11 hits (3.2/9) and walking one batter every 10 innings for a BR/9 rate of 3.5/9, a fantastic rate indeed (that is, base runners per nine innings).

Card #198, Carl Sawatski, headshot, taken in Forbes Field. Take off the glasses, and he looks like the hero in one of those omnipresent 1955–1965 Westerns.[32] He hit 202 homers in the minors in only 3,029 AB and slugged .572. Having been an SR: A man, Mr. Sawatski died at 64 in 1991.

Best game in the 1961 season: Carl hit a three-run pinch-hit home run against the Reds on June 20.

Card #199, Bob Boyd, head and shoulders shot, taken in what appears to be Yankee Stadium. He looks like one of those wise old Black men of indeterminate age in so many movies shot in the 21st century. Already 30 when he first played in O.B., Rope (short for "Frozen Rope," so named for his wicked line drives) hit .320 in a minor league career that lasted until he was 44. SR: A, Mr. Boyd passed away at 83 in 2004.

Best game in the 1961 season: Bob went 3–5 with three runs against the Tigers on May 30.

Card #200, Warren Spahn, headshot, photo taken in Connie Mack Stadium. "Say … did anyone ever tell you that you look just like Warren Spahn?" A combat engineer, he earned a Bronze Star and a Purple Heart with Oak Leaf Clusters during World War II, and he was the only Major Leaguer to receive a direct commission during

Searchin' for Toothpick Sam

the war. He famously left the Remagen Bridge just moments before it finally collapsed into the Rhine (or moments before returning to it just before it collapsed, this is unclear). Without a World War II, he might have won 400 games. He hit at least one home run for 17 consecutive seasons and totaled 35 dingers. SR: A (D: 2003). He inscribed (although it's hard to read) "Remagen 1945" for me.

Best game in the 1961 season: Mr. Spahn had a batch of very good games this season, but his best was the no-hitter he threw against the Giants on April 28.

Card #201, Pete Whisenant, headshot. Oh my gosh! Burn my boots if he doesn't look like another one of them Western stars—the unflinching gaze, the rock-solid jaw, the determined demeanor.... SR: A, he died in 1996 at 66.

Best game in the 1961 season: After going 0–6 as a Twins pinch hitter, he got his first hit for the Reds on June 2 against the Cubs.

Card #202, Al Neiger, head and shoulders shot, taken in Jack Russelll Memorial Stadium. I'll be gosh darned if he doesn't look like "Lumpy" Rutherford's brother, Schlumpy.[33] SR: A.

Best game in the 1961 season: Mr. Neiger didn't play in the majors in 1961, but he pitched two shutouts in AA ball.

Card #203, Eddie Bressoud, follow-through of a swing. The light stanchion looks like those in Connie Mack Stadium. Oddly enough, the very first thought that came to mind when I most recently looked at this card was the old Bob Dylan song "Sad-Eyed Lady of the Lowlands." It hit me so hard that I couldn't at all remember what my first reaction to this card was. Weird. Must have been the mood I was in. Anyway, he was an SR: A before his death at 91 in 2023: A. His card has "AL All Star 1964" noted on it.

Best game in the 1961 season: Eddie went 3–4 with two runs against the Pirates on June 9.

Card #204, Bob Skinner, headshot. He looked like one of Santa's elves to me. His son, Joel, played in the majors for nine years. SR: A.

Best game in the 1961 season: On August 3, against the Cardinals, he went 3–6 with three doubles, scored four runs, and drove in three.

Card #205, Billy Pierce, follow-through of a "pitch," taken in Yankee Stadium. The portrait of a man who knows his craft. Billy was the only qualifying pitcher between 1948 and 1964 with an ERA under 2.00 (1.97 in 1955). An SR: A, Mr. Pierce died at 88 in 2015. At my request, Mr. Pierce wrote, "Only sub 2.00 ERA of the '50's/1.97 in 1955" on the card.

Best game in the 1961 season: His best game was an August 11 shutout of the Athletics. At bat, Billy went 2–4 against the Athletics with two RBI on May 13.

Card #206, Gene Green, headshot. "Say, as long as we're chatting, might I interest you in some fire insurance?" He was only 47 when he died in 1981, but he had been an SR: A.

Best games in the 1961 season: On June 27, he went 3–5 with two home runs and five RBI against the Indians, and on August 12, he hit a pinch-hit grand slam against the Yankees.

Card #207, *Dodger Southpaws*, Sandy Koufax and Johnny Podres. The two lefties pause in their discussion of pitching grips to take a moment to appreciate a glorious West Coast sunset.

Card #208, Larry Osborne, Chew Crew member, "fielding" a grounder in Briggs Stadium. "Bobo," who had won the Triple Crown in the American Association in 1960 (and also led in slugging average and on-base percentage), is *sure* that *this* is the year he makes his mark in the "Show." His dad, "Tiny," won 31 games in the majors. SR: A+, he died in 2011, aged 75.

Best game in the 1961 season: On September 25, he hit a two-run homer against the Athletics.

Card #209: Ken McBride (pictured still wearing his White Sox uniform), headshot in Comiskey Park. He is giving himself a final once-over in the mirror before going into the boss's office to ask for—no, *demand*—a raise. After all, wasn't he the one who had landed the McPherson account? A good signer, SR: A. Another "1962 Miracle Angels" notation.

Best games in the 1961 season: He threw a shut-out at the Indians on May 23, allowing only three hits, and on July 18, he struck out 11 Twins in a 4–1 victory.

Card #210, Pete Runnels, follow-through on a swing in Yankee Stadium. Pete looks like the kind of guy you'd see sitting on the porch with the other regulars at any crossroads county store in an historic photo from 1934. He had been a good signer, appearances notwithstanding. A former SR: A, Mr. Runnels passed away at age 63 in 1991.

Best game in the 1961 season: Pete had a 4–4 day against the Tigers on July 6. Over a 77-game stretch from July 2 until the end of the season, Pete hit .362 to raise his average from .245 to .317.

Card #211, Bob Gibson, headshot, in Sportsman's Park. Once again, I don't recall what my first impression of Mr. Gibson's portrait on this card was, for it has been clean pushed out of my mind by Grandmaster Flash & the Furious Five's classic "The Message" ("Don't push me/'cause I'm close/to the edge"). Gibson signed a few cards back in the '70s and then went the pay for play route (not that I blame him, as he sure wasn't getting paid what he was worth when he was pitching). Bob hit .206 with 24 homers. He also stole 13 bases and will almost certainly be the last pitcher to reach double figures in career swipes. He averaged 20.2 PPG playing basketball for Creighton.[34] SR (in the 1980s): C.

Mr. Gibson was 84 when he passed in 2020.

Best game in the 1961 season: His best day at bat was against the Dodgers on July 5, when he was 2–5 with a two-run homer. He also had four RBI against the Giants on August 26. His best pitching effort was a four-hit, 11-strikeout shutout he threw at Wrigley Field on May 21.

Card #212, Haywood Sullivan, headshot, taken in Yankee Stadium. Even then, he had the look of a man on an upward trajectory. An SR: A, he was 72 when he died in 2003. His son, Marc, played 137 games in the majors.

Best game in the 1961 season: He had a career day against the Twins on April 25, going 4–4 with three runs, a double, two triples, and five RBI. On May 7, he was hitting .415 with a .467/.707/1.074 OPS. From there until season's end, he hit .217 with an OPS line of .305/.317/.622. It looks like he saved the best for first.

Card #213, Bill Stafford, follow-through after a "pitch," taken during Spring Training (but not in Al Lang Field). It's one of those third series cards on which the photo has a painterly quality to it, which makes the 22-year-old Stafford look like a Pony Leaguer. The expression is querying, "Is that how it's done, coach?" (By the way, his

2. The Quest for Fire

son, Michael, was 10–5 with a 3.15 ERA in a four-year Minor League career.) SR: A, he died in 2001 at 63.

Best game in the 1961 season: He shut out the Indians on two hits on June 7.

Card #214, Danny Murphy, headshot taken at the deep end of an empty swimming pool. In the majors at 17, the dude looks like he totally thinks he's too cool for school. Well, whatever he thought, his SR is A. The coolest thing about Danny's career is the fact that, after bombing out as a hitter, in 1965 he began transitioning to pitching, and in 1969, seven years after his last Cubs trial, he made it back to the Bigs as a relief pitcher.

Best game in the 1961 season: Against St. Louis on September 27, he went 3–4 with three runs and two homers.

Card #215, Gus Bell, swing follow-through, Crosley Field, player in background is Ken R. Hunt. Well, way back when I was 13 (shortly after the invention of the wheel and just before man went into space), he just looked like a nice old guy to me. Now, he looks like a nice young fellow. This four-time All-Star was an SR: A before his passing at 66 in 1995. Today he is most noted for the fact that his son, Buddy, and his grandsons, David and Mike, followed him to the majors. (A third grandson, Ricky, got as high as AAA ball during his 10-year OB career.)[35]

Best game in the 1961 season: On June 21, he went 2–4 with two runs, two RBI, and a homer against St. Louis.

Card #216, Ted Bowsfield, headshot, Crewcut Company platoon sergeant. Assistant coach of a high school football team, he is mainly responsible for counting laps and making sure that none of the players drink any water during practice. Nevertheless, an SR of A.

Best game in the 1961 season: On June 7, he turned in a five-hit shutout against the Orioles.

Card #217, Mel Roach, headshot, in Wrigley Field. Roach was a fantastic high school athlete and a very good college one, but his major league career was marred by injury and was also quite odd: in his eight seasons (admittedly some with very few games), he hit .300 or better twice and under .200 the other six years. Looking at his photo, I'm thinking he's part of the tire-changing crew in a NASCAR pit. He had been an SR: A until his death in 2023 at age 90.

Searchin' for Toothpick Sam

Best game in the 1961 season: Playing for the Cubs and the Braves, his best game came as a Brave, when he pinch-hit a ninth-inning, two-out, game-tying three-run homer against the Phils on April 20.

Card #218, Hal Brown, headshot. He looks like an extra in Westerns. You know, the outlaw gang member with no lines or a local hanging around the smithy, a'grinnin' and a'spittin'. An SR: A, Mr. Brown died in 2015 at 93.

Best game in the 1961 season: "Skinny" threw three shutouts in '61, his best being a four-hit, no-walk gem against the Athletics on July 7.

Card #219, Phillies manager Gene Mauch, headshot. The grin could be from Monday, September 21, 1964, before the game begins, and the collapses of the Phillies' season. SR: A.

Card #220, Giants manager Al Dark, headshot. "Looziana" all the way. SR: A.

Card #221, Red Sox manager Mike Higgins, headshot, taken just after he said that Willie Mays had no potential of being a major league ballplayer. He passed away before I started getting my cards signed, but he proved to be very difficult to find, so I'm guessing that he wasn't a great signer.

Card #222, Indians manager Jimmie Dykes, foot on dugout step. Shown here wondering what his wife is fixing for supper. Mr. Dykes also passed away before my autograph collecting days began and has also proved hard to find, plus there seem to be a lot of fake Dykes-signed cards lurking about.

Card #223, Tigers manager Bob Scheffing, headshot. Shown here on the morning of July 25, 1961. On the morning of the 25th, before their game with the Angels, the Tigers had a one game lead on the Yankees. That was the last day they were in first place. Some he signed, some he didn't. SR: B, Mr. Scheffing died at 72 in 1985.

Card #224, Athletics manager Joe Gordon, head and shoulders shot. Although he was still living when I started assembling my signed set, he passed away (at 63 in 1978) before I shifted into get-'er-done mode, so I don't know if he was a good signer or not. Cards from '61 signed by him are rather hard to come by, though.

2. The Quest for Fire

Card #225, Giants manager Bill Rigney, arms on dugout railing. Shown here wishing he were at a dog track instead. SR: A, he died at 83 in 2001.

Card #226, Twins manager Harry "Cookie" Lavagetto, headshot. Someone has just asked him about Bill Bevens. In the World Series game between the Yankees and the Dodgers on October 3, 1947, Cookie pinch-hit with two outs in ninth to face Yankee pitcher Bill Bevens, who had a no-hitter going. Cookie rapped a game-winning single, handing Bevens the loss (Bill had walked 10 batters before facing Cookie). An SR: A, he was 77 when he passed away in 1990.

Card #227, Juan Pizarro, headshot taken in Wrigley Field. That is the smile of a guy who has aces full and knows that you have kings full. SR: A. Juan won 257 games and registered 3,025 strikeouts in OB.

Best games in the 1961 season: Juan had several outstanding games that year: a three-hit shutout against Kansas City on August 20, a 3–2 victory over the Indians on August 25 in which he recorded 13 strikeouts, and a no-decision against the Orioles in which he racked up another 13 Ks on September 29.

Card #228, New York Yankees Team card. Mine is signed by coaches Earl Torgeson, Frank Crosetti, Jim Hegan, and Johnny Sain. I also have a team card signed by non-carded players Jesse Gondor and Tom Tresh, one signed by Hal Reniff and Tom Tresh, and one signed by Jack Reed and Al Downing.

Card #229, Rudy Hernandez, head and shoulders shot. I think I saw him in *West Side Story*. A SR: A, he passed away in 2022.

Best game in the 1961 season: Rudy pitched two innings of scoreless relief against the Orioles on April 29.

Card #230, Don Hoak, follow-through on swing, Forbes Field. Hard as nails, he was only 41 when he died in 1969, long before I started collecting autographs, but since his signed cards are (or were) rather plentiful, it seems safe to say that Don was a willing signer.

Best game in the 1961 season: On May 21, Don went 3–6 with five RBI (including an inside-the-park home run) in a 13—11 win against the Phillies on May 21, despite the Phillies' nine-run third inning and seven-run lead.

Searchin' for Toothpick Sam

Card #231, Dick Drott, headshot, *Crewcut Company* member, photo taken in Wrigley Field.[36] Say, didn't I see you in *Hot Rod Gang* (1958, starring John Ashley, Jodie Fair, and Gene *"Be-Bop-A-Lu-La"* Vincent)? Or was it *Hot Rod Girl* (1956), starring Lori Nelson, John (*Laramie*) Smith and Chuck (*The Rifleman, Branded,* the Dodgers and the Celtics) Connors? *Hot Rod Rumble* (1957, starring Leigh *"The Creature Walks Among Us"* Snowden and Richard "The Next James Dean" Hartunian)? Oh well, I'm sure it was one of those. He died young (at 49 in 1985) but was an SR: A.

Best game in the 1961 season: On May 21, in the second game of a doubleheader, Dick started and threw seven scoreless innings in a game the Cubs eventually lost to the Cardinals.

Card #232, Bill White, head and shoulders shot in Sportsman's Park. Looks like he's giving a public service announcement telling the youth to "Stay in School." Kinda hit and miss when I started, then turned into a complete non-signer who kept both cards and checks. SR: F.

Best game in the 1961 season: Bill had four four-hit games in '61, with the best being his 4–5 against the Dodgers on July 5, in which he drove in four runs with three home runs and a double.

Card #233, Joey Jay, headshot, still in a Braves uniform, PFC in the *Crewcut Company*. A real heartthrob, he co-starred with Dick Drott (#231) in all those movies he wasn't in. As we all know, he was the first Little Leaguer to make the big leagues. At first, he was a hit-n-miss signer, but he seemed to improve with age. SR: B.

Best game in the 1961 season: Joey shut out the Phillies on May 4, and the only hit he allowed came in the first inning, a one-out single by Johnny Callison. For the season, he was 6–0 in six starts with two shutouts against Philadelphia and a 1.65 ERA.

Card #234, Ted Lepcio, fielding crouch, photo taken in Connie Mack Stadium. He's as pleased as punch just to be wearing the uniform. He was 90 when he passed in 2019. SR: A. I also have Lepcio signed "Sold to White Sox" and "Signed by Twins" cards.

Best game in the 1961 season: Ted played for the Twins and the White Sox in '61, with his best game coming for Minnesota on July

2. The Quest for Fire

23, when he went 3–4. He also hit a grand slam against the Indians on July 13.

Card #235, Camilo Pascual, head and shoulders shot in what appears to be Comiskey Park. He looks like he's thinking about a rum and coke, an eight-inch Cohiba, and a 1959 Chrysler Imperial Crown Southampton. Dude looks chill. SR: A.

Best game in the 1961 season: On July 19, Camilo shut out the Angels and recorded 15 strikeouts.

Card #236, Don Gile, bat on shoulder. Big Don looks like he was on his way to suit up for a Boston Patriots game but took a wrong turn. SR: A.

Best game in the 1961 season: Don's best game (of eight) came on September 23 against the Yankees, when he was 2–3 with a home run off Whitey Ford.

Card #237, Billy Loes, doing "something." Actually, it looks like he got caught doing a "package check." He sure looks like this isn't the photo he wants on his card. He was 80 when he passed away in 2010 and had been an SR: A.

Best game in the 1961 season: On May 7, he shut out the Phillies.

Card #238, Jim Gilliam, headshot in the Coliseum. Been there, done that. Only 49 when he passed away in 1978, he was a good signer. SR: A

Best game in the 1961 season: On June 27, he went 3–4 against the Pirates and scored two runs.

Card #239, Dave Sisler, headshot, appears as if it *may* be Yankee Stadium. Looks like he's doing his Peter Fonda imitation. It would've worked, too, if he had 1971 hair instead of 1961 hair. SR: A, he died aged 79 in 2001.

Best game in the 1961 season: His best outing was three hitless innings against the White Sox on June 10.

Card #240, Ron Hansen, batting crouch, looks like he's in a large, abandoned warehouse (or, as with so many other AL-ers in the '61 set, Yankee Stadium). To be honest, he looks like a 60-year-old guy on a seniors slow-pitch team. (By the way, check out those guns.) SR: A. The card is inscribed "1960 A.L.R.O.Y."

Best game in the 1961 season: On August 20, Ron went 4–5

Searchin' for Toothpick Sam

against the Angels with a home run and four RBI.

Card #241, Al Cicotte, headshot, somewhere in an open pit mine near Lusk, Wyoming (actually, though, in Municipal Stadium), looks like he's in his old Cleveland uniform, or perhaps even his Yankees duds: "Well, hel-lo, ladies." He was only 52 when he passed in 1982. SR: A.

Best game in the 1961 season: In Al's best game, he went seven innings against the Cubs on July 27 and gave up only one run on three hits.

Card #242, Hal W. Smith, head and shoulders shot complete with chest protector. He looks like he could be actress Dorothy Neumann's son. A good signer, SR: A before his death at 70 in 2020. It is inscribed "All Star Ohio-Indiana/LG 1950—A.A. 1954."

Best game in the 1961 season: Hal's best game was against the Braves on May 31, when he went 2–4 and scored twice.

Card #243, Frank Lary, headshot, if, as it appears, he's wearing his whites, in Briggs Stadium. His middle name was "Strong," and boy howdy, did he ever look it. He had a brother, Al, who reached the majors as a pitcher, and another brother Gene, also a pitcher, who reached Triple A. Known as "The Yankee Killer," he was 4–2 against them in '61. SR: A, he was 87 when he died in 2017.

Best game in the 1961 season: On April 14, Frank tossed a one-hit shutout at the White Sox in his first start of the season. In that game, Frank went 2–4 at the plate with a double and an RBI.

Card #244, "Chico" Cardenas, head and shoulders shot, taken in Crosley Field with Vada Pinson behind him. Leonardo looks sooo

2. The Quest for Fire

Above and opposite: **I was struck by the uncanny resemblance between Sisler and 1960s counter-culture movie icon Peter Fonda, depicted here as Wyatt in the classic film** ***Easy Rider.***

hungry in this image, and he's imagining there's a big platter of his mother's ropa vieja on a table in the dugout. A good signer, ranked SR: A.

Best games in the 1961 season: On September 20, he went 4–4 against the Pirates, and on August 24 he went 3–4 against the Giants with three runs and three RBI.

Card #245, Joe Adcock, head and shoulders shot, taken in Crosley Field. Slow, low, and rumbly, he's asking you if you *really* "wanna step outside." SR: A, before he passed away at 71 in 1999.

Best game in the 1961 season: Against the Cubs on May 9, Joe went 3–4 with three runs, three RBI, and two homers.

Card #246, Bob Davis, head and shoulders shot, taken in Yankee Stadium. "Eleanor, do you think that that nice young man might be the new youth pastor?" SR: A, when he passed away in 2001 at 68.

Best game in the 1961 season: Instead of pitching in 1961, Bob

Searchin' for Toothpick Sam

went back to Yale, eventually winding up with a degree in clinical psychology.[37]

Card #247, Billy Goodman, batting stance in Fenway Park. Laser-focused. SR: A (he died young [58] in 1984).

Best game in the 1961 season: Billy's best game was June 18, when he pinch-hit a two-run home run against the Twins to tie the game in the ninth inning.

Card #248, Ed Keegan, head and shoulders shot in Connie Mack Stadium. "It just might be time for our Ed's voice to start changing, don't you think, Maude?" An SR: A, he was 75 when he died in 2014.

Best game in the 1961 season: He pitched a hitless inning against the Indians on April 22 with a strikeout.

Card #249, Cincinnati Reds Team card. Mine is signed by coaches Dick Sisler, Reggie Otero, and Jim Turner. Another card is signed by non-carded players Darrell Johnson, Claude Osteen, John Edwards, and Joe Gaines, and a third is signed by minor league managers Cot Deal and a gent whose signature I cannot make out.

Card #250, *Buc Hill Aces*: Vern Law and Roy Face at Spring Training in Florida. It looks like they're watching Sandy Koufax and Johnny Podres (see note on card #207) watch the sunset. (And like they might have gotten a little too much sun themselves.)

Card #251, Billy Bruton, headshot in Braves uniform in County Stadium. Billy is seen here peering into the future, watching Manny Ramirez attempt to play the outfield, and thinking, "Man, I coulda caught that wearin' buckets on my feet!" SR: A, Mr. Bruton was 70 when he passed away in 1995.

Best games in the 1961 season: On June 23 against Cleveland, he went 2–5 with three runs, two home runs and four RBI. On May 17 against the Orioles, he went 3–5 with three runs. On August 24 against the Indians, he went 4–5, and on June 16 against the Yankees, he went 4–4 and scored twice.

Card #252, Billy Short, headshot taken in Yankee Stadium. Billy has just learned that he's been farmed out to Richmond—again.[38] Despite his many disappointments, he always signed for me, hence an SR: A before his death in 2022.

2. The Quest for Fire

Best game in the 1961 season: Mr. Short did not play in the majors in 1961.

Card #253, Sammy Taylor, head and shoulders shot in Wrigley Field. He looks like he's watching his kid ride a two-wheeler for the first time. SR: B, because early on, before I got "my" three signed cards, he switched to using an agency to handle his autograph requests. Mr. Taylor was 86 when he died in 2019. Is there something of a Native American cast to his looks? I know that many South Carolinians are proud to claim such in their way-backs.

Best games in the 1961 season: On July 2, he went 3–5 with two home runs against the Cards, and on June 27, he had a 4–4 day with three RBI and two homers against the Reds.

Card #254, Ted Sadowski, head and shoulder shot in Yankee Stadium, member of the Crewcut Company (and like Ken Hunt [above], he's one more missed haircut away from being drummed out of those hallowed ranks). "Yep, that milk's turned all right." SR: A. At his passing in 1993, he was only 57. He was Ed Sadowski's (Card #163) brother.

Best game in the 1961 season: His best game was on May 24, when he pitched three scoreless innings against the Tigers.

Card #255, Vic Power, batting stance, taken in Yankee Stadium. Since he's in the stadium of the team that thought he wasn't "Yankee material"[39] despite (A) his being one of the top two or three fielding first basemen of all time and (B) having hit .340 for the Yankees' top farm club in 1952–1953 with 89 doubles, 37 triples, scoring 210 runs, and driving in 202, it would seem only human for Vic to want some payback. I may be wrong, but that is what I see on his face. He passed at 78 in 2005, and his SR had been A.

Best games in the 1961 season: On Opening Day, he had a 4–5 game with two doubles against the Tigers. His best game against the Yankees was on May 19, when he went 3–4 and scored twice.

Card #256, Billy Hoeft, head and shoulders shot, taken in Memorial Stadium. I'm thinkin' that he's thinkin', "There's three of us and one of you. Whatcha gon' do now, big man?" Mr. Hoeft (SR: A) passed away at 77 in 2020. Mr. Hoeft honored my request by adding "A.L. All Star 1955/20 wins 20 hits 1956" to his signature.

Searchin' for Toothpick Sam

Best game in the 1961 season: On August 19, he threw a one-hitter against the Senators, a fifth-inning single.

Card #257, Carroll Hardy, headshot. If he doesn't look like Jack Armstrong, All-American Boy, no one does—check this out: 12 letters in three sports for the University of Colorado, and he played in the NFL. His SR is All-American also: A+. Mr. Hardy passed away at 87 in 2020. He inscribed, "Only man to pinch hit for Ted Williams" on his card.

Best game in the 1961 season: On July 20, he went 4–5 against the Indians.

Card #258, Jack Sanford, "looking in for a sign" in what appears to be Connie Mack Stadium. It looks like he's wondering if he should shake the bullpen catcher off. A reliable returner (SR: A), Mr. Sanford died in 2000 at age 70.

Best game in the 1961 season: Mr. Sanford beat the Cubs, 2–1, on May 16, allowing six hits and walking no one.

Card #259, John Schaive, headshot (with bat cocked). "When you're in Griffith Stadium/Don't go looking for any Ivy/Who's on second for the Nats?/Our very own Johnny Schaive/Burma Shave." Mr. Schaive was an SR: A before his passing at 75 in 2009.[40] A player I believe to be his son, John Wayne Schaive, played four years in the minors.

Best game in the 1961 season: John did not play in the majors in 1961.

Card #260, Don Drysdale, headshot, Memorial Coliseum. Thinking: "Really? You're gonna dig in on me? Really?"[41] One of the great HoF signers, Don earned his SR of A. He died at only 53 in 1993.

Best games in the 1961 season: On September 28, he shut out the Phillies and went 2–5 at the plate with a home run.

Card #261, Charlie Lau, head and shoulders shot, taken in County Stadium. What you are seeing is Charlie's response when he was asked by Lüćiéñ d'Sångfreud (pronounced "Song-fwa"), ace sports reporter for *Men's Wear Daily*, which "product" he uses on his eyebrows. He signed everything I sent him, so SR: A. He was only 50 when he passed in 1994.

Best game in the 1961 season: He played for Baltimore and

2. The Quest for Fire

Milwaukee in 1961, with his best game coming for the Orioles on September 4, when he went 2–4 with a home run and three RBI.

Card #262, Tony Curry, taking a practice swing in Connie Mack Stadium. The second major leaguer from the Bahamas, Tony *knows* that he has a home in the Bigs. Always a good signer, he rated an SR: A. A member of the Bahamian Sports Hall of Fame, he was 68 when he died in 2006.

Best game in the 1961 season: On April 13 against the Dodgers, he went 2–4 with two RBI.

Card #263, Ken Hamlin, headshot in Connie Mack Field. In this image, he is caught in that age-old teenage dilemma: Which one of the Delflorio twins should he ask to Homecoming? A fine returner, he is SR: A all the way.

Best game in the 1961 season: On May 2, he went 3–3 against Baltimore.

Card #264, Glen Hobbie, follow-through on a "pitch" in County Stadium. He was deadly serious about his craft, and he had the Eye of the Cub (don-don don). Mr. Hobbie, who passed away in 2013 at 77, was counted among the SR: A elite.

Best games in the 1961 season: On May 23, he pitched 10 innings in a 2–1 loss to the Phillies, and on May 19 he pitched a shutout against St. Louis.

Card #265, Tony Kubek, batting stance in Yankee Stadium. Who wouldn't have wanted to be Tony Kubek? (Well, OK, maybe Mickey Mantle was content with the gifts God gave him, but as for the rest of us…) I believe that he was the Major Leagues' first 6'3" shortstop, and I know that his dad played in Milwaukee when it was part of the American Association. A good signer, he now asks for a charitable donation to a worthy cause, so he is still an SR: A.

Best game in the 1961 season: He had 12 three-hit games in 1961, and on August 11, he went 4–6 and scored three runs against the Senators.

Card #266, Lindy McDaniel, follow-through on a "pitch" in Sportsman's Park (I believe that is Bill White in the background). Stolid, resolute and relaxed, the Pitching Preacher appeared on both the youngest and the oldest player seasonal lists. SR: A all the way, he died at age 85 while this book was in process. He and his brothers, Von and Kerry, each received $50,000 bonuses to sign with the Cardinals.[42]

Best game in the 1961 season: His best effort was three hitless innings against the Braves on Opening Day, April 11, earning the win.

Card #267, Norm Siebern relaxing, bat on shoulder, in Yankee Stadium. Norm seems to be casting his memory back to when he sat in that first base dugout, collecting World Series checks, going to Broadway shows, and livin' large in the Big Apple. SR: A.

Best game in the 1961 season: On May 30 against the Tigers, he went 3–4 with two homers and five RBI.

Card #268, Ike Delock headshot. Mr. Delock, owner of Delock's Barrows 'n' Baskets down on Main and Maple, took his job as a Little League sponsor and coach very seriously. His older brother, Joe, spent four years in the minors, mostly in the Boston system. Before his death in 2022, Mr. Delock was good signer, SR: A.

Best game in the 1961 season: On April 15, he threw a four-hit shutout against the Angels.

Card #269, Harry Chiti, squatting in Briggs Stadium, and that may be #4, Charlie Maxwell, behind him. Harry is sporting that bemused look that can only come from a player destined to be traded for himself.[43] An SR: A, Mr. Chiti died at 69 in 2002. His son, Harry Dominic Chiti, pitched six years in the minors and also coached in the Braves' minor league system for many years.

Best game in the 1961 season: He got his only hit of the season against Baltimore on April 30.

Card #270, Bob Friend, following through on a "pitch" in Forbes Field. The Warrior (nicknamed in high school) looks ready to wrassle a bear here. Always good for a returned item, he earned an SR of A. Mr. Friend died in 2019. He was 88. Inscribed on the card is "N.L. All-Star/1956–58–60."

Best game in the 1961 season: He threw 10⅔ innings in a 1–0 loss to the Cubs on August 20.

Card #271, Jim Landis, showing batting stance in what appears to be Yankee Stadium. His piercing glare imitates the hawk-like concentration on the field that led him to five Gold Gloves. His son,

2. The Quest for Fire

Craig, was a first-round draft choice in 1977. An SR: A club member, he died in 2017 at 83. Noted on the card is "Golden Glove/1960–64."

Best game in the 1961 season: Jim had a 4–4 game against the Tigers on June 5.

Card #272, Tom Morgan, headshot, foot soldier in the Crewcut Company, taken in Yankee Stadium. Many players in this set look much younger than they are, but our Tom looks about 20 years older than his 31 years. His SR rating was an A. Mr. Morgan died young at 56 in 1987.

Best game in the 1961 season: He tossed three hitless innings against the Tigers on July 23.

Card #273, TOPPS BASEBALL CHECK LIST 4th Series, featuring Cubs manager Lou Boudreau, Ernie Banks, Glen Hobbie, Don Zimmer, and Ron Santo arguing a call at second in a game against the Pirates in Wrigley Field, with Bob Skinner on second base. I have an "A" variety signed by Boudreau, Santo, Hobbie and Zimmer, a "B" variety signed by Hobbie, Zimmer and Santo, and a "C" variety signed by Skinner. After all, it's either a *complete* signed set or it's not. (The outfielder is almost certainly Richie Ashburn [he played center in 146 of the Cubbies' 154 games in 1960], but since I could be only 95 percent sure it was he, I did not have Mr. Ashburn sign it. I should've done it anyway.)

Card #274, Gary Bell,[44] follow-through on "pitch" in Yankee Stadium. A near-perfect "Aw shucks, ma'am, 'tweren't nothin'" shot, all that's lacking in a straw stalk in his mouth and a pair of suspenders hooked onto his belt. SR: A.

Best games in the 1961 season: He threw a 10-inning shutout against Baltimore on September 3 and struck out 10 batters in a four-hit, 7–1 victory over the Angels on May 24.

Card #275, Gene Woodling, head and shoulder shot (bat casually resting on his shoulder), wearing his Orioles road grays in Yankee Stadium. Looking every bit the grizzled veteran that he was, the wily old batsman could be counted on the infuse the younger players who gathered around him in the pre-game meetings with a sense of confidence that they too would be able to decipher and maul the opposing pitchers' puny attempts at dominating them. By the way,

Searchin' for Toothpick Sam

Gene's minor league BA in 631 games was a slightly more than dismal .348, and in three of the six years he spent in the bushes, he hit at least .375. Mr. Woodling, who died in 2001 at 78, was SR: A all the way.

Best game in the 1961 season: Gene went 4–5 against the Tigers on May 9 with a triple and a home run.

Card #276, Ray Rippelmeyer, winding up,[45] Al Lopez Field (Reds Spring Training site in Tampa). This card, like the Bill Stafford card, has a watercolor quality about it, and, like the Stafford card, takes 10 years off the player's appearance. Mr. Rippelmeyer won 114 games in the minors (you don't see that happening any more). Ray looks to be warming up prior to the start of his high school's JV game, hoping to impress the coach enough with his stuff to promote him to the varsity. SR: A. He inscribed, "III All-Star 1954/PCL All-Star 1960."

Best game in the 1961 season: Ray did not pitch in the majors in '61, but he did toss three shutouts for Indianapolis in the American Association.

Card #277, Hank Foiles, head and shoulders, wearing a Pirates uni and standing in front of the Forbes Field dugout. A grizzled vet in the Crewcut Company, he fought valiantly in the Clipper Wars. Ready for any assignment, Staff Sergeant Foiles is the one the raw recruits fresh out of basic barbershop bootcamp look to for advice. Hank is SR: A-rated. I am reasonably sure that his dad played in the old Virginia and Blue Ridge leagues back in the teens.

Best game in the 1961 season: He had a 3–4 day against the White Sox on September 24.

Card #278, Don McMahon, head and shoulders shot in what appears to be Wrigley Field. Don looks willing to admit that yes, he might have possibly grooved one to Ernie Banks, but, in the immortal words of Clarence "the unwinged angel" Oddbody,[46] "You don't need to make all *that* fuss about it!" Don, who was only 57 when he passed away in 1987, was a solid SR: A.

Best game in the 1961 season: On June 18, he pitched five scoreless innings against the Dodgers, and he repeated that performance against the Reds on July 2.

Card #279, Jose Pagan, waiting for a "grounder," Giants Spring

2. The Quest for Fire

Training facility. He looks to me like a fella who just found out that the Rolex he bought for twenty-five dollars just might not be genuine. Mr. Pagan, who passed away at 77 in 2011, was an SR: A guy.

Best game in the 1961 season: On April 30 he went 4–5 with three runs scored and two home runs against the Braves.

Card #280, Frank Howard, headshot, looks like he might be in Wrigley Field. "Don't make me angry. You wouldn't like me when I'm angry."[47] As an aside, Frank still holds the Ohio State single-game rebound record with 32. An All-American in basketball, he was picked in the third round of the 1958 NBA draft. Now, I know that that doesn't sound so great, but there were only eight teams in the NBA at the time, and even though he was a third-rounder, he was the 21st overall pick, which would make him a first-rounder today. Mr. Howard has signed everything I sent him, SR: A.

Best game in the 1961 season: Big Frank went 3–4 with two home runs and six RBI against the Cubs on April 29.

Card #281, Frank Sullivan, headshot in Yankee Stadium. (In your mind, imagine a Goofy voice here) "Garsh, Miss Daisy, evvy time Ah looks at you, Ah swar my heart just goes to a'poundin' and a'thumpin'." Frank, who died at 85 in 2016, was a SR: A. He earned the CIB for his service in Korea.[48] "A.L. all star/1955–56" is written on the card.

Best game in the 1961 season: On April 23, he pitched a shutout against the Cubs, and on May 23, he beat the Cubs, 2–1, on a four-hitter, accounting for two of his victories in an otherwise lost 3–16 season.

Card #282, Faye Throneberry, head and shoulders shot, proudly balding. A high school teacher, Mr. Throneberry is pursing his lips while listening to yet another student declaim, "Last night, Leland, Legrant and myself went to Pop's Burgers to get us some burgers, a Cocola, uh, and some twirly fries too also at Pop's Burgers, uh, last night." (By the way, Mr. Throneberry teaches English.) Marv's brother, he died at 67 in 1999. SR: A.

Best game in the 1961 season: On May 3, he went 1–1 with a walk, a double, and a run against the Orioles.

Card #283, Bob Anderson, head and shoulders shot down the

left field line at Wrigley Field. Fresh from the farm, our Bob was awed at seeing his first traffic light when he got to Cedar Rapids. Reportedly a fine man, Mr. Anderson passed in 2015 at 79, having been an SR: A.

Best game in the 1961 season: His best game came in a complete-game, 7–3 win over the Dodgers on September 19.

Card #284, Dick Gernert, headshot at the Tigers' Spring Training facility. He looks like a small-town cop looking askance at the gang of teenagers hanging out at Pop's Burgers (see above). Before passing at 89 in 2017, Mr. G was an SR: A guy.

Best game in the 1961 season: Playing for the Tigers and the Reds, his best day was on April 23, when his 10th-inning, pinch-hit home run tied the game against the Angels.

Card #285, Sherm Lollar, headshot in Comiskey Park. For some reason, this particular photo of Sherm reminded me of *The Twilight Zone* episode called "Hocus-Pocus and Frisby,"[49] in which he would have been one of the old gents sitting around the pot-bellied stove.[50] A seven-time All-Star, Mr. Lollar passed before I wrote to him (at 53 in 1977), but the (at the time) easy availability of finding '61s signed by him would lead one to believe that he was, indeed, SR: A.

Best game in the 1961 season: Against the Yankees on July 15, Sherm went 3–4 with a double and a home run.

Card #286, George Witt, follow-through of a "pitch," taken in Forbes Field. I don't know why, but for some reason, this is one of my top-10 favorite cards of the '61 set, and darned if he doesn't look like a chucker of some local repute pitching for the town team.[51] Before he died in 2013 at 81, Mr. Witt signed everything I sent to him. SR: A.

Best game in the 1961 season: he pitched a scoreless inning against the Dodgers on April 16.

Card #287, Carl Yastrzemski, head "shot" (this was another one of those watercolor-like cards), background indeterminate and impressionistic, exactly the same image as the one on his 1960 card. This particular card was one of the very few that left no impression on me. I will say that, back in the late '70s when I was sending him cards to sign, he signed each time, so, for me, SR: A. His son,

2. The Quest for Fire

George "Red" Witt served in the Marines during the Korean War. He was a teacher and coach at Tustin High School (California) after his baseball days were over.

Carl Michael, "Mike," played five years in the minors and reached Triple A ball. His grandson, Mike, as readers are no doubt aware, plays for the Giants.

Best game in the 1961 season: Yaz had four four-hit games in 1961, the best coming against the Angels on June 20, when he hit a home run and had five RBI.

Card #288, Albie Pearson, head and shoulders shot taken in Griffith Stadium. Impish indeed, he looks like the elf in charge of the doll section in Santa's workshop. (And lest the reader think that this writer is mocking Mr. Pearson's relatively diminutive size, I gladly inform you that I could only aspire to his listed 5'6½" height.) Mr. Pearson was SR: A all the way until his death in 2023. He obliged me by adding "A.L. ROY 1958/ A.L. All Star 1963" on the card he signed.

Best games in the 1961 season: Albie had 4–5 games on June 13 and 23, coming against the White Sox and the Orioles.

Card #289, Ray Moore, head and shoulders shot, Municipal Stadium. The exact opposite of Albie Pearson (immediately above), Ray seems dour and vaguely threatening. He never signed a single item I sent him (but I had that initial reaction to him before I even started sending out cards to get signed), so a well-earned (and thankfully rare) SR: F. Mr. Moore was 68 when he passed in 1995.

Searchin' for Toothpick Sam

Best game in the 1961 season: He went 5⅔ innings in the first game of a doubleheader on August 6, surrendering a lone run to the Yankees. Unfortunately, it was the losing run in the bottom of the 15th inning.

Card #290, Stan Musial, head and shoulders shot, *possibly* Crosley Field. My favorite player, one of my favorite '61s, and another "good" uncle card, the kind who would say, "Hey, Fred, how 'bout I take the kids to the beach and then out for ice cream" when he came to visit. Everybody loved The Man. SR: A, he died at 92 in 2013. His brother, Ed, played in the minors for four years and hit .299.

Best game in the 1961 season: Stan went 4–4 on June 7 against the Cubs with two home runs and four RBI.

Card #291, Tex Clevenger, headshot, one of the clearest images in the entire set (in fact, so clear that it looks out of place in this series), taken in Comiskey Park. I know that the picture was taken before the deed, but boy, he looks like he just heard that he got traded to the Yankees. He was SR: A before his demise in 2019 at age 87.

Best game in the 1961 season: Tex was indeed traded to the Yankees from the Angels, and his best game was his first as a Yankee: four innings

A little-known fact: The great Stan Musial was 33–13 as a pitcher in the minors before hurting his arm. In 1959, after 17 seasons of hitting over .300 and with a .331 career average, Stan hit. .255. Coincidentally that same year, Ted Williams, after hitting over .300 17 straight seasons and with a career .344 average, hit .254.

2. The Quest for Fire

of one-hit relief against the Athletics on May 10 and an RBI double in the rally that made him the winning pitcher.

Card #292, Jim Baumer, headshot in the same pool as Danny Murphy (see above). Another of my favorite cards, mostly because I appreciated the fact that, after appearing in eight games as an 18-year-old for the White Sox in 1949 (he signed with the White Sox for $50,000 just a few days before the Yankees signed Mickey Mantle for $1,500), he toiled in the minors for 11 more years before getting a 10-game look as a 30-year-old with the 1961 Reds. Think about it—he went the entire 1950s without appearing in a major league game and yet never gave up. He is one of the very few players to have an entire decade (or more) go past between playing in major league games. He also spent two years in the service during the Korean War, but, to my sadness and embarrassment, my internet search skills were not up to the task of finding any details of his service. In all, he spent 17 years playing professional baseball, the last five in Japan. He collected 1,991 hits in the minors and Japan and hit 180 home runs. He was an SR: A, and he passed away at 66 in 1996.[52]

Best game in the 1961 season: Jim went 1–2 against the Cardinals on April 15.

Card #293, Tom Sturdivant, headshot, photo taken in Fenway Park. In this image (and none other that I have ever seen of him), he looks like a riverboat gambler, one who might have been seen matching wits with one of the Maverick boys. Before his death at 78 in 2009, he signed every card I sent, thus SR: A.

Best games in the 1961 season: Tom played for the Pirates and the Senators in '61, and his acme performance of the year was a one-hit shutout against Boston on May 13. He also pitched a complete-game, 10⅓-inning 1–2 loss to the Cubs as a Pirate on August 18.

Card #294, Don Blasingame, ready to field a grounder. I really like this card because it captures the intensity with which Don approached the game. Between the majors, the minors and Japanese ball, he collected 2,209 hits. He was an SR: A class signer who was 73 when he died in 2005.

Best game in the 1961 season: Traded from the Giants to the Reds in late April, he went 4–5 against the Cardinals on June 10.

Searchin' for Toothpick Sam

Card #295, Milt Pappas, headshot. Going into his fifth year of major league ball at only 22, he was the first pitcher to win at least 200 games without a 20-win season. In fact, his high win season was only 17 (twice), coming in his 14th and his 15th seasons in the majors. He was also one NL win away from joining the exclusive post–1901 100 wins in both leagues club. As for the photo on the card, well ... let's just say that Milt was one win away from joining the exclusive post–1901 100 wins in both leagues club. As far as his signing habits, he was SR: A to the end (he was 76 when he died in 2016). Milt had some pop in his bat and hit 20 homers during his career.

Best game in the 1961 season: On August 27, he shut out the Twins with 11 strikeouts and also hit two home runs.

Card #296, Wes Covington, taking a bat out of the rack *during a game*, the *only* in-game photo on any individual's card in the entire set. This is my favorite card in the set, partially for its honesty but mostly for the look on Wes's face. Priceless. How good a signer was he? Well, he played on four, count 'em, four, teams during the 1961 season (see below). I had cards made of him in the uniforms of the other three teams he played for, and he signed them all. Wes was an SR: A+ and passed away at 79 in 2011.

Best games in the 1961 season: Best game for

Wes Covington's high school had no baseball team, so he ran track instead. He was also twice an All-State football player and received offers from UCLA and North Carolina.

2. The Quest for Fire

Milwaukee: 2–4 against the Pirates on April 12. Best game for the White Sox: 2–4 on May 19 against Boston. Best game for the Athletics: Game-winning, ninth-inning, pinch-hit home run against the Yankees on June 19.

Card #297. Kansas City Athletics team card. My card is signed by coaches Jo Jo White, Dario Lodigiani, Ed FitzGerald, Ted Wilkes, and instructor Johnny Mize. I also have a team card signed by non-carded players Dan Pfister, Jay Hankins, Bill Kirk, and Stan Johnson, another signed by Norm Bass, Wayne Causey, and Dan Pfister, and a fourth signed by scout Hillis Layne, who hit .335 over 17 minor league seasons.

Card #298, Jim Golden, showing us his curveball grip. This man is not fooling around. It's almost as if he's showing it to the batter during a game and saying, "Hit it if you can." A terrific card, and Mr. Golden is a terrific signer. SR: A.

Best game in the 1961 season: Two scoreless innings against the Pirates on April 14.

Card #299, Clay Dalrymple, squatting, during Spring Training in Jack Russell Stadium. He doesn't look particularly anxious to receive the pitch. He was a good catcher vs. the

Selected by the Colt 45s in the postseason expansion draft of 1961, Jim Golden went 7–11 with 4.07 ERA for Houston in 1962, including 4–0 against the pitiable Mets, against whom he posted a 2.51 ERA. (He also battered them at the plate, hitting .357 with six RBI while slugging .714.) Golden was also the last pitcher to hit two triples in a game when he accomplished that feat against the Mets on June 22, 1962.

Searchin' for Toothpick Sam

steal, throwing out 49 percent of the runners who tested his arm. SR: A.

Best game in the 1961 season: On June 6, he had a 3–4 game against the Giants with five RBI.

Card #300, Mickey Mantle, bat on right shoulder in Yankee Stadium. I never looked that confident about anything on any day of my life. I got his signature on the six cards he appeared on in the '61 set (AL HR Leaders, individual card, W.S. Home Run, MVP, 565' Home Run and All-Star) at a show. Mr. Mantle died in 1995 when he was 63. His twin brothers, Ray and Roy, and his cousin, Maxie, played in the minors.

Best games in the 1961 season: The Mick had five-four-RBI games and three five-RBI games. He had eight two-home-run games. He had five three-walk games. But for pure "you are wise to fear me" Mantleness, I am choosing his game against the Senators on July 2, when they walked him four times, and then, already behind 11–2 in the eighth inning, they pitched to him and he hit a home run.

Card #301, Chet Nichols, headshot in what *looks* like Scottsdale Stadium. Perhaps the most school-teacherly image of the entire set (if this were a cricket card, I'd describe him as an "Anglican parson from North Yorkshire, serving perhaps in Osmotherley, perhaps in

Mickey Mantle, here looking much as we might imagine a Greek statue of the God of Baseball would.

Ainderby Quernhow"). Chet won the AL ERA crown as a rookie. He had his father Chet's nose (figuratively, not literally) and set of mouth, but he was definitely rounder of face. Chet Senior was 1–8 with a 7.19 ERA over his six-year career. Chet Junior was a good signer. SR: A, he was 64 when he died in 1995.

Best game in the 1961 season: He turned in an almost Ernie Shore–like[53] appearance on August 6. Replacing starter Galen Cisco with one out in the first inning, Chet went the remaining 8⅔ innings, giving up only one run to the Athletics to earn the win.

Card #302, Al Heist, headshot in Wrigley Field. Al played 11 years in the minors before finally making it to The Show at age 32. When his major league career was over, he played three more years in the minors, giving him 14 years total in the Bushes, including the last nine years in the PCL, far from his Brooklyn birthplace. Al's card is another of the (few) cards where the player looks older than he is, and in his case, he looks like one of the gunsels from the HBO series *The Sopranos*. He was a reliable SR: A type and died at age 78 in 2006.

Best game in the 1961 season: In the second game of a doubleheader against the Pirates on July 6, Al went 3–3 with two runs and three RBI.

Card #303, Gary Peters, "follow-through" in Yankee Stadium. He was a more typical opposite of Al Heist (see immediately above) in that he appeared younger on his card than he actually was. He presents as another high school JV pitcher hoping to impress the coach. Gary pulled off the unusual trick of having three rookie cards (he would have had four, but Topps didn't bother to print one of him in the '62 set).[54] Gary was quite the hitter, averaging .222 over his career with 19 homers and 102 RBI, including five seasons with double figures in RBI. He was used as a pinch-hitter 77 times, slamming four homers and driving in 13 runs. Mr. Peters had been an SR: A until his death in 2023. He added "1963 AL ROY/A.L. All Star 1964 & 1967" to his signature.

Best game in the 1961 season: On September 26, he threw three hitless innings against the Red Sox.

Card #304, Rocky Nelson, batting stance in Forbes Field, Grand Majestic Bhagwan of the Chew Crew. Now, that's what a ballplayer was supposed to look like, I tell you what. My gosh, what's not to love about this image (aside, of course, from the pukingly[55] disgusting habit itself)? Rocky won two Triple Crowns in the AAA-level International League. As far as his signing habits are concerned, he was SR: A all the way. He died aged 81 in 2006.

Best game in the 1961 season: Rocky had a 3–3 game with a three-run home run against the Reds on May 12.

Card #305, Mike McCormick, wind-up, Candlestick Park. Egads! Someone tell that boy to get out of the sun. Really, Mike looks about three minutes away from the shift from pink to rouge. He is a good signer, strictly SR: A. The note on his card reads, "Pitched @ 17 in Natl League."

Rocky Nelson won three batting titles, three RBI titles, and three home run titles in the minors, including two Triple Crowns! In 1955 he led the International League with 37 homers, 130 RBI and a .364 average; in 1957, with 43 homers, 120 RBI and .326 average. No surprise, then, that Rocky is in the International League Hall of Fame.

Best games in the 1961 season: Mike had two three-hit shutouts in '61. The first was against the Phillies on April 14, and the second was against the Pirates on May 10. In the latter game, he also fanned 10 opposing batters. The Giants also got only three hits, but they all came in the fifth inning, including a two-run single by Mike himself.

Card #306, 1960 World Series/Virdon Saves Game, Game 1 in Forbes Field, featuring Bill Virdon, Bob Skinner, Bill Mazeroski, and umpire Bill Jackowski. My card is signed by Virdon and Skinner as well as Vern Law, the winning pitcher, and Roy Face, who saved it.

Card #307, 1960 World Series/Mantle Slams Two Homers,

2. The Quest for Fire

Game 2 in Forbes Field, featuring Mickey Mantle, Smoky Burgess, and umpire John Stevens. I have one signed by the Mick and another signed by Bob Turley, Bobby Shantz, and Bobby Richardson.

Card #308, 1960 World Series/Richardson Is Hero, Game 3 in Yankee Stadium, featuring Bobby Richardson, Hal Smith, and umpire Bill Jackowski. My card is signed by Bobby Richardson and Whitey Ford.

Card #309, 1960 World Series/Cimoli Safe in Crucial Play, Game 4, featuring Tony Kubek and Gino Cimoli in Yankee Stadium. Mine is signed by Vern Law, Roy Face, Gino Cimoli, Gil McDougald, and Moose Skowron, I have another signed by Vern Law and Bill Virdon, and a third signed by Tony Kubek.

Card #310. 1960 World Series/Face Saves the Day, Game 5 in Yankee Stadium. My card is signed by Harvey Haddix and Roy Face.

Card #311, 1960 World Series/Ford Pitches Second Shutout, Game 6, featuring Whitey Ford, umpire John Stevens, and an unidentified Pirates player in Forbes Field. My card is signed by Whitey Ford, Bobby Richardson, and Yogi Berra.

Card #312, World Series/Mazeroski's Homer Wins It! Game 7, in Forbes Field, featuring Mazeroski, Hal Smith, Dick Schofield, Gene Baker, Danny Murtaugh, Mickey Vernon, umpire Bill Jackowski, and Bob Skinner. I have one signed by Bill Mazeroski, Hal Smith, Roy Face, and Moose Skowron, another signed by Mazeroski, Harvey Haddix, and Rocky Nelson, another signed by Dick Schofield, Bob Skinner, and Bob Friend, and a fourth signed Bill Mazeroski and Ralph Terry.

Card #313, 1960 World Series/The Winners Celebrate, in the Pirates' locker room. Mine is signed by Bill Mazeroski and Gino Cimoli.

Card #314, Bob Miller, follow-through on a "pitch," Bill White and Lindy McDaniel in the background. A keen young Robert is determined to show that he is worthy of the trust placed in him by his elders. (My card is signed by all three players.) Mr. Miller was only 54 when he passed in 1993. SR: B-.

Best game in the 1961 season: On June 25, he allowed only one run in seven innings against the Giants. Between April 17 and June

25, Bob had an ERA of 1.72 and lowered his ERA from 15.43 to 2.67, lowering his ERA in 14 of the 16 games he pitched during that span.

Card #315, Earl Battey, headshot in Yankee Stadium. Earl is casting a jaundiced eye on the pigeon loitering dangerously close to his catching gear. He too was an SR: A, and he passed away in 2003 at 68.

Best game in the 1961 season: On July 9, he went 3–4 against the Senators with two home runs and three RBI.

Card #316, Bobby Gene Smith,[56] head and shoulders shot in Jack Russelll Stadium. Looking more than vaguely pugilistic, Bobby Gene wants to know just exactly who it was that let the dogs out. His SR before his passing at 81 in 2015 was A.

Best game in the 1961 season: Bobby Gene had a 3–3 game against the Pirates on September 23.

Card #317, Jim Brewer, headshot taken in Rendezvous Park. In this image, I see the owner of a friendly neighborhood tavern that serves a passable brat and a noted local brew. Although he was a fine reliever for 12 years with the Dodgers (2.62 ERA in 474 games), he is most famous for being assaulted by and then suing Billy Martin. SR: A, he was only 50 when he passed away in 1987. Dave spent three and a half years as an M.P. during the war.

Best game in the 1961 season: On June 22, Mr. Brewer gave up just one hit in three innings against the Dodgers.

Card #318, Danny O'Connell, headshot. The only player who comes to mind that looks more Irish is Danny Murtaugh. Mr. O'Connell passed away before I started getting my cards signed, but since they were relatively easy to find, I'd guess that he was an SR: A. He was only 40 when he died in 1969.

Best game in the 1961 season: Danny went 3–5 with four RBI against the White Sox on September 2.

Card #319, Valmy Thomas, head and shoulders shot; the photo is from 1959, when he was a Phillie, and was taken in Connie Mack Stadium. He looks as if he has just been challenged to a limbo-off by Smoky Burgess. The first Virgin Islander to play in the majors, he called five different cities home in his five-year career (two of them being the New York–San Francisco shift). His rating is a hard one to figure. I heard that he was a virtual non-signer, but he responded to

2. The Quest for Fire

my first two mailings. After that, however, I never got a return from him, so SR: B-. He died in 2010, when he was 84.

Best game in the 1961 season: On September 30, Valmy went 2–5 with a home run against the Angels.

Card #320, Lou Burdette,[57] headshot in what looks like LECOM Park. A very good pitcher (203 wins), during one nine-year stretch, he won 157 games, including two 20-win seasons. In this photo, he looks more like an accountant, the front man at an auto-parts store, or a bank teller than a ballplayer, but that just goes to show you. His name was Selva *Lewis* Burdette, so his card should have said Lew Burdette. Oddly, up until the 1959 set, he *was* referred to as Lew, but then Topps shifted to the incorrect Lou for some reason. He signed his name Lou. I wonder why. Easier to write? He was a solid SR: A. Mr. Burdette was 80 when he passed in 2007.

Best game in the 1961 season: Selva pitched a two-hit shutout against the Reds on July 25. He got two hits in a game five times in '61, his best coming against the Dodgers on May 15, when he went 2–4 with a home run and three RBI.

Card #321, Marv Breeding, batting stance. He looks like the "thin but wiry" type, the fellow who will not go too far out of his way to afford a fight. I can picture him in cuffed jeans and an oil-stained tee shirt working on a '54 Pontiac. His SR was A, and he passed away in 2006 aged 72.

Best game in the 1961 season: On September 24, Marv went 3–4 in the first game of a doubleheader against the White Sox.

Card #322, Bill Kunkel, "looking for a sign" in what appears to be Centene Stadium in Great Falls, Montana, one of the watercolor-like images. The not-so-well-defined look on his face appears to be registering skepticism at his catcher's choice of pitches. Bill was an A.L. umpire from September 1968 until August 1984 and was behind the plate for two no-hitters, Nolan Ryan's third and the 1975 Oakland oddity in which four pitchers (Vida Blue, Glenn Abbott, Paul Lindblad, and Rollie Fingers) combined to complete the gem. He was one of the last umpires to wear his chest protector outside of his uniform. In addition, he was a ref in the NBA during the 1966–1967 and 1967–1968 seasons, as well as in the ABA for the 1968–1969 season. His son, Jeff, played in the majors, and he had two grandsons (Jeff and Kevin) who played minor league ball. He was an SR: A guy who was only 48 when he died in 1985.

Best game in the 1961 season: Mr. Kunkel threw four innings of one-hit ball at the Indians on May 27.

Card #323, Sammy Esposito, follow-through on a "swing" in Yankee Stadium. I know that readers may think that I was influenced solely by his last name, but the face on this card belongs to an Italian fisherman from one of the islands south of Sicily. By the way, Sammy once scored 81 points in a high school basketball game. Jim Rivera was in the background of the card, and he signed it also. Esposito's SR rating was A.[58] He died aged 86 in 2018.

Best game in the 1961 season: He went 1–3 with a home run against Boston on September 26.

Card #324, Hank Aguirre, follow-through on a "pitch" in Yankee Stadium. A serious-looking young man, he was well-known in his day for being a terrible hitter, as he struck out in 61 percent of his at-bats. Hank was an SR: A sendee until his death at 63 in 1994.

Best game in the 1961 season: Mr. Aguirre pitched three innings of hitless relief against the White Sox on May 7.

Card #325, Wally Moon, follow-through on swing. Frida Kahlo in a baseball uniform, he was an SR: A until his death in 2018 when he was 87.

Best game in the 1961 season: Wally had four four-hit games in 1961, the best of which came in the first game of a doubleheader against the Reds, when he went 4–5 with two doubles and four RBI.

Card #326, Dave Hillman, head and shoulder shot, probably taken in Yankee Stadium. He looks like a dryland farmer in Kansas during the Dust Bowl Era on the day his well ran dry. He was an SR: A until his death at age 95. He pitched two no-hitters in the minors, a fact he mentioned on his card.

Best game in the 1961 season: On two occasions, Dave pitched 6⅔ innings of three-hit, scoreless ball. The first was against the White Sox on April 23, and the next was April 27 against the Tigers.

Card #327, Matty Alou, waiting for a "play" in Scottsdale

2. The Quest for Fire

Stadium. Forget the JV high schoolers—this young man has dreams of going to Williamsport![59] Matty was an SR: A returner until passing away in 2011, when he was 72.

Best game in the 1961 season: On July 25, Matty went 4–4 with four RBI against the Pirates, against whom he hit .459 in 1961.

Card #328, Jim O'Toole, windup, Crosley Field. A veritable picture of concentration, young master James had his mind set on dispatching the opposing batsman or fail with grit and a steely resolve to do better next time. (His brother, Denny, got a near-record five cracks at sticking with the Chisox from 1969 to 1973, but his 15-game totals included a 5.04 ERA and a 1.74 WHIP.)[60] Jim was an SR: A. He was 78 when he died in 2015.

Best game in the 1961 season: Jim tossed a two-hit shutout against the Dodgers on August 16—and a 10-hit shutout against the Phillies on June 18.

Card #329, Julio Becquer, head and shoulders shot, probably in Yankee Stadium. A sober and self-contained Julio reflects on what he could have done better when he took the mound for the Senators.[61] Mr. Becquer passed away at 87 while I was working on this, having been an SR: A.

Best game in the 1961 season: Julio played for the Twins and Angels in '61. with his best game coming as a pinch-hitter on June 20 when he hit a ninth-inning, walk-off home run against the Orioles.

Card #330, Rocky Colavito, batting stance. Like a cobra, Rocky was ready to unleash his whip-like swing as soon as he saw a pitch he liked. The Rock made female fans swoon and opposing pitchers swallow their gum. He was the owner of an absolute gun. I remember seeing him at one of the old Crackerjack Old Timer games in RFK Stadium, and when a ball was hit out to him with a man on base, the crowd as one held their breath, waiting for his cannon to fire. Alas, poor Rocky threw it straight into the ground, and you could feel the crowd deflate. He signed the first few times I sent items to him, but then quit, period. SR: D.

Best game in the 1961 season: In a career season, the Rock had many good games, but his best in '61 was a 3–5 game against the

Senators on August 27 in which all three hits were home runs and he drove in six runs.

Card #331, Ned Garver, headshot in Yankee Stadium. "Yes sir, for just $50 down and $35 a month for 10 months, you could drive this little beauty right off the lot."[62] In 1951, Ned became the first pitcher to win 20 games for a team that lost 100 games (while also hitting .305).[63] Former Reds and Mets pitcher Bruce Berenyi is his nephew. An SR: A man, Garver was 93 when he passed away in 2017. He added "20 wins .305 BA/Last place 1951 St. Louis Browns."

Best game in the 1961 season: On April 30, he threw 5⅔ scoreless innings against the Athletics.

Card #332, Dutch Dot-terer, headshot, taken during Spring Training. Actually, it's not Henry "Dutch" Dotterer, it's his brother, Tommy. Dutch's dad played pro ball for a couple of years, and Dutch's brother, also a catcher and the one pictured on the card, played in the Reds' system for eight years, reaching AAA ball. Pretty slick, if you ask me. Dutch (and Tommy) both signed everything I sent them, and I often wonder how many other collectors have a '61 Topps Dutch Dotterer signed by Tommy.

Best game in the 1961 season: Dutch went 2–4 against the Indians on April 16.

As they used to say in Cleveland, "Don't knock the Rock." Rocky Colavito finished in the top ten in MVP voting four times and played in nine All-Star Games. Cleveland's attendance dropped by 541,000 after he was traded, then rose by 282,000 when the Indians reacquired him.

2. The Quest for Fire

Card #333, Fritz Brickell, fixin' to toss the old pea, looks like in, I wanna say Central Park? Definitely looking like another Little Leaguer, he stood a towering (to me) 5'5". His dad played in the majors and, after his father passed away at the comparatively young age of 54, his mother (eventually) married Hall of Famer Burleigh Grimes. Fritz himself, an inveterate plug chewer, was only 30 when he died in 1965 of jaw cancer. As can be well imagined, finding a signed '61 Brickell is *extremely* difficult. In my 45 years of trying, I've only managed to procure two such cards.

Best game in the 1961 season: Fritz went 1–3 with a run scored and an RBI against the Yankees on April 20.

Card #334, Walt Bond, head and shoulders shot. Bond. Walt Bond. He left pitchers shaken, not stirred. The look on his face says that not only can I take you yard, but I can take you to the hoop as well. The 6'7" Bond was second only to Gene Conley on the 1961 Height Parade. He was only 29 when he died of leukemia in 1967.[64] As to his signing habits, I cannot comment, because I have had four Bond signed (?) '61s, all identical, garnered over a period of two decades, and I have seen two others, also identical. I have the above "(?)" because either they were signed by Mr. Bond or someone, back in the '70s, got himself a bunch of 1961 T #334s and signed them, hoping to make a killing 30 years down the road.

Best game in the 1961 season: In the first game of a season-ending October 1 doubleheader against the Angels, Walt had a career day, going 4–5 with a triple, a grand slam, three runs, and five RBI.

Card #335, Frank Bolling, head and shoulder shot, taken in Briggs Stadium: "I assure you, madam, your husband will feel very comfortable resting in eternal peace in his plot in Holy Angels Blissful Heavenly Rest Memorial Gardens." His uncle Jack and his brother, Milt, both played in the majors. Mr. Bolling passed away in 2020 aged 88, having been an SR: A club member. Frank added "all-star 1961–62" to his signature.

Best game in the 1961 season: Frank had nine three-hit games in '61. He also had a four-hit game against the Giants on September 19 with a home run included.

Card #334, Don Mincher, head and shoulder shot, unidentifiable location: "Ya know, there's a heckuva lot more to raisin' chickens than jes' throwin' some feed about." At one time (and possibly still), Don held the record for fewest RBI despite 200 or more career home runs. Don (SR: A) was 73 when he passed away in 2012.

Best game in the 1961 season: On May 11 against Baltimore, Don went 3–3 with a home run and scored three runs.

Card #335, *Al's Aces*, Early Wynn, Al Lopez, and Herb Score, taken in Comiskey Park. All three were good signers.

Card #335, Don Landrum,[65] head and shoulders shot, taken in Sportsman's Park. This photo makes it look like Don may have lifted weights, but I doubt it, since managers, coaches and trainers were so dead set against it. Don died at 66 in 2003 and had been SR: A rated. He wrote on his card, "Eastern League All-Star 1956/Int'l League All-Star 1960."

Best game in the 1961 season: On May 12, Don went 2–5 with a home run and scored two runs against the Phils.

Card #339, Gene Baker, follow-through on a swing, down the left field line in the single-stanchion field that has me stumped. In this image, he looks like the Babe watching one of his mammoth shots leaving, not just the field, but the stadium itself. (Of course, I know that the Babe was a lefty, but you get the idea.) Gene and Ernie Banks were the first black DP combo in the majors back in 1953, and he became the first (or possibly the second, as Nate Moreland *may* have managed Mexicali in the Southwest League for a spell back in the early 1950s) black manager in OB when he took over the reins in Batavia in 1961. In '62, he became the first black coach in OB for the Columbus Jets, and a year later he became the second black coach in the Majors, following in the footsteps of the beloved Buck O'Neil, who coached for the Cubs. Mr. Baker was 74 when he passed away in 1999. SR: A.

Best game in the 1961 season: Mr. Baker went 1–2 against the Cubs on April 19.

Card #340, Vic Wertz, taking a low "throw" in an unidentified stadium/field/park. Take away the glove, put him in overalls, and exchange the baseball cap for a straw hat, and he's hoeing his garden. Change the overalls for waders, the straw hat for a nor'wester,

2. The Quest for Fire

and he's clamming in Maine. Lose the hat altogether and put him in a cheap suit and he's playing pool on a table with six-inch legs. I believe that he still holds the record for the fewest runs scored (45) in a season with 100-plus RBI. Mr. Wertz died in when he was only 58 in 1983, but he had been an A+ signer.

Best games in the 1961 season: On June 15, against the Tigers, Vic went 1–3 and hit a grand slam off Jim Bunning. On July 22, he went 4–5 with two doubles against the Yankees.

Card #341, Jim Owens, looking in for the "sign," Connie Mack Stadium. He can't believe that his catcher is calling for an eephus pitch with Eddie Mathews at the plate with the bases loaded and no outs. Strange tale about my adventures trying to get Mr. Owens to sign my cards: For many years, nothing I sent him got returned, and I mean each member of the famed vaudeville trio of Nada, Zippo, and Zilch. Then, after perhaps a decade of saying that I was not going to send anything to him again, I sent one last '61 to get signed. Well, not only was my card signed, but he also included a signed '62 and a signed '64, which hadn't even been in the envelope I sent, so SR: ?.

Best game in the 1961 season: On September 9, he beat the Cubs, 6–2, allowing five hits.

VIC WERTZ
First Base
Boston Red Sox

Vic Wertz had the most typewriter-friendly last name in baseball until his record was broken by Don Wert in 1963. He was a four-time All-Star who finished in the top ten in MVP voting four times. He spent three years with the 81st Infantry Division, but like many baseball players during the World War II, he mostly just played baseball.

Searchin' for Toothpick Sam

Card #342, Clint Courtney, Chew Crew member, head and shoulder shot in Briggs Stadium. Addressing Billy Martin (they did not get along): "You got a problem?" "Scrap Iron" may (or may not) have been the first catcher to wear glasses, but he was in far more fights than sucker-puncher Billy Martin (see the Earl Torgeson blurb above). In 1954, he struck out only seven times in 437 plate appearances. Mr. Courtney died at 48 in 1975, before I started my collection, but his cards are not hard to find, so he must have been a good signer.

Best game in the 1961 season: On June 6, he went 2–4 against the Angels. In 46 at-bats in '61, he struck out only three times while drawing 10 walks.

Card #343, Earl Robinson, batting stance, wearing Dodgers uniform, in Holman Stadium. This card made no lasting impression on me but, by golly, that face looks familiar. Mr. Robinson died in 2014 at 77. SR: A.

Best game in the 1961 season: On June 20, he went 3–4 against the Twins with two runs, a double, a home run and three RBI.

Card #344, Sandy Koufax, follow-through, Charlie Neal behind him, looks like it was taken during Spring Training. He looks a lot more intelligent than most of the players in the set. He also looks like what a Brooklyn cabby *used* to look like. For many years, he held the Major League record for "most consecutive strikeouts at bat to start a career" with 12, a record that was broken 52 years later by Daniel Cabrara, who struck out his first 17 at-bats in the majors. He got a basketball scholarship to the University of Cincinnati when the school was a national powerhouse, and he had monster dunking ability. Early on, he was a willing signer, but the deluge must have gotten to him. Now, I understand he does one show a year and also signs at the Hall of Fame. SR: B+ in the past.

Best games in the 1961 season: He struck out 15 Cubs in a 13-inning, 3–2 win on September 20. On June 20, he two-hit the Cubs and registered 14 strikeouts. On August 29, he pitched another two-hitter against the Cubs and struck out 12. In 1961, Sandy had a 1.70 ERA against the Cubs, allowing just 20 hits (3.9/9 IP) and striking out 60 (11.7 K/9 IP) in 47⅔ innings. Domination, anyone?

2. The Quest for Fire

Card #345, Jim Piersall, warding off a potential mugger with a bat in Cleveland's Municipal Stadium. Mr. Piersall was 87 when he died in 2017, having been SR: A rated.

Best game in the 1961 season: Jim had 10 three-hit games and five four-hit games. I would pick the game against the Athletics on July 26, when he went 4–6 with three runs.

Card #346, Howie Nunn, head and shoulders, in what appears to be County Stadium, and I think the man seated over Howie's left shoulder might be D.B. Cooper. Most people don't realize this, but "Howie Nunn" was the name Wally Cox used to keep his amateur status while attending the Cincinnati College of Mortuary Science (founded 1882). Mr. Nunn (SR: A) died in 2012 at 76.

Best game in the 1961 season: He went 7⅔ innings against the Phillies on June 18 without giving up a run. He must have hurt his arm in July, because he didn't pitch from July 18 until September 4 and threw only 1⅔ innings after his return.

Card #347, St. Louis Cardinals Team card. Mine is signed by coaches Darrell Johnson, Harry Walker, and Vern Benson. I also have a team card signed by non-carded players Ed Bauta and Craig Anderson, another signed by Tim McCarver and Ed Olivares, and another signed by minor league managers George Kissell and Eddie Lyons.

Card #348, Steve Boros, follow-through on a swing in Henley Field. Like Sandy Koufax, Steve looks a lot brighter than the average ballplayer. In fact, as many readers will know, he was smart enough to be the first manager to rely heavily on computer-generated sabermetric stats to plan for a game. Mr. Boros passed away in 2010, having been rated SR: A.

Best game in the 1961 season: On May 21 against the Athletics, Steve went 3–5 with a double, a home run, and four RBI.

Card #349, Danny McDevitt, headshot in an unidentified park. It was just this look of stern reprobation that had quelled many a whisper in Mr. McDevitt's classroom countless times before, but it wasn't working on young Joey Ramone. So, while his face said locked and loaded, Danny's mind was filled with butterflies and little chirping birds. Danny pitched a shutout for the Dodgers in front of only 6,702 fans in the last game at Ebbets Field (and, in fact, his card has

Searchin' for Toothpick Sam

written on it, "Won last game/at Ebbets/Field"). Mr. McDevitt passed away in 2010 at 76. He was an SR: A signer.

Best game in the 1961 season: He was traded from the Yankees to the Twins in June. On July 16, he pitched the last four innings of a 7–5 loss to the Indians, giving up two hits and one run and striking out four.

Card #350, Ernie Banks, head and shoulder shot. My, what a pleasant-looking fellow. Mister Banks passed away aged 83 in 2015, having been, of course, a solid SR: A just about forever.

Best games in the 1961 season: On May 9 against Milwaukee, he went 2–3 with two home runs and four RBI. On August 17 against the Pirates, he went 3–5 with a double and two home runs.

Card #351, Jim King, follow-through of a swing, an old photo of him in a Giants uniform in Candlestick Park. Although devoid of hope and worn to a nub by the cares of the world, Jim, with a heavy sigh, trudged wearily up to the plate. Mr. King was 82 when he passed away in 2015. SR: A.

Best game in the 1961 season: On May 30, Jim went 3–4 with two runs against Cleveland. From May 11 until June 2, Jim hit .387 to lift his average from .125 to 361. He hit .221 over his last 81 games to wind up at .270.

Card #352, Bob Shaw, head and shoulders shot. Coyly arching an eyebrow, Bob let the waitress know that he *might* be available for a discussion of current events *après le jeu*. Mr. Shaw, a reliable signer, died at 77 in 2010. His card has the inscription "NL all star pitcher/1962."

Best game in the 1961 season: Traded from the White Sox to the Athletics in June, Bob's best game for Chicago was a complete-game, 7–1 win over Boston on April 23, and his best for Kansas City was a four-hit, 2–1 win over Washington on July 29.

Card #353, Howie Bedell, head and shoulders, in what appears to be McKechnie Field at the Braves' Spring Training facility in Bradenton. The Man with the Richard Widmark Grin, Howie spent five years in the minors before getting a trial in the Show. He spent five more years there before getting another shot (he was 32 at the time) and then played two further years before retiring. In toto, he had 1,599 hits in the minors and hit .294. He is rated SR: A.

2. The Quest for Fire

Best game in the 1961 season: Howie did not play in the majors in '61 but had a very good year at Louisville, leading the American Association in hits and triples and finishing in the top 10 in runs and doubles.

Card #354, Billy Harrell, an older headshot of him in an Indians uniform (ID markings excised) in Yankee Stadium. The man just looks plum worn out, almost as if he can see that his future is the same as his past, except that he'll be older and more tired. Just as with virtually every Big Leaguer, he was a superstar athlete in high school and did as well in college. In fact, he is in the Siena College Hall of Fame (where he was the first Golden Hurricane athlete to have his number retired), as well as the MAAC Hall of Fame. He could have played in the NBA[66] (he averaged over 12 rebounds a game at Siena), but he chose instead to play baseball. Just as with Howie Bedell (immediately above), his shots at The Show were preceded, interspersed with, and followed by stretches in the minors (in which he accrued 1,560 hits). He was an SR: A+. He passed away in 2014, when he was 85.

Best game in the 1961 season: Billy's best game was a 1–3 outing against the White Sox on April 23 with a run scored.

Card #355, Bob Allison, bat on shoulder, taken in Griffith Stadium, Zoilo Versalles in background. Ruggedly handsome, check. Athletically gifted, check. Personable, check. Rookie of the Year, check (1959). All-Star, check. Bob was no Mickey Mantle—heck, Al Kaline was no Mickey Mantle—but he sure was everything I wanted to be when I was 13. Mr. Allison was only 60 when he died in 1995, and his SR: A rating was well-earned.

Best games in the 1961 season: On April 16, he hit two home runs and had seven RBI against the Orioles. On July 19, he went 4–5 with two home runs against the Angels. On May 13, he also punished the Angels by going 3–4 with two home runs and five RBI.

Card #356, Ryne Duren, shown here attempting to find something in his glove without looking, in Yankee Stadium with Yogi Berra in the background. Ryne was the first flame-thrower reliever to have (A) spectacular back-to-back seasons and to (B) average over a strikeout per inning. Mr. Duren was 81 when he passed in 2011 after being an SR: A man forever.

113

Searchin' for Toothpick Sam

Best game in the 1961 season: Traded from the Yankees to the Angels early in the season, this erstwhile reliever threw a three-hit shutout at the Indians on August 12. He faced his old Yankees team twice after being traded, and in 13⅓ innings, he struck out 20 batters (13.5 K/9) and gave up only 4.9 H/9. With the Angels, he faced his former teammate Mickey Mantle seven times. He gave up a homer but also struck him out four times.

Card #357, Daryl Spencer, headshot, I believe during Spring Training. In this photo, he is standing on second base, trying to read an eyechart in the dugout (Ted Williams could've done it). Daryl was the first major leaguer to have a 20-home run season and bat under .210 (he was also the first to do it batting less than .220 and only the second to do it hitting under .230, the first being Pat Seerey in 1946, when he hit .225 and was fourth in the league with 26 homers [which would make him a $4,000,000 man in today's game]). He hit 336 homers in pro ball, the last when he was 43 and playing in Nishinomiya for the Hankyu Braves. Mr. Spencer (SR: A+) died at 88 in 2017. I have two cards signed by him, one on which he added, "All Star SS/Class D 1949 Sooner State League/Class AAA 1952 Amer Assoc" and the other which states, "Traded to the Dodgers/May 30 1961."

Best game in the 1961 season: His best game for St. Louis was on April 20, when he went 3–4 with two home runs against the Dodgers. He also had a five RBI game on April 17 against the Dodgers. His best Dodgers game was a 3–4 showing against the Phillies on July 27.

Card #358, Earl Averill, son of Hall of Famer Earl Averill, headshot, executive officer of the Crewcut Company, shot in Comiskey Park. Wasn't he the offensive line coach for the 1967 Quinnipiac Quaggas? I'll bet his kids didn't leave his dining table without asking permission and saying excuse me. Mr. Averill, SR: A, was 83 when he died in 2015.

Best games in the 1961 season: he went 3–4 and scored three runs against the Twins on August 20 with a double and two home runs. On May 3, he had a 4–4 game against the Orioles.

Card #359, Dallas Green, headshot, Connie Mack Stadium. Trying to contain his sense of pride and accomplishment, Dallas mentally prepares himself to receive the perfect attendance award at

2. The Quest for Fire

Richey Elementary. Incidentally, he was one of the few signatures I got in person when, as a bigwig in the Phillies organization, he came to Eugene to watch an Ems game in classic Civic Stadium. Mr. Green passed away at 82 in 2017, having been an SR: A man.

Best game in the 1961 season: On April 15, he threw a five-hit shutout against the Giants.

Card #360, Frank Robinson, head shot in Crosley Field. He looks like the class valedictorian going over his speech moments before going to the podium at graduation (minus the cap, of course). Baseball lost a class act when he died in 2019 at age 83. SR: A, at least back when I sent him cards before all my F. Robby needs were filled.

Best game in the 1961 season: On July 9, he was 4–4 against the Dodgers with three runs, a double, two home runs, and seven RBI. In the 50 games between June 4, when he was batting .265, and July 24, he hit .415 and raised his average to .349. He also scored 55 runs and drove in 54, both more than one per game.

Card #361, TOPPS BASEBALL CHECK LIST, 5th Series. Ted Lepcio gets the throw too late to tag a sliding Ernie Banks. Both players have signed my card (on both varieties).

Card #362, Frank Funk, head and shoulders shot. Coming off a rookie year during which he had an ERA of 1.99 in his nine-game trial, young Frank was facing the future with stars in his eyes. Still signing, Mr. Funk is an SR: A+.

Best game in the 1961 season: On May 22, Frank held the Twins scoreless over the last eight innings of a 15-inning game, giving up only two hits.

Card #363, John Roseboro, head and shoulders shot in the Coliseum. When asked whether he'd rather get beaned by Sandy Koufax or Don Drysdale, John had to take a minute to decide.... Mr. Roseboro passed away, aged 69, in 2002. He had always been SR: A.

Best game in the 1961 season: On July 25 against the Phillies, he went 3–4 with a double, a triple, and two RBI.

Card #364, Moe Drabowsky, headshot, Wrigley. Ever the prankster, Moe watches the paint-filled balloon he had paid the batboy to toss from the second tier descend into the "college of coaches"[67] assembled by the dugout. Moe, an excellent signer, died at age 70 in 2006. My card has the added notation, "Six Cons Ks Oct 5/1966 World Series."

Best game in the 1961 season: On May 14, he hurled three hitless innings at the Giants, striking out three.

Card #365, Jerry Lumpe, headshot in Comiskey Park. Jerry knew his mom would be thrilled to learn that Mr. Fishbracker had just promoted him to be the prestigious Assistant Night Manager at Fishbracker's In-n-Out Burger Barn (the one on Main, *not* the one out on Walnut). Mr. Lumpe, who passed away in 2014 at 81, was a solid SR: A guy.

My card has "A.L. All Star '65'" noted on it.

Best game in the 1961 season: Jerry went 4–4 against Boston on August 29.

Card #366, Eddie Fisher (again, not the Eddie Fisher referred to tangentially in the Sherman Jones blurb), headshot, squad leader in the Crewcut Company, taken in Wrigley Field. Eddie, recalling his days as a Boy Scout, was justifiably proud of his 15 merit badges. Now, here's something you won't ever see again: in 1965, Eddie pitched 165⅓ innings and won 15 games *in relief.* In all of the many color variations this card has (and there are many), Eddie's hair is almost always light yellow-greenish. Eddie rates a SR: A mark.

Best game in the 1961 season: His longest scoreless outing was two innings on May 20 against the Dodgers.

Card #367, Jim Rivera, batting stance in Comiskey Park. Livin' large and enjoyin' every minute of it, Jungle Jim is ready to rock and roll. Jim's late start in pro ball was due to the fact that he had spent five years in the Atlanta Federal Penitentiary for attempted rape. He finished in the top 10 in steals in the AL seven years in a row, 1952–1958. Mr. Rivera died aged 91 in 2017, having been an SR: A man.

Best game in the 1961 season: he went 3–3 against the Tigers on September 14.

Card #368, Bennie Daniels, headshot. Straight outta Compton, I can picture him with a porkpie hat, a toothpick in his mouth, and some dice in his pocket. Bennie could whack-a-mole, and he hit .250 with 19 home runs in the minors, plus five dingers in the Bigs. SR: A.

2. The Quest for Fire

Best game in the 1961 season: On July 30, Bennie shut out Kansas City.

Card #369, Dave Philley, headshot taken in Yankee Stadium. Chiseled from stone, he was a real-life cowboy. He set the record for most pinch-hits in a season when he came through 24 times in 1961, driving in 18 runners. Dave was still playing in the majors at age 43, and over his career in pro ball, he collected 2,218 hits. His brother, Noel, played in the minors for a few years after World War II. Dave and his wife, Nell, had been married for 66 years when he passed away in 2012 at 91 years of age. SR: A.

Best game in the 1961 season: On June 11 he went 2–4 with a triple and a home run against the White Sox.

Card #370, Roy Face, looking for the "sign" in Forbes Field. Leaning nonchalantly back against a hitching post, Elroy hoped that no one noticed that he had taken his big brother's glove instead of his own when he went out to play. When he retired, he ranked in the top five all-time in games pitched; now he is 24th. Times have changed. Roy is an SR: A responder. On my card he noted, "NL All Star/1959–60–61"/"3 Saves 1960/World Series."

Best game in the 1961 season: On June 25 against Philadelphia, he pitched four scoreless innings with four strikeouts to earn the win.

Card #371, Bill Skowron, bat resting on shoulder in Al Lang Field. I'll bet that when young men came a'callin' on his baby girl, it was all "Yes, sir, I will" and "No, sir, I won't." What a tough looking gent! Apparently, he was a teddy bear in real life. "Moose," an SR: A fellow, passed away in 2012 at 81.

(By the way, card #371 is one of the places where the appearance of the cards changed and also one of the famed '61 "Short Prints." Another thing—why, following the pattern used almost everywhere else in this set and given the year he had in 1960, did Moose's card not end in a five or a zero?)

Best game in the 1961 season: He went 3–3 with four RBI against the Angels on August 23.

Card #372, Bob Hendley, holding the ball in his glove in an undisclosed location. He looks like a high school ace just about to

Searchin' for Toothpick Sam

face the 0–17 St. Zita School for Future Butlers and Footmen. Bob, in my experience, has been a spotty signer. I did, eventually, get my three '61s signed, but it took a while. SR: B-.

Best game in the 1961 season: On August 31 he beat Don Drysdale and the Dodgers, 2–1.

Card #373, Boston Red Sox Team card. My copy is signed by coaches Sal Maglie, Billy Herman, and Len Okrie, as well as by Bobby Doerr. I also have a team card signed by non-carded players Galen Cisco, Arnold Earley, and Lou Clinton, another signed by Don Schwall and Galen Cisco, and another signed by minor league managers Johnny Pesky and Don Lenhardt.

Card #374, Paul Giel, headshot, wearing his Pirates uniform. As good as the other athletes in the '61 set were, very few were in Paul's league. He was the first-ever two-time All American in two sports (baseball and football), and he finished third in the Heisman Trophy voting as a junior and second (by a whisker) as a senior—and he played for team with a losing record! As you probably know, he never came close to stardom in the big leagues. In fact, he rarely even approached mediocrity. He was a reliable SR: A, however. Mr. Giel died at 69 in 2002.

Best game in the 1961 season: On May 4, he threw two scoreless innings against the Yankees.

Card #375, Ken Boyer, taking a swing in Al Lang Stadium in St. Pete. Here, he looks every bit as steady as he was in real life on the field. He drove in at least 90 runs and hit at least 20 home runs[68] seven consecutive years (1958–1964). He also hit over .290 in six of those years, and the one time he didn't, he hit .285. Ken is still rated as the 14th-best third baseman ever. For me, though, the most incredible thing about Mr. Boyer is his family. In addition to having two brothers who played in the majors (Clete [see above] and Cloyd), four more brothers, Wayne, Lynn, Ron (who stalled out in Triple A) and Len (who reached Double A), played in pro ball. Mr. Boyer was only 51 when he passed in 1982, but while he lived, he signed every single thing I ever sent him. SR: A.

Best game in the 1961 season: On September 14, in the second game of a doubleheader, Ken went 5–6, hitting for the cycle against

2. The Quest for Fire

the Cubs. That, of course, can't be topped, but on May 26 against the Pirates, he went 3–5 with four runs, two homers, and six RBI.

Card #376, Mike Roarke, full catching gear (save the mask, as that doesn't work well on a baseball card), taken at Henley Field in Lakeland during Spring Training.[69] He looked like a grizzled veteran, and he was, almost 30 when he played his first major league game. Mr. Roarke, SR: A, passed away in 2019 at 88. My card has the notation "All Star/'54 Sally/'60 A.A."

Best game in the 1961 season: Mike had two 3–4 days: July 14 against the Twins and July 20 against the Orioles.

Card #377, Ruben Gomez, headshot taken in Connie Mack Stadium. I have to report that this was one of the very few cards that never spoke to me. There are, however, two things I remember about Ruben. First, him running for his life while being chased by big (6'4", 230-pound) Joe Adcock, who charged the mound after Ruben hit him with a pitch. The second thing is that, after not pitching in the States since 1962, he came back at age 39 in 1967 and performed adequately in seven games for the Phillies. SR: A, Mr. Gomez died at 77 in 2004.

Best game in the 1961 season: Ruben did not play in the majors in '61.

Card #378, Wally Post, batting stance, taken in Al Lopez Field during Spring Training. The vibe I got from this card was one of good humor. Of Native American heritage, Wally once hit a ball off the top of the 60-foot-high clock atop the left field fence in Sportsman's Park. In 1947, when Wally and his brother, Edward, were both on the Muncie Reds of the Class D Ohio State League, Edward went 19–8 to Wally's 17–7. Wally (SR: A) was only 52 when he passed away in 1982.

Best game in the 1961 season: Wally went 3–4 against the Cards on April 14 with a double, a triple, and a two-run home run.

Card #379, Bobby Shantz, headshot, Yankee Stadium. In 1949, in his second major league game, Bobby took over for Carl Scheib (at 22, already a six-year veteran) in the fourth inning and proceeded to throw nine innings of no-hit ball. He gave up two hits in the 13th inning but won the game. Just as with Wally Post (immediately

119

above), he appears a pleasant sort. No slouch at the plate, he hit .195 over his 16 years in the Bigs. Still chooglin' along at 97, he's SR: A.

On his card he noted, "A.L. All Star 1951–1952/Won Houston's first game/1952 A.L. MVP."

Best game in the 1961 season: Bobby, who hit .438 in 1961, had two 2–2 games at bat on June 3 against the Phils and July 2 against the Giants, a game in which he just happened to pitch a seven-inning shutout.

Card #380, Minnie Miñoso, batting stance in Comiskey Park. One of my favorite players of all time, Saturnino Orestes didn't find a permanent home in the Bigs until he was 25, and then he became a star of the first magnitude for the next 10 years. He led the A.L. in HBP 10 times (the last six consecutively), and his 192 HBP is 10th all-time. After his last year in the majors, he went down Mexico way and played nine more years, hitting .317 over that span. In 1973, at 47, he played in 120 games and hit 12 home runs. Not counting his gimmick at-bats, he played pro ball for 28 years. All told, he had 3,252 hits, scored 1,521 runs, drove in 1,321 runs, and hit 301 home runs. Eighty-nine when he died in 2015, he was an SR: A all his life.

Best game in the 1961 season: On April 27, he went 3–5 and drove in five runs against the Athletics.

Card #381, Dave Wickersham, follow-through on a "pitch," taken at Connie Mack Field in West Palm Beach during Spring Training. He is one of the most ordinary-looking fellows in the entire set. I could see him as a pump jockey, a warehouseman, or a clerk in the town's only men's wear store. Mr. Wickersham told me that he lost his only shot at a 20-win season on the last day of the 1964 season when, after two errors were committed behind him in the seventh inning, he lost it and got tossed from the game. The Tigers (he had been traded to Detroit after the 1963 season) scored three runs in the ninth inning and won the game. Mr. Wickersham was 86 and still an SR: A when he died in 2022.

Best game in the 1961 season: Against the Twins on September 10, he threw three hitless innings with four strikeouts.

Card #382, Frank Thomas, headshot in Wrigley Field. Here, he

2. The Quest for Fire

looks as if he's gently admonishing one of his eight children.[70] This three-time All Star is most famous for two things: his fight with Richie Allen in Philadelphia and his ability to catch anybody's throw barehanded. Mr. Thomas was an SR: A+ fellow until his passing at 93 in 2023. On my card he added, "NL All Star/1954–56–58."

Best game in the 1961 season: His best game as a Cub occurred on April 22, when he went 3–5 against the Phils, and his best game as a Brave was June 22 against the Giants, when he went 3–3 with two home runs and four RBI.

Card #383, *Frisco First Liners*, featuring Mike McCormick, Jack Sanford, and Billy O'Dell in Candlestick Park. All three gents were SR: A.

Card #384, Chuck Essegian, headshot in Miami Stadium, the Orioles' Spring Training park. Eye of the tiger, baby, eye of the tiger. Mr. Essegian, perhaps the preeminent ballplayer ever of Armenian heritage, is primarily known for his two pinch-hit home runs in the 1959 World Series. He is a fine SR: A gentleman who played for three A.L. teams in 1961. I have a card on which he added, "2 PH HR 59 WS/.All Star Cal 1954/All Star NW 1956," and another upon which he wrote, "Traded to Indians/May 3." He had 201 homers in pro ball.

Best game in the 1961 season: He played one game for Baltimore, four for Kansas City, and 60 for Cleveland. His best game was June 11 against the Athletics, when he was 2–2 with two home runs and five RBI.

Card #385, Jim Perry, follow-through on a "pitch" in Municipal Stadium. Perry was lean and lanky, and his coastal plain farmer roots are easily discernable in his visage. Funny thing about Jim, he *didn't* make the All-Star team in 1960 when he was 11–4, 3.23 at the break, but he *did* in 1961, when he was 8–8 with a 4.24 ERA. Mr. Perry gets an SR: A insofar as this collector is concerned.

Best game in the 1961 season: In the second game of a September 2 doubleheader against the Orioles, Jim pitched a four-hit shutout and went 2–3 at bat.

Card #386, Joe Hicks, "Sox" on cap blotted out, batting stance in Yankee Stadium. If David Bowie had collected baseball cards in the early 1960s (which is *extremely* doubtful), this card could have been

121

the inspiration for his song "All the Young Dudes." When the White Sox brought him up, his five-year batting average stood at .337. He remains an SR: A fellow. He wrote, "All Star 1958 Western League" on my card.

Best game in the 1961 season: On May 2, he hit a home run against Detroit's Jim Bunning.

Card #387, Duke Maas, follow-through after a "pitch" in Yankee Stadium.[71] The Duke looks tired in this image, and I'm not just saying that because I know his fate. Arthritis, which had plagued him his entire career, finally forced him out of the game, and '61 would be his final year in baseball. He died in 1976, when he was only 47, with rheumatoid arthritis being a contributing factor. Apparently, he was not a prolific (or even average) signer, because his signed cards are *extremely* difficult to come by (and watch out for fakes).

Best game in the 1961 season: Duke pitched in only one game in 1961, the final game of his career on April 23 against the Orioles, when he got one out and gave up two hits, both of which resulted in runs.

Card #388, Bob Clemente, head shot, probably in Forbes Field. "Bob"? Really? Well, at least some things have changed for the better. In my opinion, the look on his face typifies his approach to the game: intense and focused. All of his cards, regardless of year, are very hard to find with his signature.

Best games in the 1961 season: Roberto had 18 games with three hits, four games with four hits, and two five-hit games. The first was on July 6 against the Cubs (5–5, four runs, five RBI), and the other was on August 3 against the Cardinals (5–6 with four runs). He hit .413 against the Dodgers, getting hits in 20 of 22 games against them.

Card #389, Ralph Terry, head and shoulders shot taken in Yankee Stadium. That is the look of a stubborn man. Ralph was one of the last, if not *the* last (U.S.-born) player born in a log cabin with a dirt floor.[72] Mr. Terry was an SR: A. He died in 2022.

Best game in the 1961 season: On August 20, he pitched a four-hit shutout against the Indians.

Card #390, Del Crandall, bat on shoulder in Country Stadium. If this photo were taken during a game, I would say that he is intently

2. The Quest for Fire

Roberto Clemente, here presented as "Bob," an unwelcome Anglicization of his name. At least he wasn't labeled "Chico" Clemente.

studying the pitcher he's about to face. He is a good signer, SR: A. On my card, he also wrote, "8x All Star/4 Gold Gloves."

Best game in the 1961 season: Del was out with an injury for most of the year, getting into just 15 games, but on April 15, he went 4–5 against the Cubs.

Card #391, Winston Brown, headshot, McKechnie Field, the Braves' Spring Training facility. Winston would have been the fourth Major Leaguer born in Panama, *if* he had made the team out of Spring Training. He won a total of 191 games in the Minors over his 15-year career, striking out 1,745 batters and walking 1,446. The only impression that this card made on me was one of general nonchalance, gently layered over a natural-born wisecracker. I was never able to locate him to write to, but apparently other folks were able to, for over the decades I have managed to acquire three signed Brown cards. Mr. Brown passed away in either 2019 or 2020, and he was 87 or 88 when he died.

Best game in the 1961 season: Mr. Brown was the only player in the '61 Topps set who *never* played in the majors.

Card #392, Reno Bertoia, headshot in Griffith Stadium. He was one of the few players born in Italy (there are only seven such, and Reno was the last one before Alex Liddi in 2011). Oddly enough, his next-door neighbor in Windsor (Ottawa, Canada) just happened to be Hank Biasatti, another of the Italian-born major leaguers. In this photo, I can see him giving the "mano a borsa" to a heckler ragging him about his bonus. An iffy signer (SR: B), Mr. Bertoia passed away in 2011 when he was 77.

Best game in the 1961 season: On April 24, he went 3–4 against the Athletics.

Card #393, *Batter Bafflers*, featuring Don Cardwell and Glen Hobbie. Don is telling Glen how sorry he feels about pulling the old "Atomic Balm"[73] prank on him, but Glen is still tempted to whop him upside the head. Both are SR: A.

Card #394, Ken Walters, batting stance in Connie Mack Stadium. He appears to be thinking about taking that job teaching high school shop and assistant coaching he had been offered during the off-season. SR: A, Mr. Walters died at age 76 in 2010.

Best game in the 1961 season: On May 21, he went 3–4 against the Pirates with two doubles and a triple.

Card #395, Chuck Estrada, follow-through on a "pitch." After tying for the league lead in victories as a 22-year-old in his rookie season, the only A.L. pitcher to pull off that feat, Chuck had every reason to think that he had the world by the tail. Mr. Estrada is an SR: A signer.

Best game in the 1961 season: Chuck threw a two-hit, 12-strikeout shutout against the Angels on June 6.

Card #396, Bob Aspromonte, head and shoulders shot, taken in Holman Stadium in Vero Beach. Fresh-faced and full of spunk, grit, vim, pluck, sand, and moxie, young Robert looked forward to a long career in the dynamic yet challenging field of "Base Ball." Well, if this *were* the case, he would have been correct. In fact, he was the last Brooklyn Dodger to play in the majors, 15 years after breaking in with his hometown club. Bob is one of those SR: A+ players autograph hounds love so much. Besides Ken, his other brother, Charles, also played pro ball. On my card, he has also written (of course and as noted above), "Last Brooklyn Dodger active/in the Major Leagues."

Best game in the 1961 season: On June 5, pinch-hitting against the Pirates, he singled in a run and came around to score.

Card #397, Hal Woodeshick, another squadron leader in the Crewcut Company, in Griffith Stadium. Hal *cannot* believe the kid

2. The Quest for Fire

who just came to the door to pick up his daughter for a movie date—the kid's hair is touching his ears! Mr. Woodeshick, an SR: A+, passed away in 2009. He was 76. My card also has the notation "N.L. All-Star 1963."

Best game in the 1961 season: On April 30, he pitched eight innings of a 2–1 Senators victory over the mighty Yankees.

Card #398, Hank Bauer, headshot, Connie Mack Park in West Palm Beach. Make no mistake, this old dude could walk the walk. A Marine, he fought on Guam and Okinawa, earning two Bronze Stars and two Purple Hearts. (His brother, Herman, also a ballplayer, was killed in Normandy.) Mr. Bauer, who passed away in 2007 aged 84, always signed and returned every item I sent to him.

Best game in the 1961 season: On June 8, he went 3–4 against his old Yankees team. He was named manager of the Athletics on June 19 and played in six more games after taking over the reins. In his last game as a player on July 21, he went 2–3 against the Tigers.

Card #399, Cliff Cook, ready to "field" a grounder. That is one determined look, seasoned perhaps with a soupçon of trepidation. Cliff hit 195 homers in the minors. I never got a signature from him without a fee, but he did at least answer one of my letters, telling me that he charged a fee, so there's that.... SR: B-. His card also has "All Star SALLY Lg 1959/A.A. 1961" written on it.

Best game in the 1961 season: He was hitless in five September games for the Reds after hitting 32 home runs for Indianapolis with 119 RBI.

Card #400, Vern Law, follow-through on a "pitch" in Connie Mack Stadium. Just as nice as he looks in this card, Vernon and his wife, VaNita, raised six children: Varlin, Vaughn, Veryl, Vance, Veldon, and VaLynda. As one would expect, he ranks as an SR: A returner, and his card has the notation "C.Y. 1960."

Best game in the 1961 season: In an injury-plagued partial season, his best outing was five scoreless innings against the Cardinals on May 16. On May 27 against those same Cardinals, he went 2–2 at the plate.

Card #401, Baseball Thrills subset, *Babe Ruth Hits 60th Homer*. I wish that I had started getting my cards signed in the 1960s while

Searchin' for Toothpick Sam

Tom Zachary was still alive, but by the time I thought about it, only two of the pitchers Ruth hit home runs against in '27 were still alive, so at least I got them (Paul Hopkins and Willis Hudlin) to sign the card.

Card #402, Baseball Thrills subset, *Larsen Pitches Perfect Game*. Mine is signed by Larsen, Yogi Berra, and Sal Maglie. I don't know why I didn't get Dale Mitchell and Gil McDougald as well, and I *really* wish that I had started collecting autographs in time to get Babe Pinelli to sign the card.

Card #403, Baseball Thrills subset, *Brooklyn-Boston Play 26 Inning Tie*. Leon Cadore had already passed by 1961, but I did get Joe Oeschger's signature.

Card #404, Baseball Thrills subset, *Hornsby Tops N.L. with .424 Average*. I have managed to acquire two of these cards signed by Hornsby, who died in 1963.

Card #405, Baseball Thrills subset, *Gehrig Benched After 2,130 Games*. It didn't occur to me to get Babe Dahlgren's signature until it was too late.

Card #406, Baseball Thrills subset, *Mantle Blasts 565 Ft. Home Run*. I have two signed by the Mick, but Chuck Stobbs, who signed everything else I sent him, wouldn't sign this card.

Card #407, Baseball Thrills subset, *Jack Chesbro Wins 41st Game*.

Card #408, Baseball Thrills subset, *Mathewson Strikes Out 267 Batters*.

Card #409, Baseball Thrills subset, *Johnson Hurls 3rd Shutout in 4 Days*. Again, by the time I thought to get this signed, only one of Johnson's former teammates was still alive to sign it, Paul Hopkins, who added "My Idle [sic]."

Card #410, Baseball Thrills subset, *Haddix Pitches 12 Perfect Innings*. Mine is signed by Harvey Haddix and Joe Adcock.

Card #411, Tony Taylor, headshot. Unfortunately, this is another of the (few, very few) cards which failed to evoke any memorable response. I do know that Tony had a brother who played in the minors and that Tony was probably the most popular Phillie between when Richie Ashburn was traded to the Cubs and the blossoming

2. The Quest for Fire

of Mike Schmidt. Mr. Taylor died in 2020, age 84, and was a reliable signer.

Best game in the 1961 season: On August 16 against his former team, the Cubs, he went 4–5 with three runs.

Card #412, Larry Sherry, head and shoulders shot, taken in Wrigley Field. "Look, Mrs. Shapiro, how 'bout if I just give you the extra half-ounce of chopped liver no charge?" One of the more interesting facts about Larry is that he overcame being born a taliped. Mr. Sherry (SR: A) passed away at 71 in 2006. His card also has "2 Wins 2 Saves/ 1959 World Series" written on it.

Best game in the 1961 season: His best stint was the last 5⅓ innings of a 13-inning win against the Cubs on August 5 in which he gave up one hit and struck out six.

Card #413, Eddie Yost, headshot, taken in the Polo Grounds[74] in Palm Springs. A Brooklyn boy, he never spent a day in the minors. Vastly underrated while he was a player, he led the league in walks six times while both Ted Williams and Mickey Mantle were playing (!) and drew at least 100 free passes eight times (with anywhere from 123 to 151). With enough power to hit 139 home runs (including 28 leadoff dingers), he had a skill set that would have him making $10 million a year today. Mr. Yost (SR: A) died at age 86 in 2012. He added "The Walking Man/1614 BB" to my card.

Best game in the 1961 season: Eddie went 3–4 with a walk against the Tigers on September 24.

Card #414, Dick Donovan, headshot taken in Comiskey Park. After 12 years of working in the offices of Worthingham and Shropington Mercantile, Dick was still thrilled when he off-handedly mentioned to his wife over dinner that Mr. Shropington himself had said, "Nice work on the Sashimi broadcloth deal, Donovan." (I should here mention that this was the first time in those 12 years that either Messrs. W. or S. had acknowledged his existence.) Mr. Donovan, an SR: A signer, died in 1997 at 69 years of age.

Best game in the 1961 season: On June 9, he pitched a complete 10-inning shutout against the White Sox, giving up just six hits.

Card #415, Hank Aaron, shown here playing fetch with his dog in County Stadium. When I first started sending cards to Mr. Aaron,

Searchin' for Toothpick Sam

it was shortly after he finished playing and before the heinous, charge-for-a-signature craze began. The first several items I sent ('60 T, '62T, '60T #415, NL Batting Leaders, MVP, All-Star), I got back signed. By the mid–1980s, however, this stopped. After either getting cards sent back sans signature or not getting them back at all, I had to resort to shows and pay first $30, then $50, and finally $100 to get the third '61 signed. This, by the way, was not at all uncommon with the big "stars." Given these circumstances, I feel that any SR I gave Mr. Aaron would be irrelevant.

Best game in the 1961 season: Mr. Aaron had 13 three-hit games but, surprisingly, no four-hit ones, a lot of good games but no spectacular ones. My choice for his best game is the July 21 game against Pittsburgh when he went 3–4 with two homers and three RBI.

Card #416, Dick Howser, preparing to "field" a ball in Connie Mack Field in West Palm Beach. My gosh, is it *totally* my age, or do so many of these fellows really look like Little Leaguers? This image makes you wonder if the logo on the back of his shirt doesn't say something like "Luby's Sporting Goods." Only 51 when he died in 1987, Mr. Howser was an SR: A man.

Best game in the 1961 season: Mr. Howser finished second in the Rookie of the Year race, scoring 107 runs and walking 92 times. His best game was against the Twins on September 10, when he went 5–5 with a double, a triple and three runs.

Card #417, Juan Marichal from the waist up, somewhere (I'm assuming) in America. This may be the happiest any player looks in the entire '61 set. It's as if he just heard that he won a new Dodge Polara or that he was going be the father of twins. I haven't sent him anything to sign in quite a while, but he was SR: A back in the day. He is José Rio's father-in-law and José Acevedo's cousin.

Best game in the 1961 season: Juan shut down the Dodgers with a one-hit shutout on August 2, striking out 11 batters, the only hit a Tommy Davis single in the fifth inning.

Card #418, Ed Bailey in the batting cage in Crosley Field. You *do not* wanna mess with Ed. In 1959, he was part of a rare "Brother Battery" for all three games of brother Jim's major league career.[75] Mr. Bailey was an SR: A, and he passed at age 75 in 2007.

2. The Quest for Fire

Best game in the 1961 season: Ed was traded from the Reds to the Giants in late April. His best game as a Red was a 3–3 day on April 13 against the Cubs. His best game as a Giant occurred on June 14, when he went 4–4 with two home runs against the Braves.

Card #419, Tom Borland, head and shoulders shot in Fenway Park. Give him a shapeless hillbilly hat with some holes in it and some scraggly facial hair, and he could be a Hatfield *or* a McCoy. He was 30–2 and an All-American playing for Oklahoma in 1954–1955.[76] Tom's son pitched a season in the Pirates' system. An SR: A fellow, Mr. Borland died in 2013 at age 80.

Best game in the 1961 season: Tom pitched in one game for Boston in '61 on April 23, throwing one inning and allowing three hits and two runs.

Card #420, Ernie Broglio, headshot. I don't recall what my original impression was, but that's because since then, I have seen *Fawlty Towers*. Take off the hat, give Ernie a mustache, and he's Basil Fawlty doing what he hates the most, talking to a prospective client. An SR: A, Mr. Broglio died at age 83 in 2019.

Best game in the 1961 season: On August 14, he pitched a five-hit shutout against the Dodgers.

Card #421, Ty Cline, batting stance out in the great wide open (under a sky of blue).[77] My, doesn't he look quite the cocky young man. Well, I guess I would've been too if I had QB'd my high school football team to a state championship, received a basketball-baseball scholarship to a major Division I university, been named an All-American and, after just a half-season in the minors, came up for a September trial in 1960 and hit .308. Mr. Cline is SR: A.

Best game in the 1961 season: On September 29, he went 2–4 against the Angels.

Card #422 Bud Daley, headshot. "Oooo—does anyone else smell that?" Mr. Daley, who is 90, is an SR: A fellow.

Best game in the 1961 season: All of his dreams came true when he was traded from the abysmal A's to the Mighty Yankees on June 14. My card also has "All Star 59–60" on it.

His best game as an Athletic was May 2, when he defeated

Searchin' for Toothpick Sam

Boston and struck out nine batters. His best game as a Yankee was July 16, when he beat the O's, 2–1, on four hits.

Card #423, Charlie Neal, shown here either "fielding" a ball or trying his hand at rattler snatching in the Coliseum. An SR: A, Mr. Neal died in 1996 at age 65.

Best game in the 1961 season: His best game was April 16 against the Phillies, when he went 3–4 with a double, a run and an RBI.

Card #424, Turk Lown, either in a follow-through or playing catch with his son, Craig, before the game in Yankee Stadium. Turk was wounded in the Battle of the Bulge and was awarded the Purple Heart. Since he was an 11B, he should also have received a Bronze Star and the CIB.[78] Mr. Lown (SR: A) died in 2016. He was 92.

Best game in the 1961 season: Turk had a three-hit, scoreless, $5\frac{2}{3}$-innings stint against the Tigers on June 6.

Card #425, Yogi Berra grinning at the camera in Yankee Stadium before a game. What can you say about Yogi that hasn't been said a hundred times before? Try this: Yogi looks like a Psammead (minus the horns, of course). Mr. Berra, who took part in the D-Day invasion on an LCT(R),[79] was 90 when he passed away in 2015.

Best game in the 1961 season: On June 2, Yogi went 2–3 with two homers against the White Sox.

Card #426, Milwaukee Braves Team card. Funny story about this card. It was supposed to be card #429, but it was printed as card #463, the same number as the Jack Fisher card. Mine is signed by coaches Whit Wyatt, George Myatt, and Andy Pafko. I also have a team card signed by manager Birdie Tebbetts, one signed by non-carded players Sammy White and Tony Cloninger (and back-signed by Phil Roof), another signed by Bob Boyd, Gino Cimoli, and Phil Roof, and another signed by Neil Chrisley.

Card #427, Dick Ellsworth, "pitching" in Rendezvous Park in Mesa. He only looks about four years younger than he actually was. After going 15–0 in his senior year for Fresno High School (where his teammates were Jim Maloney and Pat Corrales) and regarded as the Number One pitching prospect in the country, he signed for with the Cubs for $60,000 and started a game for them as an 18-year-old

2. The Quest for Fire

before serving (a short) time in the Bushes. He was back in the Bigs for good when he was 20 and stayed another 12 years. SR: A.

Best game in the 1961 season: He threw a three-hit shutout against the Cardinals on May 20.

Card #428, Ray Barker, head and shoulder shot in Miami Stadium. He looked to me like the owner of a small-town bank. (He also looked like a young Tol Avery.) The first Yankees' first baseman of what has become known to history as the "Horace Clark Era," Ray had more than 1,400 hits and 180 homers in the minors. He was SR: A before passing in 2018 at 82.

Best game in the 1961 season: Ray, who had had a five-game trial in 1960, would not appear in another Big League game until 1965.

Card #429, Al Kaline, headshot in Briggs Stadium. He wound up with 399 career home runs, and he told me that he had four homers rained out over the years. On his way to what would have been his most productive home run season in 1962, Al broke a collarbone making a catch on May 26. In only 36 games, Al already had 13 home runs.[80] He was another one of those (used to be) rare players who made both the league's top 10 youngest and top 10 oldest while he was playing. Mr. Kaline passed away in 2020 at the age of 85. For me, he had always been SR: A.

Best game in the 1961 season: Al had 13 three-hit and three four-hit games in '61. His best game came in a 12–10 win over the Yankees on June 17, when he went 4–5 with three runs and five RBI.

Card #430, Bill Mazeroski, recreating waiting for the "pitch" for the camera in Forbes Field. One of the nicer-looking cards in the set, our Bill looks quite the steely-eyed hero here. (And check out those guns!) Sad story—up until he was elected to the Hall of Fame, he was an SR: A. Ever since, he has been (for me) an F, even not returning a World Series card already signed by other players and keeping a $30 check, so…

Best game in the 1961 season: Against the Dodgers on September 13, he went 4–5 with two homers and three RBI.

Card #431, Chuck Stobbs, headshot (mostly) in Comiskey. Remember when I wrote that Tom Borland looked like a person who could have been involved in the Hatfield-McCoy feud? Well,

Searchin' for Toothpick Sam

whichever side Tom was on, Chuck was on the other. Aside from the Mantle Home Run card (see #406 above), Mr. Stobbs signed everything I sent him (SR: A). He passed away at 79 in 2008.

Best game in the 1961 season: On April 25 against the Athletics, he pitched two scoreless innings.

Card #432, Coot Veal, headshot (mostly). Coot Veal! Coot Veal! Coot Veal![81] SR: A.

Best game in the 1961 season: Coot went 3–4 against the White Sox on June 9.

Card #433, Art Mahaffey, wind-up in Jack Russell Memorial Stadium, Clearwater. After a 14-game, 7–3, 2.31 ERA 1960 half-season, the best Phillies rookie pitching since Ray Semproch way back in '58, Art knew that "big things" were expected of him this year. Mr. Mahaffey is an SR: A grade returner. He added, "N.L. All Star/1961–1962" to his signature.

Best game in the 1961 season: In the second game of a doubleheader against the Cubs on April 23, Art pitched a four-hit shutout and struck out a team record (and 1961 season-high) 17 batters.

Card #434, Tom Brewer, follow-through on a "pitch" in Yankee Stadium. "Fierce of countenance, strong of jaw/Our Tom was not one to hem and haw/He pitched them brave and pitched them bold/Beloved was he by the Fenway fold/He challenged the mighty with vim and grit/ until '61 when his arm went pffft." Mr. Brewer, who was SR: A rated, died at age 86 in 2018.

Best game in the 1961 season: On April 23, he gave up five hits and one run against the White Sox in eight innings, hitting a two-run double in the victory.

Card #435, Orlando Cepeda, batting stance in Scottsdale Stadium. The cast on Orlando's game face is just about the opposite of the one he presented off the field, a face that struck fear into opposing pitchers for 17 seasons. Mr. Cepeda started out as a good signer, but as his life went downhill, so did his signing habits. I don't know what his present stance is, but for me, SR: C+.

Best games in the 1961 season: On May 15, the Baby Bull went 3–4 with a double, two home runs, three runs, and five RBI versus the Cubs, and on the Fourth of July he topped that with a 5–5 game

2. The Quest for Fire

and the N.L.'s single-game 1961 high of eight RBI against those same Cubs. He had 15 games with at least three RBI.

Card #436, Jim Maloney, follow-through on a pitch in Tampa's Al Lopez Field, one of the famous '61 "Short Prints." Another most definitely Irish-looking fellow, this cat could flat out bring it. In fact, he was only the third pitcher in major league history to have more strikeouts than innings pitched in a season with at least 154 innings,[82] when he struck out 265 batters in 250⅓ innings in 1963. Since he was on the same high school team as Dick Ellsworth (see above), he only got to pitch twice for Fresno High School for a total of 18 innings. Perhaps you're wondering how he did in those two games, because I certainly did. Well, thanks to Gregory Wolf's biography of Maloney at the SABR bio site,[83] I now know: 41 Ks in those innings. Using my trusty slide rule, I was able to come up with a figure of 22.8 K/9 IP. That means that fewer[84] than seven batters per game on batted balls (assuming that there were no caught-stealings or pick-offs)! That is just insane, even at a high school level. He was an iffy signer, hence SR: C. (Had he not had frequent [and ultimately career-ending] arm woes, I have no doubt that he would have been ranked among the all-time greats.)[85] On my card he added, "3 No Hitters/39 10K games."

Best game in the 1961 season: On June 4, he hurled a three-hit, 3–1 victory against the Cubs.

Card #437, TOPPS BASEBALL CHECK LIST, Sixth Series. Play at third base, it looks as if the runner just got clocked on the back of the head by a thrown ball. Mine is signed by Gene Freese and Frankie Crosetti, although I am no longer sure if I identified the player correctly.[86]

Card #438, Curt Flood, "fielding" a grounder. More than looking like just another high school player trying to make varsity, as so many other players in this set do, Curt Flood did what none of the others did: He changed baseball, perhaps more so than any other player other than Babe Ruth. But there is something else that sets him apart from all the other players. After his career was over, he became an artist, a *real* artist and not just a dabbler. Mr. Flood's signing habits seemed to depend a lot on how his life was going (and in that, he is certainly no different from most of us). Given the vicissitudes of that life, I feel that it would be unfair of me to give him a rating. By the way, I would strongly suggest that the reader check out his paintings, especially his portrait of Bob Gibson. The man was an artist of rare talent. Mr. Flood was only 59 when he passed away in 1997.

Best game in the 1961 season: Mr. Flood went 5–5 against the Pirates on September 2.

Card #439, Phil Regan, headshot taken during Spring training. This photo was clearly taken the day he got his job selling vacuums door to door (do people still do that?) and not a week later. He is SR: A.

Best game in the 1961 season: He beat the Orioles, 9–1, on May 17.

Card #440, Luis Aparicio, head and shoulders shot taken in the visitors' dugout in Yankee Stadium. I'd say that he looks just a slick as he was sly. Nice photo, though. Back in the day, he was SR: A, but you should go through a signing to get his autograph today if you want to be sure of a return.

Best games in the 1961 season: Luis had three four-hit games in '61, the best coming against the Senators on August 5, when he was 4–5 with two runs, a double, a home run, and two RBI. He also had a 3–4 day against the Athletics on August 13 in which he scored four runs.

Card #441, Dick Bertell, fixin' to throw an imaginary runner out at an imaginary second base. ID-ing the park is a toughie. Even though there is the appearance of some sort of plant-like growth or mesh on the fence in the background (it is definitely not a "wall"), there is what appears to be a palm frond in the background also, so despite Mr. Bertell being a Cub, it is obviously *not* Wrigley Field. My first (and most logical) thought was that the photo was taken at the Cubs' Spring Training facility in Mesa, Arizona, Rendezvous Park, but I have been unable to find a photo of that park with a fence so vestured. So, park unidentified.

So, where were we? Oh, yeah, Dick's card. Well it *almost* looks like an actual action card, so there's that. I like the card. What I see is the little boy in Dick's mind playing catch with his dad in the back yard and imagining that he's throwing Maury Wills out at second base. SR: A, Mr. Bartell died in 1999, age 64.

2. The Quest for Fire

Best game in the 1961 season: On August 26, he went 4–4 against the Pirates with a home run.

Card #442, Gordon Jones, headshot in Miami Stadium. Another in the small-town businessman subset, Mr. Jones is shown here talking to a potential customer who is inquiring as to whether "Jonesie's One-Stop Septic Tank and Well Drilling Services" is the right company for him.[87] Mr. Jones was SR: A before his death at 64 in 1994.

Best game in the 1961 season: Appearing in only three major league games in 1961, the best was a scoreless inning against the Twins on May 10.

Card #443, Duke Snider, in his mind, watching the ball sail over the fence onto Bedford Avenue. This is a very nice card of a man who, for five glorious years (1953–1957), absolutely deserved to be mentioned in the same breath as Willie and Mickey. The Duke, who died in 2011 at 84, was a prince when it came to signing.

Best game in the 1961 season: The Duke went 3–4 with three runs scored and a two-run home run in a game against the Braves on August 8.

Card #444, Joe Nuxhall, headshot: Say hello to Guff, the fellow who works the late shift down at Wally's garage down by the state highway exit. If you look at a picture of him when he broke into the Majors as a 15-year-old and compare it to this photo, he looks like he's been rode hard and put away wet. That aside, however, he is in the Reds' all-time top 10 in games, wins, innings pitched, strikeouts, starts, walks and shutouts. I believe that he also holds the record for most career home runs hit by a Reds pitcher with 13. A last point of interest about him: Joe pitched in the Majors for 16 years, 15 of them with the Reds. The one and only year he *wasn't* a Red was 1961, the first year since 1940 that the Reds won the pennant. He had his best year in the Majors when he was 34, 19 years after his debut. After retiring from pitching in 1967 he was immediately hired as a Reds broadcaster, a job he held until 2004. Mr. Nuxhall (SR: A) passed away in 2007 at 79.

Best game in the 1961 season: Joe pitched his only 1961 complete game against the Senators on May 25, beating them 4–3.

Searchin' for Toothpick Sam

Card #445, Frank Malzone, headshot (with bats). He looks like a Maine fisherman, the good-natured kind, not the crochety old sorehead type. A six-time All-Star, Mr. Malzone passed at 85 in 2015. SR: A.

Best game in the 1961 season: On August 15, he punished the Indians for their flagrant effrontery by going 5–5 with two home runs and three RBI.

Card #446, Bob "Hawk" Taylor, head against a background of sky. In this photo, he looks like a competitor in a strongman contest. (That neck! Those shoulders!) A super athlete in high school, he won 14 letters in four sports and was offered a basketball scholarship at a Big Ten school. His incle Benny played for the Browns, Tigers, and Braves (that last in 1955, just two years before Bob joined the team). He was an SR: A before his death at age 73 in 2012. He added "IM @18" ("In Majors at 18") to my card.

Best game in the 1961 season: On October 1, in the last game of the season, Hawk tied the game in the ninth inning with a pinch-hit home run against the Giants.

Card #447, Harry Bright, "fielding" a ball at Spring Training in Pompano Beach. He looks like he's flinching. Harry played in pro ball for 24 years, including 11 before he reached the majors. He had 1966 hits and hit 167 homers in the Minors, and he was SR: A before passing away at age 70 in 2000.

Best game in the 1961 season: On April 19, he went 3–4 against the White Sox.

Card #448, Del Rice, squatting at the Polo Grounds during Spring Training. To be honest, he looks like he is falling asleep and is just about ready to tip over. He played in pro ball from 1941 until 1961, and then in four games in the minors as a player-manager when he was 46 and 47 years old. In 1945, he played with the Rochester Royals in the old National Basketball League, the predecessor of the NBA. He told me that his high game was 14 points, but since he only scored 22 points in 11 games, his memory may have been a little sketchy. Mr. Rice was only 60 when he passed away in 1983, having been an SR: A+ man.

Best game in the 1961 season: On June 18 against the Athletics,

2. The Quest for Fire

in his 17th season, 38-year-old Del Rice had his first two-home run game, going 2–2 with three RBI against the Athletics.

Card #449, Bobby Bolin, follow-through in Scottsdale Stadium. He looks so much like a young Norman Leavitt that I can only picture him as a yokel kibitzing around a pot-bellied stove in a small-town feed and seed. Mr. Bolin was a kind of spotty signer, although I did eventually get all the cards that I needed signed by him signed. An SR: B, he passed away in 2023.

Best games in the 1961 season: On the 3rd and 4th of September, Bob pitched four innings against the Dodgers (two in each game) allowing three hits and no runs and striking out six batters.

Card #450, Jim Lemon, headshot. Man, was there ever a name that more matched a face? Boy howdy, that is one sour look. Appearances aside, Mr. Lemon was an SR: A signer before his death in 2006 at 78.

Best game in the 1961 season: Against the Yankees on June 24, Jim went 3–5 with a double and two home runs.

Card #451, *Power for Ernie* featuring Daryl Spencer, Bill Whit,e and Ernie Broglio. The three gents appear to be puzzled by what it is that they're looking at, like the cops (Henry Brandon and Bobby Sommers) and the forest ranger (Robert Rockwell) around the crater in the original (and vastly superior) 1953 version of *War of the Worlds* or the tramp (Olin Howland) in the original (and vastly superior) 1958 version of *The Blob*.

Card #452, Bob Allen, head and shoulder shot. He looks like he knows something you don't know, and not only is it about you, it's also something not very nice. After leaving The Show, he pitched five more years in the minors before retiring. Ballplayers used to do that kind of thing. They used to have to. He is an SR: A.

Best game in the 1961 season: Jim hurled six scoreless innings against the White Sox on June 20.

Card #453, Dick Schofield, going to his left. This canny old vet (even though he was only 26 years old, 1961 was his ninth season in the Bigs) has got it down pat—crouch, inhale, exhale, inhale, react! Dick's father, John, played in the minors for 10 years, his son, Richard, played in the majors for 14 years, and his grandson, Jason

Werth, spent 15 years in the Show. He was SR: A ranked before his death in 2022. On my card, he added, "In Majors at 18/19 Year Major Leaguer."

Best game in the 1961 season: He went 2–4 against the Dodgers on June 28 with two RBI, his only two that season.

Card #454, Pumpsie Green, feigning a fielding chance in Fenway. Elijah labored in the minors for seven and a half years before finally getting the gracious opportunity[88] to become the Red Sox's first African American player in 1959 (you read that right—1959). His other main (but very secondary) claim to fame is getting off the team bus (stuck in New York traffic) on June 25, 1962, with Gene Conley (see above) when Gene tried to talk him into flying to Israel. Mr. Green (SR: A) passed away at 85 in 2019. His brother, Cornell, played in the NFL for 13 years.

Best game in the 1961 season: On August 20, he went 3–3 against the Tigers with two runs, a double, and a triple.

Card #455, Early Wynn, smirking at the camera in Yankee Stadium. Famous for saying that he'd brush back his own mother if she tried to crowd the plate, I'll be dadgummed if he doesn't look like he would do just that.[89] Early hit .217 with 17 homers and had nine seasons with 10 or more RBI (and five with 10 or more walks[90]). He stole his only base (on his only attempt) when he was 36. He was among the ten youngest players as a rookie in 1939 and among the 10 oldest his last six years.

Best game in the 1961 season: He beat the Athletics 2–1 on May 12, giving up just four hits.

Card #456, Hal Bevan, daydreaming between pitches. He appears to be casting his memory back to when he was a fresh-faced and hopeful 21-year-old. The 1961 season was Hal's 13th season in pro ball. In those 13 years, he had had two tiny bites of the Major League macaroon. He played in the minors for 15 years, amassing 1,582 games and 1,618 hits, walked more often than he struck out, and accrued a fine .295 batting average.[91] Mr. Bevan proved to be a very hard-to-find "get." He died when he was only 37 in 1968, and at this late date, I can't tell if he was a hard "sign" or if there just weren't many folks back in the late 1960s looking for his autograph. In the

2. The Quest for Fire

event, I did not acquire a signed '61 Bevan until the mid–1990s and only found and purchased my third one in 2018.

Best game in the 1961 season: On May 12, Mr. Bevan pinch-hit against the Pirates and hit a home run. He had a perfect "three perfect outcomes" season, striking out twice and hitting a home run in his other at-bat.

Card #457, Johnny James "pitching" in Al Lang Field. Meaning absolutely no disrespect, but in this image, Johnny looks like a disgruntled (but very slim) oompa loompa.[92] He was only the 12th major leaguer born in Idaho (even though he grew up in SoCal). He told me that one of his classmates at Hollywood High was Carol Burnett, whom he remembers as (surprise!) a sweet and funny girl. SR: A+

Best game in the 1961 season: On May 24, he pitched 3⅔ scoreless innings against the Athletics.

Card #458, Willie Tasby, head shot with bat on shoulder, Memorial Stadium. Dude looks pleased as punch. Another McClymonds High product,[93] it took Willie nine years to reach the majors, and by then he had already hit 139 homers in the minors. He was an SR: A returnee before his passing in 2022.

Relaxed, confident, and stalwart-looking on his card, Hal Bevan endured a litany of injuries over the course of his career—1948, fractured jaw; 1949, injured ankle; 1950, beaned, missed 10 games; 1952, fractured ankle; 1961, broken finger, dislocated thumb. He was only 37 when he died of a kidney infection.

Best game in the 1961 season: On April 22, he went 3–4 with a home run against the Twins.

Searchin' for Toothpick Sam

Card #459, Terry Fox, head and shoulders shot, another of those photos apparently taken in an empty swimming pool. Although he looks like he worked in an auto-parts store, Terry was in fact the first reliever with at least 50 innings pitched to record back-to-back seasons with an ERA below 2.00, beating Hoyt Wilhelm by two years. In fact, on my card he wrote, "83 games/61–62 1.57 ERA."[94] SR: A.

Best game in the 1961 season: On April 9 against Cleveland he pitched three scoreless innings with four strikeouts.

Card #460, Gil Hodges,[95] batting stance in Wrigley Field. He looks just like every description of him I have ever read: stolid, strong, and self-contained, but definitely not a man you want to get upset with you. You may not have noticed, but the card has him as a "First Base·Catcher," even though he had only caught in two games since 1948 and would never play that position again. A battle-hardened Marine (he served on Okinawa and earned a Bronze Star), he passed away in 1972 when he was only 47 and before I started getting my cards signed, so I cannot comment on his signing habits, but I can state that I was not able to find one to purchase until sometime in the 2000s, and I didn't get my third signed '61 Hodges until 2018.

Best game in the 1961 season: On July 27 against the Phils, Gil went 4–5 with a home run and three RBI.

Card #461, Smoky Burgess, head shot in Forbes Field, Rocky Nelson in the background. It is possible that no player in the entire set (with the exception of Jack Curtis [see below]) looks less like a major league ballplayer than does Forrest, shown here eyeing the ribs being munched on by a fan behind the dugout. He hit .286 in 504 ABs as a pinch-hitter with 16 homers and a terrific 147 (!) RBI. Since he was used as a pinch-hitter a total of 606 times and rarely struck out (once every 16.5 at-bats) and in his entire career had only 13 sacrifice hits and 39 sac flies, when we add in 75 walks as a pinch hitter, he wound up with a very good .374 OBP. Others may have surpassed his totals, but he is still the greatest pinch-hitter in MLB history. Smoky passed away rather young (he was 64 when he died in 1991), but he had been SR: A all the way.

Best game in the 1961 season: Smoky went 5–5 with a home run and four RBI against the Phillies on August 8.

2. The Quest for Fire

Card #462, Lou Klimchock, head and shoulders shot in Connie Mack Field in West Palm Beach (but I wouldn't bet my cards on it). Lou looks like a Shavetail (or, if you prefer, Butter Bar) addressing his platoon for the first time. Lou (SR: A) got what might be a record nine tries to stick in the majors. He hit .136 in 162 at-bats as a pinch-hitter. My card has "Pioneer League All Star 1959/Souther Assoc All Star 1959" added to his signature.

Best game in the 1961 season: On April 25, Lou went 2–2 with two runs and two RBI against the Twins.

Card #463 (see note after card #426), Jack Fisher, follow-through after a "pitch" in Municipal Stadium. Another in the 1961 *Looks Like a High Schooler* subset, he is an SR: A. In September of 1965, he went 0–6 with a 3.38 ERA and a WHIP of 1.22, giving up more than three runs only once in five starts. The Mets were not fun to pitch for from 1962 to 1968.

Best game in the 1961 season: Jack beat the Yankees, 5–3, on September 21, all of the Yankees' runs being unearned.

Card #464, LeRoy Thomas, follow-through on a swing in Al Lang Field. From the expression on his face, he appears to have "hit" the ball into the dirt directly in front of the batter's box. (Remember, this was in the days when all batting coaches were preaching the "swing down and don't hit the ball in the air" gospel.) SR: A for Mr. Thomas who passed away in 2022.

Best game in the 1961 season: An early-season trade brought LeRoy from the Yankees to the Angels. For the Angels against the Athletics on September 5, LeRoy went 4–5 with three home runs and eight RBI, second-most for an A.L. batter in the 1961 season.

Card #465, Roy McMillan, headshot in County Stadium, Vada Pinson in the background. No player looked more like a professor than Roy. Still rated highly in many defensive metrics, Roy was SR: A before he passed at 68 in 1997.

Best game in the 1961 season: On April 26, Roy went 3–6 with a home run and two runs scored against the Cardinals.

Card #466, Ron Moeller, head and shoulders shot in an unidentifiable park, and the uniform is neither that of the Angels nor the Orioles, his former team. He looked more like a boxer than a ballplayer, as in "Ronnie 'The Whirlwind' Mō-ō-ō-ō-ō-ler." In the majors at 17 (he went 33–2 in high school and American Legion ball), he was out of baseball by 24. Mr. Moeller passed away at 71 in 2009 and was an SR: A guy.

Best game in the 1961 season: On June 5, Ron pitched a six-hit shutout against his former team, Baltimore, striking out a career-high nine batters.

Card #467, Cleveland Indians Team card. Mine is signed by coaches Luke Appling, Mel Harder, and Mel McGaha. I also have a team card signed by non-carded players Sam McDowell, Al Luplow, and Jack Kubiszyn, and one signed by minor league managers Herman Franks and George Strickland.

Card #468, Johnny Callison, taking his ease somewhere in the vicinity of the on-deck circle in Connie Mack Stadium. Holy Cowfish, does he look like an athlete or what? Possessed of every tool a ballplayer needs, he, like so many supremely gifted young men, didn't live up to his advance notices. It must be said, however, that he came closer than most—after all, he made three All-Star teams, finished second in the 1965 MVP vote, led his league in triples twice (and had at least 10 triples five consecutive years), hit 226 homers, and is still ranked 12th all-time in assists by a right fielder (he led in assists five times *during* the Clemente era). In fact, he was considered the 50th-best right fielder of all time by Baseball-Reference's Hall of Fame statistics at the time of this writing, and that's something (he has since declined to 53rd). Mr. Callison was an SR: A+ before passing at 67 in 2006.

Best game in the 1961 season: Against St. Louis on August 4, Johnny went 4–5 with a double, a home run, and three runs.

Card #469, Ralph Lumenti, head and shoulder shot taken In Tinker Field, Orlando. He was the possessor of an intense, near-monobrow look, and I'll bet he made the ladies go all a-quiver in the classroom if they caught his eye. He was the only player in the '61 set with the same birthday as mine. I think that it took four cards to get my three signed (although he did sign the '60 Leaf first shot), so I'm giving him an SR of B+. He died in 2018 at age 81, another Bonus Baby brought up too soon and who flamed out early.

2. The Quest for Fire

Best game in the 1961 season: Ralph did not pitch in the majors in 1961.

Card #470, Roy Sievers, batting stance taken in Yankee Stadium. He was probably my third- or fourth-favorite player in the early 1960s, and by all accounts, he was a very nice man. An SR: A before his passing at 90 in 2017, he looks particularly steely-eyed in this photo. My card has the added notation, "R.O.Y. 49/All Star 56–57/59–61."

Best game in the 1961 season: Roy went 4–5 against the Orioles on June 11. On June 12, he went 3–5 against the Orioles with a double and two home runs, scoring and driving in three runs each. On June 21 against the Indians, he went 3–4 with four runs. On May 7 against the Tigers, he went 2–4 with two home runs and six RBI.

Card #471, Phil Rizzuto, headshot, Most Valuable Player subset. An absolutely terrific signer, SR: A+.

Card #472, Yogi Berra, bat on shoulder, Most Valuable Player subset, see above.

Card #473, Bobby Shantz, looking for the sign, Most Valuable Player subset, see above.

Card #474, Al Rosen, headshot, Most Valuable Player subset. An SR: A man until his passing at 91 in 2015. He manned an assault boat during the invasion of Okinawa and left the service as a Navy lieutenant (which is the equivalent of an Army captain).

Card #475, Mickey Mantle, headshot, Most Valuable Player subset, see above.

Card #476, Jackie Jensen, headshot, Most Valuable Player subset, see below.

Card #477, Nellie Fox, batting stance, Most Valuable Player subset, see above.

Card #478, Roger Maris, swinging, Most Valuable Player subset, see above.

Card #479, Jim Konstanty, headshot, Most Valuable Player subset, SR: A. He earned 16 letters in four sports while at Syracuse University, including four in boxing (he may be the only major keaguer to letter in boxing). Mr. Konstanty was only 59 at the time of his passing in 1976.

Searchin' for Toothpick Sam

Card #480, Roy Campanella, head shot, Most Valuable Player subset. Obviously, Mr. Campanella was unable to sign this card. He did, however, very occasionally go to shows and hand stamp cards, and that's how I got mine "signed."

Card #481, Hank Sauer, headshot, Most Valuable Player subset, SR: A.

Card #482, Willie Mays, batting stance, Most Valuable Player subset, see above.

Card #483, Don Newcombe, headshot, Most Valuable Player subset, SR: A+.

Card #484, Hank Aaron headshot, Most Valuable Player subset, see above.

Card #485, Ernie Banks headshot, Most Valuable Player subset, see above.

Card #486, Dick Groat, headshot, Most Valuable Player subset, see above.

Card #487, Gene Oliver, squatting in Al Lang Field in St. Petersburg. He certainly looked the part as his card is unique in that his position is listed as "Catcher-Infield-Outfield." In the event, during his career he played 201 games at first base, 91 in the outfield, and 381 as a catcher. He was also used as a pinch-hitter 172 times. Gene hit 151 home runs in the five and a half years he spent in the minors before gaining a permanent spot in The Show. Mr. Oliver (SR: A) passed away at age 71 in 2007.

Best game in the 1961 season: Against the Pirates on September 16, he went 2–4 with a home run and two RBI. He also scored twice.

Card #488, Joe McClain, looking for a sign in Pompano Beach Municipal Park. Unfortunately for Joe, this is one of the goofiest-looking cards in the entire set. In one of those watercolor-like cards which make this set so cool,[96] Joe looks like a cross between a squirrel and the squinty kid in class who eats paste. (No offense, Mr. McClain. You didn't take the picture, and you weren't the one who decided to use it on a card.) He pitched a lot better than his eventual 8–18 record would indicate, for in 20 of his 30 starts, the Senators scored three or fewer runs. Something must have happened to his arm or elbow or shoulder in either the 1961–1962

2. The Quest for Fire

off-season or Spring Training, because whatever ability and promise he showed in '61 was gone like Ozymandias in '62.[97] He is SR: A.

Best game in the 1961 season: he shut out Boston on five hits on May 14.

Card #489, Walt Dropo, batting stance in Memorial Stadium. Another avuncular gent, he looked like the uncle that taught you how to play ball. The Moose from Moosup was one of the more amazing of the amazing athletes who populate these pages. Scouted personally by George Halas and drafted by the Bears, drafted #4 in the 1947 NBA draft (he averaged a for-the-time phenomenal 20.7 PPG as a senior), he was Dave Winfield before Dave Winfield was born.[98] During *the* War, he served as a 12B (combat engineer), one of the most dangerous wartime jobs in the Army. As mentioned in the Introduction, this card was the gateway to a whole new world for me, and I just love it. Mr. Dropo was SR: A all the way. (I even sent the taped-together card to him to sign, and he did.) He was 87 when he died in 2010. On my card he added the notations, "1950 AL ROY/12 Consecutive Hits July 1952." (In the 17 games between July 5 and 25, 1952, he went 33–70 [.471] and raised his average from .262 to .304.)

Best game in the 1961 season: On April 30, he went 2–2 against the Tigers with a home run.

Before steroids and HGH, this is what a slugger looked like. In this photograph, Walt Dropo also looks as if he is very much aware that his career is drawing to a close.

Searchin' for Toothpick Sam

Card #490, Jim Bunning, headshot in Henley Field, Lakeland. He does look extremely self-confident in this photo, and he doesn't appear at all crazy. Jim and his wife Mary had nine children, Barb, Joan, Cathy, Bridget, Amy, Jim Jr., Bill, Mark, and David, and 35 grandchildren. The first cards that I sent to him were signed by him, but his signings in the 20 years preceding his demise at 85 in 2017 were done by a secretary. SR: F (See Card #150).

Best game in the 1961 season: he pitched a four-hit shutout against the White Sox on August 8.

Card #491, Philadelphia Phillies team card. Mine is signed by coaches Al Vincent and Bob Lemon. I also have a team card signed by non-carded players Chris Short, Frank Herrera, Charlie Smith, George Williams, and Jack Baldschun, another signed by Cal Neeman and Darrell Johnson, another signed by minor league manager Andy Seminick, and another signed by minor league manager Stan Benjamin.

Card #492, Ron Fairly, batting stance in Holman Stadium. In my opinion, in this image, he is the most collegiate-looking of all the ballplayers in this set. His father played in the minors, getting as high as what today would be Triple A and collecting over 1,300 hits. Add him to the short list of those who were among the 10 youngest players at the start of his career and the 10 oldest by the time it ended. Ron, who was recruited by John Wooden to play basketball for UCLA, died in 2019 at 81, having been an SR: A. He was another player from the set who became a long-time broadcaster. Some Ron Fairly trivia: He is the only player with at least 200 home runs who never had a 20-home runs season, and I believe that he is one of only two players to have at least 1,000 RBI without an 80-RBI season (the other being Tim Raines).

Best game in the 1961 season: He went 4–5 with four RBI against the Braves on September 16.

Card #493, Don Zimmer, Chew Crew sergeant major, taking a breather in Wrigley Field. Don is shown here practicing Zen Yoga, of which he was so fond, demonstrating the correct hand to knee position when contemplating a cheek full of dip. He was an SR: A before he passed at 83 in 2014. Note that his card has both the Brooklyn and

2. The Quest for Fire

Los Angeles Dodgers as being in the *American* League. That fact gets a great big "[sic]."

Best game in the 1961 season: He went 3–4 against the Phillies on July 23, scoring four runs, hitting two home runs, and driving in four runs.

Card #494, Tom Cheney, headshot in Forbes Field. He looks like he just got called on in class to name the capitol of New Jersey.[99] He died in 2001 at 67, and he had been SR: A. His card also has "21 Ks—2-12-62," obviously an error as he certainly didn't strike anyone out on February 12 of any year. He should have written 9-12-62.

Best game in the 1961 season: Tom's best performance was a two and a third inning stint against the White Sox with three strikeouts.

Card #495, Elston Howard, batting stance in Yankee Stadium. That might be Harry, my second cousin once removed on my father's side, in the background.[100] Mr. Howard, the first Black man to play for the Yankees, died in 1980, when he was only 51. He signed the items I sent him before his passing. SR: A.

Best game in the 1961 season: He had 15 games in 1961 with at least three hits. On June 4 against the White Sox, he went 3–4 with three RBI.

Card #496, Ken MacKenzie, shown here demonstrating his take-down move to the photographer at McKechnie Field in Bradenton. Ken was the only Yale Eli in the majors between 1960 and 1979. SR: A.

Best game in the 1961 season: Against the Giants on April 30: one inning, no hits, no runs, one strikeout.

Card #497, Willie Jones, calling the team cat in Al Lopez Field, Tampa. It looks like his back just went out. Willie never signed anything I sent (see story re: Willie above), hence SR: F. He died at 58 in 1983.

Best game in the 1961 season: In his last game in the majors on May 7 against the Braves, he walked as a pinch-hitter and later scored.

Card #498, Ray Herbert, headshot in Yankee Stadium. Mr. Herbert was so proud when he heard that his prize pupil had been accepted at Morton College (founded 1924) in faraway Cicero. Mr.

Searchin' for Toothpick Sam

Herbert had been an SR: A before his passing in 2022. My card also has "A.L. All Star '1962.'"

Best game in the 1961 season: with the Athletics, one run in six innings against Boston on April 11; with the White Sox, a 4–1, complete-game win against the Angels on June 14.

Card #499, Chuck Schilling, watercolor-style head and shoulder shot taken in the swimming pool which was mentioned earlier. In this image, he looks a lot like a painting by Tibor Gergely in an LGB.[101] A fine signer, SR: A.

Best game in the 1961 season: He went 3–4 with four runs against the Angels on June 20.

Card #500, Harvey Kuenn, Crewcut Company and Chew Crew member. Although it hurts him to have to do it, he knows that he has to turn down another extension on Emil "Spud" Andersen's farm loan. Harvey, a lifelong SR: A, was only 57 when he died in 1988. Mr. Kuenn added, "2092 [hits]—303 [batting average]."

Best game in the 1961 season: Harvey went 4–6 with four RBI against the Pirates on July 25.

Card #501. John DeMerit, headshot taken in McKechnie Field. Here seen looking back on his life and wishing that he had been able to start his pro career in Class B ball instead of sitting on the bench in Milwaukee for two years. Johnny, who earned 16 letters in high school, is an SR: A man.

Best game in the 1961 season: He went 3–4 against the Pirates on April 23.

Card #502, Clarence[102] Coleman squatting insouciantly in Clearwater's Jack Russelll Stadium. Clarence liked to take little catnaps between pitches, and he spent the 1957 season barnstorming with the Indianapolis Clowns. Until he was located in 2011 or 2012, he had been lost in the mystic for almost 50 years, at least as far as answering his mail was concerned. *If* the addresses I had for him over the years were correct, then he was an SR: F. By the way, my all-time favorite Choo Choo story is the one where a reporter asked him what he called his wife and he answered "Mrs. Coleman."

Best game in the 1961 season: May 9 was Choo Choo's premier 1961 effort. He got 25 percent of his season's RBI, 33 percent

2. The Quest for Fire

of his runs, 50 percent of his walks and 100 percent of his extra base hits.

Card #503, Tito Francona, Chew Crew member, using the dugout roof to hold up his bats, in what I think is Yankee Stadium. Here he is shown trying to see if he can steal the Indians' third base coach's signs. Terry's dad, he was an SR: A+ before passing away in 2018 at 84. Tito added, "A.L. All Star/1961" to his signature.

Best game in the 1961 season: Against the Indians on July 20, he went 4–4, hit a home run, and drove in three runs.

Card #504, Billy Consolo, bat on shoulder in Orlando's Tinker Field. Billy, a barber in the off-season,[103] is looking at Dan Dobbek's head (see above) and wondering what he could do with Dan's 'do. Mr. Consolo, an SR: A, died at 73 in 2008.

Best game in the 1961 season: Used as a pinch-runner on May 18, he scored a run against the Athletics.

Card #505, Red Schoendienst, noted lentiginous ginger, head and shoulder shot, still wearing his Braves uniform, taken during Spring Training. "Are you lookin' at me? Are you lookin' at me? I don't see anyone else here—are you lookin' at me?" He had three brothers (Julius, Elmer, and Joseph) who also played pro ball, as did his son, Kevin. I also believe that minor leaguers Louis and Paul Schoendienst were his cousins. Red (SR: A) passed away at 95 in 2018. His card has "10 Time All Star/Hall of Fame 89" written on it.

Best game in the 1961 season: On April 23 against the Giants, he went 3–5 with a home run and two RBI.

Card #506, Willie Davis, taking a serious cut in Holman Stadium. Tell them Willie Boy is here.[104] He looks as if he's warning the N.L. that he's a'comin'. If he had played his entire career after they lowered the mound in 1969, he might very well have been in the Hall of Fame conversation. He was one of the fastest major leaguers ever, running a 9.5 100-yard dash in high school, just one-tenth of a second slower than Herb Washington. He also long jumped 25'5", second only to Jackie Robinson's 25'6", all-time among major leaguers (and the high school record at the time). The only major leaguers in the past 70 years who hit more triples than Willie are Roberto Clemente, Willie Mays, Lou Brock, and Willie Wilson.

Searchin' for Toothpick Sam

Best games in the 1961 season: On July 26, he went 4–4 against the Phils, and on May 27, he went 3–5 against the Braves with a triple, two home runs, and five RBI.

Card #507, Pete Burnside, head and shoulders shot in Pompano Beach Municipal Park. A proud Ivy League graduate, Pete, in his mind, is basking in the adulation and respect he imagined he would be receiving from his hayseed teammates. (Paraphrasing the immortal Bugs Bunny, he don't know them very well, does he?) Pete, who passed away in 2022, was an SR: A club member.

Best game in the 1961 season: he shut out the A's on September 16 and again on September 29. He pitched 22 innings in six games against Kansas City in '61 without giving up a run and allowed just eight hits, 3.3/9.

Card #508, Rocky Bridges, Grand Panjandrum of the Chew Crew, taken in Palm Springs Stadium, Ken Hunt in the background. Now that, my friends, is a ballplayer—or what used to be one, anyway. One might even say that he was the physical embodiment of a John R. Tunis character. John R. was the most popular author of kids' baseball books ([an actual one-time niche] in the 1940s and 1950s). Mr. Bridges (SR: A) passed at 87 in 2015.

Best game in the 1961 season: Rocky went 3–4 against the Athletics on July 4 with the game-winning, three-run home run.

Card #509, Camilo Carreon, upper body outlined against, for some reason, a wall of rich,

If baseball cliches had dictionary entries, this photograph would run alongside "just happy to be here." Rocky Bridges managed for 21 seasons in the minor leagues, including 11 consecutive years for the Giants' Triple-A Pacific Coast League team. He won a championship with Phoenix in 1977.

2. The Quest for Fire

creamy butter. Unafraid, our steadfast young hero gazes into a future bright with promise, already visualizing the rich fields of clover upon which his winged feet shall soon be treading. Would that the fates had somehow ordained that he and Camilo Pascual had, for one glorious season, been teammates, they would have formed the major leagues' only All-Camilo battery. His son, Mark, also played in the Bigs. Mr. Carreon died young and was only 50 when he passed in 1987. He had been SR: A.

Best game in the 1961 season: Cam went 4–4 against Baltimore on July 22.

Card #510, Art Ditmar, headshot. Most ill-fated of all the players in this set *whose card ended with a zero*, Art would win only two more games in his major league career. He is SR: A, or at least has been for me.

Best game in the 1961 season: he split his season between the Yanks and the A's. He beat Cleveland, 4–3, with a complete game for New York on April 27. For the Athletics, he had two four-inning, scoreless relief appearances, against the White Sox on August 13 and against the Angels on September 4.

Card #511, Joe Morgan, headshot, Hi Corbett Field in Tucson. He looks like a farmer looking out over a field of hay ruined by a hard, early rain. Joe was an All-American in hockey. SR: A.

Best game in the 1961 season: On May 2, he went 2–5 against the Indians.

Card #512, Bob Will, headshot. One of the most teacherly-looking (probably geometry) of the 1961 Topps players and owner of a minor league batting average of .333 and an on-base percentage well over .400, Bob never became the big leaguer the Cubs spent seven years waiting for. An SR: A man, Mr. Will passed at 80 in 2011. Mr. Will added, "All Star 54 Pioneer/55 III 56 Texas 58 AA" to his signature.

Best game in the 1961 season: On May 13, he went 3–4 against the Dodgers.

Card #513, Jim Brosnan, head and shoulders shot in Crosley Field. Even more teacherly than Mr. Will immediately above, I would even go so far as to say that Mr. Brosnan looked professorial. He was unceremoniously cut after four straight seasons of being in the top 10 in saves (with a 2.91 ERA) because baseball had neither place nor patience for a player who wrote books (and precious little for those who read them either, a situation that has changed very little since then). SR: A, he died at 84 in 2014. His card also has the notation "The Long Season/Pennant Race," his two best-sellers.

Best game in the 1961 season: The Professor pitched four scoreless innings against the Braves on July 2 to get the win.

Card #514, Jake Wood, head shot, apparently somewhere in the grain belt of the Ukraine. At 13 and in what used to be called junior high, I thought he looked like a cool 18-year-old. Now that I have grandkids who have graduated from high school, I think he looks 13 and cocky. His brother, Richard, spent 10 years in the NFL. SR: A.

Jake was a minor league whiz and added "1957 NYP All Star/1958 Pioneer All Star/1959 SALLY All Star/1960 AA All Star" to his signature.

Best games in the 1961 season: Jake went 5–5 against the White Sox on August 8 and 3–3 with four runs against them on June 28. He hit .408 (29/71) against Chicago in 1961.

Card #515, Jackie Brandt, batting stance in Memorial Stadium. He looked like the second baseman on Theodore "Beaver" Cleaver's Little League team in Mayfield. He is an SR: A guy. His card also has "61 All Star/59 Gold Glove" inscribed on it.

Best games in the 1961 season: Against Chicago on May 30, he went 4–4, and against the Yankees on April 22, he went 3–4 with two home runs, three runs and three RBI.

Card #516, TOPPS BASEBALL CHECK LIST, 7th Series. Featuring (and signed by) Johnny Logan and Chuck Cottier in Wrigley Field, it looks as if Johnny has flubbed a potential double play.

Card #517, Willie McCovey, kneeling in Scottsdale Stadium. He appears to be deeply contemplating the number 42. Big Mac passed at 80 in 2018. He had been SR: A all the way.

Best games in the 1961 season: On April 29, he went 3–5 with two home runs and four RBI against Milwaukee.

Card #518, Andy Carey, head and shoulder shot in Yankee Stadium. Stuck on the dreadfully bad Athletics, Andy, like Norm

2. The Quest for Fire

Siebern and Jerry Lumpe above, is remembering when *he* used to sit in the first base dugout in the Stadium. An SR: A, Mr. Carey died at age 80 in 2011.

Best game in the 1961 season: Andy played for the White Sox and Athletics in '61. His best game for Kansas City was on May 9, when he went 2–3 with two doubles against Whitey Ford of the Yankees, and his best game for Chicago was a 3–4 game against Detroit on June 27 in which he hit two triples and scored three runs.

Card #519, Jim Pagliaroni, about to shuck his mask in the Scottsdale sun. In this photo, he is shown failing in his attempt to pat his head and rub his stomach concurrently. A Hawaiian shirt devotee, Mr. Pagliaroni (SR: A) passed away in 2010. He was 72. At my request, he added, "On deck batter when Ted Williams hit his last home run" to his signature.

Best game in the 1961 season: he went 3–4 with a double, a home run, five RBI, and three runs against Detroit on September 8.

Card #520, Joe Cunningham, head and shoulder shot in Sportsman's Park. Here, Joe is transfixed by a plane flying by overhead, pulling a banner promoting *Herbie* comics.[105] SR: A, he wrote, "1959 All Star" on the card.

Best game in the 1961 season: On April 17, he went 4–5 with three runs against the Dodgers.

Card #521, Brother Battery, featuring Norm and Larry Sherry, taken in County Stadium. Norm did not have a card of his own in the '61 set.

Card #522, Dick Farrell, headshot, taken in Jack Russell Memorial Stadium (notice that Dick is pictured wearing his Phillies uniform). Shown here is the photo he sent to the William Morris Agency in his attempt to become the next Tab Hunter. He died in a car accident in England in 1977, shortly after I began my autograph odyssey and before I had a chance to write him, so I can't rate him as a signer, but the scarcity of cards signed by him (I didn't get my third signed "61T Farrell until into the 2010s) may mean that he was a hard get.... He was only 43 at the time of his demise.

Best game in the 1961 season: On May 28 for the Dodgers, he threw six scoreless innings against the Braves.

Searchin' for Toothpick Sam

And then the change came...

...Behold! The vaunted, fabled, storied, legendary myth-enshrouded 1961 Topps Highs.

Card #523, Joe Gibbon, doing something to something from Area 51 that somehow made its way to Connie Mack Stadium. (Well, let's see now, a chunk of pure Osmium [the heaviest naturally occurring substance on Earth] that size would weigh right around 16 pounds, and since whatever Joe is lifting is clearly at least four times that, it is therefore obvious that whatever is in his left hand is ... not of this earth.) His senior year playing hoops at Ole Miss, Joe, a 6'4" forward, averaged 14.1 rebounds and was second in the nation with a 30 PPG average. An SR: A man, Mr. Gibbon passed on at age 83 in 2019.

Best games in the 1961 season: On May 31 he beat the Braves 9–1 and had 10 strikeouts and on July 20 he shut out the Cubs with nine strikeouts.

Card #524, Johnny Logan, ready to fling the ol' pea. In this instance, Johnny appears to be feinting a chimerical runner caught in a phantasmic rundown back to a notional bag. Mr. Logan, who died in 2013 at 87, always was SR: A.

Best game in the 1961 season: he played for the Braves and the Pirates in '61, pinch-hitting 31 times in his 45 games. His best appearance was against

Joe Gibbon averaged 22.6 points and 11.4 rebounds over his last three years playing basketball at Ole Miss. In the 1956 NCAA baseball championship tournament, he hit .396 and slugged .909 for the university, then hit .425 for the 1957 regular season.

2. The Quest for Fire

the Phillies on June 25, when he got a hit, drove in a run and later scored.

Card #525, Ron Perranoski, headshot in front of a giant block of Velveeta. Another of the few (fewer than 10) cards which didn't instantly bring a thought about itself and/or the player thereupon depicted. I did notice that, on this card, the left side of his face looked like a surfer dude, while the right side looked more bowling league-ish. Note that this rookie got one of the coveted ending-in-five numbers. Mr. Perranoski, who passed away in 2020 at the age of 84, was an off-and-on signer, hence his SR: C rating. (It might have been higher, but those '61 high replacement cards don't come cheap.) He did add "737 Games/2.79 Lifetime ERA" to my set #1 card.

Best game in the 1961 season: His best appearance was a four-inning, one-hit, four-strikeout game against the Reds on August 16.

Card #526. R.C. Stevens, headshot, somewhere on Earth, probably somewhere in the Northern Hemisphere/Western Hemisphere quadrants of the oblate spheroid we call home. Note that, although the card has R.C. on it, plain old R C was his given name. He was a basher in the Bushes, where he hit 191 homers. An SR: A club member, he died at 76 in 2010.

Best game in the 1961 season: R C went 2–4 against the White Sox on April 20.

Card #527, Gene Leek, taking five after bending down to pick up a loose ball in Palm Springs Stadium. SR: A.

Best game in the 1961 season: He went 3–4 against the Senators on May 22 with two doubles.

Card #528, Pedro Ramos, Chew Crew jemidar, head and shoulders shot. He may well have had the longest hair in the majors in 1961, and he wasn't bashful about using "product." Pedro made 120 appearances as a pinch-runner, and he also led the AL in losses for four consecutive years, 1958–1961. He was a gun-totin' wild man for many a year during and after his time in the majors, but he was always good for a signature. SR: A.

Best game in the 1961 season: He went 3–3 at the plate with a home run and scored three times against the White Sox on May 16.

Searchin' for Toothpick Sam

On the mound, he pitched a three-hit shutout against the Yankees on April 11.

Card #529, Bob Roselli, batting stance in Payne Park, Sarasota. This is a photo of a man just happy to be wearing the uniform. He was an SR: A before his passing at 77 in 2009.

Best game in the 1961 season: On June 29 against Detroit, he went a career-best 3–4.

Card #530, Bobby Malkmus, follow-through on a swing in Jack Russell Memorial Stadium in Clearwater. A nice fellow and an SR: A, he told me that his best friend in baseball (and still today) was Don Demeter. A real puzzle to me as to why he got a card ending in zero, however.

Best game in the 1961 season: Against Milwaukee on August 17, he went 3–4 with three RBI.

Card #531, Jim Coates, doing his Imhotep imitation[106] in Yankee Stadium. Nicknamed "the Mummy," he toiled in the minors for 15 seasons before, during and after his time in The Show, winning 139 games. He only very rarely returned a card I sent (1–7, .143 in baseball terms), and then stopped altogether (although later on, he would sign for a fee). SR: D-/F+.

Best game in the 1961 season: He shut out the Angels on four hits on August 9.

Card #532, Bob Hale, head and shoulders shot in Hi Corbett Field, Steve Demeter in the background. Shown here in the guise of "concerned citizen," he was a consistent .300 hitter in the minors. However, he had little power and thus could not win a regular job in the Bigs. Of his 376 games in the majors, almost three-quarters (278) were as a pinch-hitter. He hit .247 with no home runs and 58 RBI as a pinch-hitter, and .294 in non–PH roles. An SR: A, Mr. Hale passed at 78 in 2012.

Best game in the 1961 season: Playing for the Indians and the Yankees in '61, he hit a pinch-hit home run for New York against the Senators on September 6.

Card #533, Jack Curtis, headshot. Oh my gosh, if any proof was needed that back in the day, the players had no say over what their baseball cards looked like, one need look no further. Is this where

2. The Quest for Fire

an eight-year-old Matt Groening got the idea for Nelson Muntz?[107] Is this a photo of a fifth-grader who already weighs 180 pounds and wants to know why he has to share his birthday cake? Why is Jack standing in front of a huge Andy Warhol painting of an egg yolk? So many questions, so few answers.... Despite the unflattering picture, Jack is SR: A all the way down the line. His card has "All Star Northwest 1959/Texas 1960" on it in addition to his signature.

Best game in the 1961 season: he beat the Giants, 6–1, on August 31.

Card #534, Eddie Kasko, batting stance, park unidentifiable, Ed Bailey in the background. Although I like this card, sadly, it never spoke to me. Even looking at it now, six decades later, I am receiving no messages from either my own (formerly) nimble mind or The Great Beyond. Mr. Kasko was SR: A until his death at 88 in 2020. "N.L. All Star 1961" is also written on his card.

Best game in the 1961 season: Eddie went 4–5 against the Dodgers on August 15.

Card #535, Larry Jackson, windup in Connie Mack Stadium. By the look on his face, you can tell that he's not thinking about pitching to Willie or Hank, and it's more likely that Bob Buhl is at bat (see above). I asked Mr. Jackson if he was ever sorry that he retired before reaching 200 wins (he retired with 194 wins after going 13–17 with a fine 2.77 ERA for the seventh-place Phillies in 1968), and he told me that he had no regrets at all. A solid SR: A, Mr. Jackson was only 59 when he passed away in 1990.

Best games in the 1961 season: He twice shut out the Giants on three hits, on August 17 and 27.

Card #536, Bill Tuttle, Chew Crew Nabob, headshot at Connie Mack Field in West Palm Beach. He looks like a rancher who just got news that his cattle have blackleg.[108] Mr. Tuttle died at 69 in 1998, having been an SR: A from when I started getting cards signed.

Best game in the 1961 season: He played for the Athletics and the Twins in '61. His best game for Kansas City was on April 25, when he went 3–5 with three runs and four RBI against his future team, and his best game as a Twin was on September 27, when he went 3–3 with two runs against the Indians.

Searchin' for Toothpick Sam

Card #537, Bobby Locke, follow-through after unleashing a real whizzer in Municipal Stadium. If all it took was grit, according to this photo, Bobby was destined to be a star. He was a good enough athlete to go to Arizona State on a football scholarship. A good hitter for a pitcher, his MLB batting average was a very respectable .255. A solid SR: A, Mr. Locke passed at 86 in 2020.

Best game in the 1961 season: He threw 6⅔ shutout innings to beat the Red Sox on May 17.

Card #538, Chuck Hiller, ready to pounce on a dribbler in Candlestick. The coach is going to tell him to decide if he wants to be a ballplayer or a beatnik (and to lose those JD sideburns too). SR: A, he was 70 when he died in 2004.

Best game in the 1961 season: he went 3–6 with two doubles against the Braves on April 30.

Card #539, Johnny Klippstein, headshot in Yankee Stadium. Shown here checking himself out in the barbershop mirror, Johnny was 33 years old going into the '61 season and was already in his 17th year of pro ball (he had also missed two seasons while serving in the Army). His career lasted 23 years, from 1943, when he was a 16-year-old pitching in the Class D Ohio State League, to 1967, when he rung down the curtain with the Tigers in his 18th major league season at 39. Always an SR: A, he passed away at age 75 in 2003. His card says, "started pro career at 16/23 years in O.B." in addition to his signature.

Best game in the 1961 season: There were four different games in which he threw two scoreless innings.

Card #540, Jackie Jensen, headshot in Fenway Park. Baseball's most noted aviophobe, he already looks worried about the team's next flight. (He had sat out the entire 1960 season after ranking in the top 10 in 10 different A.L. batting categories in 1959.) Jackie, an All-American football player (and member of the College Football Hall of Fame), received a $75,000 bonus from the *Oakland Oaks* (!) of the Pacific Coast League after his junior year at Cal-Berkeley.[109] He married high-school sweetheart (and Olympic diving silver medalist) Zoe Ann Olsen.[110] He always signed whatever I sent him (SR: A) and died young in 1982, when he was only 55.

2. The Quest for Fire

Best game in the 1961 season: On August 24, Jackie went 3–4 with two home runs against the Senators.

Card #541, Roland Sheldon, head and shoulder shot in Al Lang Field. Rollie, shown here practicing his "too cool for school" look, made the improbable (and never to be repeated) jump from Class D ball in 1960 (15–1 for Auburn in the New York-Pennsylvania League) to #4 starter for the World Champion New York Yankees. Mr. Sheldon can be counted on to sign your items (SR: A), or at least he could when I was sending cards out.

Best game in the 1961 season: On July 5, the Indians bowed before Rollie's masterful pitching and succumbed, runless and baffled by the young man's wizardry.

Card #542, Minnesota Twins team card. Mine is signed by coaches Ed Lopat, Sam Mele, and Clyde McCullough. I also have a team card signed by non-carded players Ed Palmquist and Joe Altobelli and by traded-for players Ted Lepcio and Danny McDevitt, and another signed by minor league managers (and former big leaguers) Frank Verdi and Gene Verble.

Card #543, Roger Craig, wind-up, Holman Stadium. Here shown trying to mesmerize the batter with his fabled "Mystic Eye." In 1962, when he went 10–24, the Mets "backed" him by averaging 3.78 runs in the games he started, including three or fewer runs 16 times (one or fewer eight times); in 1963, when he went a miserable 5–22, his "support" amounted to 2.27 (!) runs a game, and in his 31, starts his teammates scored three runs or fewer 23 times, including 15 times where they either scored one or no runs. Nine times, the Mets were shut out when he started, and he lost five 1–0 games.[111] Anyway, he was an SR: A before his death at 91 in 2023.

Best game in the 1961 season: On April 23, Mr. Craig beat the Reds, 5–1.

Card #544, George Thomas, batting stance in Henley Field, Lakeland. "Bring it!" Self-assured and full of confidence as only the young and gifted can be, George is ready for anything the imaginary pitcher will throw him. His brother, Gerald, also played pro ball (they were teammates at Augusta in 1958). Versatile, he played every position but pitcher in the majors. In 1962 and '63, he was fourth and

Searchin' for Toothpick Sam

third in errors by a right fielder even though he played only 45 and 34 games in right field those seasons. SR: A

Best game in the 1961 season: George played in 17 games for the Tigers before being traded to the Angels. On July 21 against the hapless Senators, he went 4–4 with three runs and three RBI.

Card #545, Hoyt Wilhelm, demonstrating his grip in Comiskey Park. This is how Rembrandt must have looked when he finished a painting. As most everyone reading this book knows, Hoyt hit a home run in his first at-bat in the majors and then went 20 years without hitting another one.[112] Hoyt was on the oldest player list 15 times (tied with Jack Quinn), including eight as *the* oldest. He was already 30 when he reached the majors and had won 107 games in the minors even though he lost three years while serving in World War II. Hoyt was in the 395th IR and fought in the Battle of the Bulge, where he earned a Purple Heart. *If* he was an 11B (see Turk Lown), he should also have received the CMB and a Bronze Star. He was SR: A all the way before passing on at 80 in 2002.

Best game in the 1961 season: On August 2, he pitched the last five innings of a win over the Twins and held them scoreless while registering eight strikeouts.

Before finally getting his shot at the big leagues in 1952, Hoyt Wilhelm won 107 games in the minors, with back-to-back 20-win seasons for the unaffiliated Mooresville Moors in the Class D North Carolina State League.

160

2. The Quest for Fire

Card #546, Marty Kutyna, headshot in Pompano Beach Municipal Park. Shown here getting his first look at a miniskirt, Marty pitched for 12 teams in 10 leagues in the Bushes before sticking in the Bigs. He struck out in his fifth at-bat for the A's and then went 42 ABs before striking out again. He struck out only twice in his 47 ABs in the majors. SR: A "1954 Pony LG-All Star" is also on his card.

Best game in the 1961 season: He held the White Sox scoreless for six and a third innings on April 19.

Card #547, Leon Wagner, headshot in a Dick Cheney–like "undisclosed location." "Cool cat lookin' for a kitty…"[113] He never signed anything I sent before disappearing completely for a few decades, I didn't get a signed 1961 Wagner until sometime in the 2000s, and I have never found another. SR: F-.

Best game in the 1961 season: On September 8, he lambasted the Senators in a 13–4 crushing by going 3–4 with two doubles and a grand slam, driving in a season-high eight runs.

Card #548, Ted Wills, headshot in Scottsdale Stadium. He looks like another small-town preacher in this photo. SR: A.

Best game in the 1961 season: He held the Angels scoreless for four innings on June 8 while striking out four men.

Card #549, Hal R. Smith, head and shoulder shot. "You certainly do look lovely today, Mrs. Cleaver." Mr. Smith was a solid SR: A until his passing at 82 in 2014. He added "All-Star 1957–1959" to his signature.

Best game in the 1961 season: Hal R. went 3–4 against Milwaukee on June 2.

Card #550, Frank Baumann, headshot in an unidentifiable park/field/stadium somewhere in Florida. That's the smile of a man who had "just showed 'em." A former Red Sox "Bonus Baby," he was traded to the White Sox for Ron Jackson, who proceeded to hit .226 with no RBI in ten games for the Red Sox while Frank set about winning the A.L ERA crown. SR: A.

Best game in the 1961 season: Frank shut out the Tigers on June 5.

Card #551, George Altman, batting stance in Wrigley Field. A void is opening up beneath me. I cannot remember what I thought of the image before, and no neurons are being activated as I look at the card now. After his big league career ended, he spent eight seasons in Japan, playing until he was 42 and accruing 205 homers and a .3106 career BA in the land of samurai, sake, and sushi. SR: A.

Best game in the 1961 season: On June 28, in the first game of a doubleheader, George went 4–5 with two doubles and a home run against the Reds.

Card #552, Jim Archer, follow-through on a "pitch" in Connie Mack Field in West Palm Beach. He looks determined to show he belongs in the Bigs. Jim waited 10 years from his first pitch as an 18-year-old in Class D baseball to his first pitch in the majors. In '61, his rookie season, he finished ninth in the league in ERA while compiling a 9–15 record. During one stretch, he lost six games in a row despite compiling a 3.15 ERA over those games. He is a solid SR: A.

Best game in the 1961 season: On June 4, Jim surrendered a stunning 15 hits to the Senators but walked away with an 8–5 victory, facing nine batters in the ninth inning, giving up five hits and walk before nailing down the complete-game W. Oh, he also hurled two shutouts.

Card #553, Bill Fischer, headshot in Yankee Stadium. Bravely displaying his rapidly balding pate, Bill only chuckled when asked if women found it attractive. Did he know something he wasn't telling? Mr. Fischer (who died at 88 in 2018) was always SR: A.

Best game in the 1961 season: He held the Yankees scoreless for three innings on May 14, giving up only one hit.

Card #554, Pittsburgh Pirates team card. Mine is signed by coaches Bill Burwell and Sam Narron, the only coaches still alive when I started my Quest. I also have a card signed by Larry Foss, Vinegar Bend Mizell, and Al Jackson, and another signed by Roman Mejias.

Card #555, Sam Jones, follow-through in Candlestick Park. Arrrrrgh. I could have bought a signed #555 once for $50, back in 1984, but we didn't have $50 to spare back then[114] so I took a pass. I have neither seen nor heard of another since. Arrrrrgh. You are my White Whale, I am your Ahab. "To the last I grapple with thee; from hell's heart I stab at thee."[115]

Well, okay, perhaps that is a bit overstated. Of course, I bear no

2. The Quest for Fire

personal animus toward the departed "Toothpick" Sam, and I don't believe that my life has been consumed in this damned chase, this folly, this search for my own personal Grail. But man ... 45 years before the mast, crawling through the desert towards Cibola and through the jungle for the Lost City of Z. And for naught, all for naught. I fear that I shall enter The Big Sleep[116] Samless.

As for his signing proclivities, I am not qualified to speak. He was quite young when he died (only 45 when he passed in 1971). I recommend that any interested reader check out Rory Costello's biography of Sam Jones at the SABR bio site.

Best game in the 1961 season: he lost 1–0 to the Braves on April 28, striking out 10 and suffering an unearned run.

The Final Aside

Just a note on my attempts to find a signed Sam Jones '61 via ads in the *Sports Collectors Digest*, if I may. When I placed my first ad in the Collector-to-Collector section, I got just two responses, and they led to the purchase of one of the two cards (the Nellie Fox All-Star card) which I still needed at the time for my #1 set (as well as eight or nine of the cards I still needed for set #2). When, a year later, I placed another add seeking only Sam and three other cards I needed for the second set, I got but a single response, this from a fellow who said that yes, he had the cards I wanted (including The Sam) but that he did not want to sell them. Now, why would anybody send such a message? Fortunately (for both of us) he also sent images of the card through email, and I was able to inform him that the Sam Jones card he had was indeed signed, but that, alas, it was most definitely *not* signed by Mr. Jones, so I didn't really lose anything, and he got bit by karma.

Card #556, Ken R. Hunt, wind-up in an unidentifiable park (probably Al Lopez Field). The image on the card is that of a young man facing a bright future. In the event, that was not to be, at least insofar as baseball was concerned (although he was a highly successful high school coach after he retired). The Reds went 0–12 in Ken's

Searchin' for Toothpick Sam

final 12 appearances in 1961 (he himself was 0–6), and his nine-win total ranks high on the list of "Most Wins, One Year Career."[117] Mr. Hunt died, aged 69, in 2006. Over the years, I sent him six '61T cards to get signed, and he returned one. SR: F+.

Best game in the 1961 season: Ken beat the Giants, 5–1, on May 29. On June 21 he was 8–3 with a 2.73 ERA. From then to season's end, he was 1–7 with a 5.11 ERA, and he never threw another pitch in the majors.

Card #557, Jose Valdivielso, headshot in what is likely Yankee Stadium. Shown here looking quizzically at a fan wearing a cheese wedge cap on his head. There were two highlights to Jose's career. The first (and most noteworthy to baseball triviots such as I) is that he was the all-important pivot man in the major leagues' only all-Cubano triple play, Pedro Ramos to Valdivielso to Julio Becquer, which took place on July 23, 1960. The second is that, in the 1955 AL MVP voting, he got one vote, despite playing in only 95 games for a last-place team, hitting only .221 with 28 RBI, and scoring just 32 runs. He is an SR: A-ranked signer.

Best game in the 1961 season: he went 2–3 with a home run on June 4 against the Tigers.

Card #558, Don Ferrarese, head and shoulders shot, in a White Sox uniform with the cap altered, taken in Comiskey Park. Don, who was a Korean War–era vet, started a foundation which honors vets and awards scholarships to local high schoolers. His wife of 68 years died in September of 2020. SR: A+.

Best game in the 1961 season: Best game in the 1961 season: he threw a five-hit shutout at the Pirates on June 4.

Card #559, Jim Gentile, batting stance, in an unidentifiable park (probably Yankee Stadium). Jim has that "see, I told ya I could do it if you'd only give me a chance" look on his face. He hit 208 home runs in the Dodgers' farm system, waiting for Gil Hodges to age.[118] SR: A.

Best game in the 1961 season: Jim had a majors-leading ten games with at least four RBI. He topped the charts with his nine-RBI game against the Twins when he hit grand slams in back-to-back innings on May 9. In fact, he set the American League record with

2. The Quest for Fire

five grand slams that year, and get this—they all came when Chuck Estrada was on the mound!

Card #560, Barry Latman, follow-through on a "pitch" in Municipal Stadium. he was the second-best Jewish pitcher in the majors in 1961, and you can see from whence came his sobriquet of "Shoulders." Barry started off the 1961 season 9–0 and was named to the All-Star team. Mr. Latman had an SR: A mark before passing away at 82 in 2019.

Best game in the 1961 season: Barry pitched a four-hit shutout against the Twins on September 16.

Card #561, Charley James,[119] head and shoulder shot in an unknown ballpark (although I suspect it's Wrigley Field). Here shown is his incredulous look when he was told that the Cardinals expected him to be the "next Stan Musial." At my request, he inscribed, "Texas Lg. ROY 1958/Int. Lg. All Star 1959." SR: A. (By the way, he spelled his name Charlie.)

Best game in the 1961 season: On June 22, he went 3–4 against the Reds with three RBI.

Card #562, Bill Monbouquette,[120] headshot in Comiskey Park. Darned if he doesn't look like a '70s TV detective in this photo ("Book 'em, Danno"[121]). An SR: A fellow, Mr. Monbouquette passed away in 2015 aged 78.

Best game in the 1961 season: He three-hit Baltimore on September 17.

Card #563, Bob Cerv, follow-through on a swing in Yankee Stadium. Man, what a tough-looking character. During World War II, he served on the destroyer U.S.S. *Caxton*, which received eight battle Stars and a Presidential Unit Citation in addition to the American Campaign Medal, the European-African-Middle Eastern Campaign Medal, the Asiatic Pacific Campaign Medal, the Navy Occupation Service medal, the Combat Action Ribbon, the Philippine Republic Liberation Medal (with two stars), and the Philippine Republic Presidential Unit Citation Ribbon. Mr. Cerv, who lettered four times each in basketball and baseball (even though he *really* looked like a footballer) at Nebraska, was 91 when he died in 2017. Over the years, I sent him eight '61T cards to sign, and none were returned. I didn't get a signed Cerv until the 2000s, when I found out he was doing a signing. SR: F-.

Best game in the 1961 season: His best game for the Angels was a 2–4 game with two doubles against Detroit on April 23. and his best Yankees game was a pinch-hit grand slam against the White Sox on May 28.

Card #564, Don Cardwell, follow-through on a "pitch" in Wrigley Field. He looks like a redneck tobacco farmer in this image. He wasn't a particularly good hitter, but he went up hackin' (he hit 15 homers). SR: A, he passed away at 72 in 2008.

Best game in the 1961 season: Don pitched an 11-inning, six-hit shutout against Pittsburgh on August 20, the longest shutout of the year.

Card #565, Felipe Alou, demonstrating his swing in Candlestick Park. He looks like he's still happy to have gotten out of Lake Charles.[122] Felipe took part in the 1954 Central-American Games, throwing the discus and javelin as well as running the sprints.[123] He was part of an athletically gifted family, with two of his brothers (Matty and Jesus), his son (Moises), one of his cousins (Jose Sosa) and a nephew (Mel Rojas) reaching the majors. On September 15, 1963, the three Alou brothers played together in the outfield for the Giants in Forbes Field, something they did twice more before the season ended. SR: A, 100 percent.

Best game in the 1961 season: On September 17, Felipe went 4–4 against the Cubs with a double, a home run, and four RBI.

Card #566, Paul Richards—Mgr, All-Star subset, headshot, park indeterminate. He is on this card because Casey Stengel had been fired by the Yankees via a Trumpian-announced "resignation."

Card #567, Danny Murtaugh—Mgr, All-Star subset, headshot, park indeterminate.

Card #568, Bill Skowron—1B, All-Star subset, batting stance, Al Lang Field.

Card #569, Frank Herrera—1B, All-Star subset, head and shoulders shot, Connie Mack Field. Oddly, Frank (more commonly known as "Pancho") did not appear on a regular card in this set. He hit 321 home runs in the minors and won the Triple Crown in the International League in 1959 (and also the quadruple slash championship:

2. The Quest for Fire

329./.608/.410/1.018). An SR: A guy, he passed away at 70 in 2005. (Frankly, I'm surprised that he is on this card instead of Gordy Coleman, who got off to a terrific start in '61.)

Card #570, Nellie Fox—2B, All-Star subset, headshot, indeterminate park.

Card #571, Bill Mazeroski—2B, All-Star subset, follow-through on swing, indeterminate park.

Card #572, Brooks Robinson—2B, All-Star subset, headshot.

Card #573, Ken Boyer—3B, All-Star subset, headshot.

Card #574, Luis Aparicio—SS, All-Star subset, fixin' to fling the pelota antigua.

Card #575, Ernie Banks—SS, All-Star subset, shown here shying away from a swarm of bees.

Card #576, Roger Maris—RF, All-Star subset, taken in AL Lang Field. Roger is here shown doing his George Sanders imitation.[124]

Card #577, Hank Aaron—RF, All-Star subset, headshot, pictured here reacting to his first whiff of kimchee.

Card #578, Mickey Mantle—CF, All-Star subset, headshot. A look that only The Mick could pull off—dominant insouciance with a smidgen of godhood.

Card #579, Willie Mays—CF, All-Star subset, headshot. More like the old Willie this shot is.

Card #580, Al Kaline—RF, All-Star subset, after a swing in Henley Field in Lakeland.

Card #581, Frank Robinson—RF, All-Star subset, batting stance, probably in Al Lopez Field.

Card #582, Earl Battey—C, All-Star subset, squatting, possibly in Tinker Field. He is programmed to receive.

Card #583, Del Crandall—C, All-Star subset, in the on-deck circle. A strange choice for this card, since he played in only 15 games all year and hit just .200 with one RBI.

Card #584, Jim Perry—Pitcher (R), All-Star subset, standing by the dugout, staring at the camera man (whom he suspects of being a communist).

Card #585, Bob Friend—Pitcher (R), All-Star subset, warming up. Another odd choice for an All-Star card.

Searchin' for Toothpick Sam

Card #586, Whitey Ford—Pitcher (L), All-Star subset, follow-through on a "pitch" in Yankee Stadium.

Card #587, not issued.

Card #588, not issued.

Card #589, Warren Spahn—Pitcher (L), All-Star subset, head-shot of a smiling Spahnie.

3

Bringing It All Back Home[1]

Here, at the end of all things, when all the cards and their tales and impressions have been, both finally and for the first time, put to paper. (An archaic formulation, I know. Future generations will ask "What is this 'paper' to which this ancient one is referring?") What deeper memories and emotions are stirred by these cards? Surely, there must be more psychic (here meaning "relating to the psyche" and most definitely not having anything at all to do with mind reading, fortune telling, levitation, spirit writing, apparitions, Ouija boards, pyramids, crystals or goop products) connotations connected to a larger interior world than the mere baseball cards themselves that bring forth a deeper resonance in my mind, some sweeter song which must release and diffuse endorphins that in turn engender that odd mixture of joy and melancholy upon which we all thrive.[2]

And so, while writing this, for the first time I tried to piece together other memories of that time and place to see if any dulcet tones reverberated in my memory which were related to the summer of '61 and yet were unrelated to the Joy of Baseball. Not surprisingly, I discovered that there were.

What else happened in my life that year? Well, in ascending order of importance (rated on ye olde 1 to 10 scale, with 1 being vanishingly insignificant but greater than none and 10 being permanently life-altering), they are as follows, as best as I can recall.

1.7 In the world that 12- to 14-year-olds inhabit today, it may seem silly to even mention this, but for me (and likely most

Searchin' for Toothpick Sam

others of my age group), the switch from Harvey Comics'[3] *Richie Rich/Baby Huey/Little Lotta/Little Audrey/Little Dot* comics to American Comics' *Forbidden Worlds* and *Unknown Worlds* and Marvel's *Tales to Astonish, Journey into Mystery* and *Tales of Suspense* was indeed akin to the crossing over from one world to another.[4] Darker, certainly, but much more exciting.

5.9 My parents stopped using corporal punishment on me and my younger siblings. (Although it may shock some younger readers, the use of corporal punishment back then was the rule rather than the exception. In fact, most elementary school teachers were not reticent on using the ruler on malefactors and transgressors for such evil deeds as passing notes, laughing and/or staring out the window in spring.)

7.5 I acquired my first sports hero, a Black high school kid who lived across the parking lot in our family housing unit (Benjamin Franklin Village) in Mannheim. His name was Raymond Ash, and he was a football player and track athlete attending Mannheim American High School. To me, he was larger than life, and I so much wanted to be just like him. He was a sprinter, a broad jumper (now known as the long jump), and a pole vaulter, setting the school record in the latter. I still remember how proud I was that he picked me to catch his vaulting pole, another thing that is not done anymore. I seem to remember there being a rule at the time that if the pole went into the pit, the effort was a failure whether or not you cleared the bar, but I am probably misremembering that.

9.5 I discovered sports. As mentioned above, my father was not into sports. Well, not real sports—he did watch wrestling, roller derby, and bowling. (In fact, the only sporting event he ever took me to was a wrasslin' match when we were stationed at Fort Benning.) For the first time ever, I was playing baseball, football, and basketball, and I loved 'em all. (Of course, I was absolutely terrible at all of them, never having played any "sport" other than kickball before,[5] but I didn't know that, since none of us kids were really very good

3. Bringing It All Back Home

at anything other than Hide-and-Seek, Red Light-Green Light, Tag [and of course Freeze Tag], Red Rover, British Bulldog, Capture the Flag, and Swing the Statue.)

9.7 Girls discovered me. Ray (see 7.5 above) had a sister named Beatrice, an absolutely beautiful girl who, for some reason, decided that I was the boy for her.

10 I discovered girls (unfortunately, this happened after the Ashes had rotated back to the States [see 9.7 above]). Her name was Sue Davis, and I fell madly in limerence with her because she could beat me in a race, the only person in our grade (7th) who could. This was back at a time (oh days of innocence and wonder) when that was enough for me to lose my head over a girl, days which lasted until I met my wife seven years later, when all seeking stopped.

So there was indeed more to '61 than just the cards, but nothing else from that Golden Age has remained truer and caused less pain. I would guess that I have gone through the set hundreds and hundreds of times over the years, like Uncle Scrooge taking a dip in his money bin, and they are as familiar to me as any inanimate thing in my life. Being inanimate, they have never disappointed me or spurned me, and they, like my wife, are as beautiful to me as the day I first saw them.

4

Just the Facts, Ma'am[1]
Or the Devil Is in the Details

I feel that it is incumbent upon this would-be/wanna-be quasi-historian to both point out and elucidate upon some pertinent and quirky facts about the '61 Topps set itself, a stand-alone exploration into some of the incidentals of the actual corporeal magic rectangles themselves, so...

The cards were printed in sheets of 264 which were then cut vertically in half. Half sheets still very occasionally show up for sale, full sheets orders of magnitude more rarely.

The first fact to note about the individual cards themselves is the remarkable difference in their appearance, if not exactly along Series lines, then surely along the lines of the actual printing of the sheets. For example, Series 1 runs from card #1 (Dick Groat) to #88 (Richie Ashburn), but insofar as the cards' general appearance, the break clearly occurs at card #110 (Vada Pinson), 12 cards into Series 2 and most assuredly not at card #89 (Billy Martin). The next shift in appearance occurs not at the end of Series 2 (card #176, Ken Aspromonte) but between cards #196 (Ed Bouchee) and #197 (Dick Hall), 20 cards into Series 3. There is another, but less discernable, shift between card #370 (Roy Face) and #371 (Bill Skowron). The final (and most well-recognized) appearance change occurs 16 cards into the seventh and final series, between card #522 (Dick Farrell) and #523 (Joe Gibbon), where the fabled "Topps Highs" begin.

The hardest split to discern (by far) is that between #288 and #289, and it may be possible that there is no split, but then there would be a super-group of 174 cards smack in the middle of the set. The other splits are quite obvious even to the most undiscerning eye,

4. Bringing It All Back Home

and examining the differences in color quality and richness, gloss and sheen, and the general look of the cards should be enough to convince sceptics that the split is real and not the imaginings of a fevered mind.

Another oddity is the fact that several cards can have some rather remarkable color shifts. This occurs most spectacularly on cards #278 (Don McMahon), in which Don's face runs from an almost normal flesh color through severely sunburned on to Trumpian orange, #281 (Frank Sullivan), on which his face runs from almost genuinely colored through pink to an odd pinkish orange, and #293 (Tom Sturdivant), whose face can appear from greyish pink to jaundiced, but there are others, including (as far as I've noticed) from as low as #156 (Ken Hunt) to as high as #366 (Eddie Fisher). Nearly all of the color differences occurred in the third series, however.

Another quirk of the '61 set, but not one limited to it, is the use of numbering to pick the cream of the crop (mostly). #1 is NL MVP Dick Groat, and #2 is AL MVP Roger Maris. #100 is Harvey Haddix (an outlier, sort of), #200 is Warren Spahn, #300 is Mickey Mantle, #400 is Cy Young Award winner Vern Law, and #500 is Harvey Kuenn, who may seem today like an outlier but who had a .313 BA coming into the 1961 season. The 50s also have major (at the time) stars, and a lot of All-Stars and/or stars whose careers are mostly in the rearview mirror (e.g., Gil Hodges, Robin Roberts and their contemporaries) have cards that end with a zero. The numbers ending in five are also well-stocked with the likes of Yogi Berra, Hank Aaron, and a lot of younger All-Stars and fading former All-Stars like Gene Woodling and Sherm Lollar. The two most egregious examples of overlooked players in the set numbering are Al Kaline (#429) and Duke Snider (#443), and one must wonder how players of such quality were overlooked while lesser players were honored with a "special" number.

Three of the cards have no background, à la the '58 set, and they are all in the Seventh Series. The three are #509, Cam Carreon (Mark's father), which has a light cream-colored background; #525, Ron Perranoski, which has a washed-out orange background; and #533, Jack Curtis, which has a pale-yellow background. The Curtis

Searchin' for Toothpick Sam

photo has to be one of the worst ever put on a card, as it makes poor Jack look like a 270-pound[2], fin-de-siècle Viennese butcher. Fortunately, he appears in several other sets, affording the Youth of America a chance to see the *real* Jack Curtis. A fourth card, #459 (Terry Fox), also appears to have a fake background, but if you look at card #514 (Jake Wood), you will notice that both were taken at the same spot, most likely on the same day. There is a fence in the background of the Wood card, which means that the reason Fox's card has a monochromatic background is because of the closeness and the angle of the shot and not some photo lab trickery.

It should also be noted that *many* of the '61's are extremely hard to find centered, with several nearly impossible to find even close to evenly centered.

It was not a great year for star cards. Yogi Berra looks Yogi-riffic. Willie McCovey also has a fine card, showing a relaxed Stretch kneeling in the on-deck circle. Roberto Clemente looks good, as usual (was there ever a bad Clemente card?). The Mick looks stolid, as if he were cut from stone. Willie looks annoyed about something, and Hank looks terribly bored by it all. The Hoyt Wilhelm card shows a great shot of his knuckleball grip, a fact I didn't discover for some years, wondering instead why the photographer didn't wait to snap the photo until Hoyt's knuckles were on the ball instead of his fingertips.

Another sign of my dotage: Nowadays, it seems as if there are about 50 "Superstars" and at least three or four "stars" per team. Back in the day, a player had to maintain a certain level of excellence over a period of at least five (usually more) years before the "Super-Star" appellation would even be considered. In 1961, there were five recognized Superstars in baseball: Joe DiMaggio, the recently retired Ted Williams, and three active players: Stan Musial, Mickey Mantle and Willie Mays. There were about a dozen players who could legitimately be called Stars: Hank Aaron, Yogi Berra, Whitey Ford, Duke Snider, Rocky Colavito, Al Kaline, Eddie Mathews, Ernie Banks, Nellie Fox, Minnie Miñoso, Warren Spahn, and maybe Frank Robinson and Don Drysdale. In today's game, the "star" designation is bestowed on one-year-wonders or guys who have been pretty good for three or four years.

4. Bringing It All Back Home

Sixty years ago, old-timers were disappearing from the celestial firmament, and the players who would take their place were too early in their careers to be mentioned in the same breath as the real stars. Just as with everything else in this modern era, the idea of stardom has been devalued, and celebrity has now become conflated with actual achievement. In the debased lingo of today, "great" has come to mean "slightly above average." I liked it better when "great" meant "of an extent, amount or intensity considerably above the normal." I liked it better when a player could have a great year without being an instant "superstar" or a great career but could not throw a "great" pitch or have a "great" at-bat (when the end result is an out). It is not uncommon today to hear announcers claim that both teams have four, five or even more "great" players. Hey—if they're so great, why are they in fifth place?

It's the same with individual games, though not so much in baseball as in other sports, especially basketball. I no longer watch basketball, mostly because of statements like "He had a monster game!" for a player with 24 points, six rebounds, and eight assists. If that's a "monster" game, what would you call a Wilt Chamberlain game with 50 points, 30 rebounds and 20 blocks, or the one in which he had at least 20 points, rebounds, *and* assists? In fact, he had 442 games with at least 30 rebounds and 20 points, including 126 30–30 games and 50 with at least 30 boards and 50 points—and that's not including playoff games.

Six of the seven checklists had varieties. The 2nd series CL had three: A, where the word "Checklist" on the front is yellow and the number on the back is white in a black circle; B, where the word "Checklist" on the front is yellow and the number in the back is black in a white circle; and C, where the word "Checklist" on the front is red and the number on the back is black in a white circle. On the 3rd series CL, variety A has the copyright symbol adjacent to #264 and on B, it is adjacent to #263. The two 4th series CLs had two similar tiny (but slightly more readily apparent) variations: A, the copyright symbol is adjacent to #336, and B, with the copyright signal adjacent to #339. The varieties on CL 5 are so large that even I noticed them in when I was 12 back in 1961. Variety A did not have an ad stating (in

Searchin' for Toothpick Sam

all caps) "Special Feature in Next Series/Most Valuable/Players/From 1950 To 1960/Coming in the/6th Series" with the type in three different sizes, while variety B did. The 6th series CL had two varieties also. On type A, Luis Aparicio's name was misspelled as "Louis," and on type B, the mistake had been rectified. Finally, on the 7th series, on type A , the letter "C" of check list is obscuring part of Chuck Cottier's hat, and on type B, it isn't.

There are also several other unforced and uncorrected factual errors on the cards which were not mentioned above. #14 has Don Mossi's birthdate as 1930 instead of 1929. Card #29 has Hector Lopez's birthdate as 1932 instead of 1929. Card #52 has George Crowe's birthdate as 1923 instead of 1921. On Alex Grammas's card (#64), his birthdate is 1927 instead of 1926. Joey Amalfitano's card (#87) has an incorrect number of games for him in 1955 (45 instead of 36). On Al Neiger's card (#202), his name is misspelled ad "Nieger." Danny Murphy's card (#214) says that he debuted at 18, but he was actually only 17. On card #220, Al Dark's birth year should be 1922 instead of 1923. Camilo Pascual's name in misspelled on the back of his card (#235) as "Camilio." Finally, Vic Power (Card #255) was born in 1927, not 1931. (All of the error facts [save the Neiger/Nieger error] are from the Baseballcardpedia.com site, as I caught none of them.)

The '61 Topps set also included some inserts. One set was called "Magic Rub-Offs," which, since I rubbed all the rub-offs on, I have none of (and which, thankfully, I had no desire to reacquire since, as can well be imagined, the vast majority of kids who had them followed the same course of action as I did, making them quite pricey). A second insert was a set of "Baseball Stamps" which was great, because I was also a stamp collector (however undiscerning I may have been) at the time. One hundred four players were on green stamps, and 104 were on brown stamps. Some players appeared in both colors. I even sent a dime to Topps to get an "album" to keep them in.

My collection also includes three wrappers and two (empty) boxes. I was amazed to see what these extremely disposable items of ephemerata were going for on eBay, but I guess that's *because* they were so easily disposable.

4. Bringing It All Back Home

Which brings us to the notorious '61 "short prints." There are canonical SPs and others which should also be included in the "official" list. The "accepted everywhere" cards are as follows: #371, Bill Skowron; #402, Larsen Pitches Perfect Game; #408, Mathewson K's 267; #417, Juan Marichal; #421, Ty Cline; #423, Charlie Neal; #428, Ray Barker; #430, Bill Mazeroski; and #436, Jim Maloney. The only one of those that I ever had trouble finding is the Jim Maloney card, but that may well just be pure chance. The non-stars in this group appear to be selling, ungraded, for a bit more than the SPs, but that may well be because a lot of folks selling their cards on eBay aren't aware that they are selling their cards for eight to ten dollars less generally than do dealers who seem to be in the know.

Having seen a photo of the sheet which has the SPs on it, it does appear that they were indeed printed in half the number as the other cards on the sheet. But, since that is so, why are not the other single-printed cards also included in the "official" SP subset? (The other cards are #361, CL 5, #372, Bill Hendley, #389, Ralph Terry, #399, Cliff Cook, #400, Vern Law, #405, Lou Gehrig Streak, #407, Jack Chesbro Wins 41, #412, Larry Sherry, #413, Eddie Yost, #415, Hank Aaron, #463 [misnumbered], Milwaukee Braves TC, #441, Dick Bertell, and #446, Bob Taylor. It seems that these cards should be just as difficult to find as The Nine.) On my part, it all seems hit and miss, for, as astute readers may recall, I was never able to get Bob Davis or Rudy Hernandez in a pack (nor indeed did I ever get either of them until the "terrific" Mantle for Davis and Hernandez deal I made after getting out of the Army and coming back to Oregon).[3]

Finally, there are four other details about the '61 set to which I would like to call the reader's attention. First, 12 carded players did not indeed appear in a major league game in 1961. These include Winston Brown (who, as stated above, never did grace a major league lineup),[4] Danny Kravitz, Johnny Kucks, Ralph Lumenti, and Bob Davis, none of whom appeared in a major league game after 1960, Ray Barker, Ruben Gomez, Dave Nicholson, Al Neiger, Bill Short, Johnny Schaive, and Ray Ripplemeyer.

Second 6'7" Frank Howard and 6'6" Frank Sullivan were carded back to back, making them the tallest such players in baseball card history at the time (and perhaps still—I stopped paying attention around 30 years ago).[5]

Third, 6'7" Walt Bond and 5'5" Albie Pearson were also carded back-to-back, and I am sure that the 14" difference is still the largest between subsequent cards ever (if one does not count the 3'7" Eddie Gaedel and the 6'5"Chuck Connors cards in the 1977 Fritsch One Year Wonders set, in which they were #s 1 and 2. In this instance, the difference was 34", or approximately one Eddie Gaedel). By the way, active players named Walt (Bond, Dropo and Moryn) and carded in the set averaged 6'4½", not so unusual today but unusually tall for the time.

Last, cards 175 (Gene Freese) and 176 (Ken Aspromonte) feature back-to-back players who had brothers who also played in the majors in '61, the uncarded George Freese and the carded Bob Aspromonte. I know that this particular circumstance (the adjacency of brothers who had brothers who played the same year) had never occurred before, and, although I am not positive, I would be willing to wager that it hasn't happened since.

A Final Point

A Note on Pre-Investigatory Prejudice

After I had written all my impressions, I decided to include each player's best day of the 1961 season, something I had planned to do before I started writing but which I forgot about once I actually got started. As I got further and further along in my card descriptions, I began to notice the seeming frequency with which certain teams appeared to be popping up as the "victims" of players' best days, two in each league.

Those teams were the Cubs and the Phillies, the teams which finished seventh and eighth in the National League, and the Athletics and the Senators, who tied for last in the American League. I must confess that, once that thought popped into my head, I thought, "Well, yeah." It made sense that it turned out that way. I went back through all the "Best Day" results and found the following numbers.

Number of Times Victims of Player's Best Day

Phillies	*Cubs*	*Athletics*	*Senators*
30	30	34	32

It all seemed so right.

But as I was compiling these totals, I noticed that the Dodgers and the Tigers seemed to be popping up quite frequently also, and now that my preconceived notion had been empirically tested but *only for those four teams*, it seemed to me that the "Best Day" victim was more random than I thought. I didn't want to go back through all 500-plus players and find each team's victimization

Searchin' for Toothpick Sam

number, but I figured that I could just do the pennant winners and compare those with the tail-enders. If the totals were reasonably close, then that would be conclusive evidence that randomness ruled, as it so often does in the real world.

I went back through all the players a second time, in this instance looking for best games against the pennant winners, the Reds and the Yankees.

Reds	*Yankees*
15	15

So my initial impression (that it's all random) of my first impression (that the worst teams should have the most "best days against") was also wrong. That left only one option: Find the results for every team to look for a correlation between the number of best games against and final standings. Therefore, it was once more into the breach, doing what I should have done at the start of this exercise but, unfortunately, that's not my *modus operandi*. I mean, why do something once when you can do it three times?

So the *final* final results are in, in order from fewest to most times victimized and then by how they finished.

See table on the following page.

It becomes apparent that while the number of victimizations and the position in the final standings roughly align and that the majority of the teams' total victimizations fall within a very small window, there are a few anomalies.

Let us examine those statements. In the American League, whose teams played eight more games than did the National League teams, seven of 10 fell between 30 and 34 victimizations, or with a 90 percent correspondence (30.7 losses apiece, with a lower than 11.3 percent difference between the highest number in that group and the lowest), and an eight-team average of 30.3 victimizations with the eighth team just 11 percent below the average.

There are two outliers in the AL victims: New York, with over 50 percent fewer victimizations, and Boston, with only 62 percent of the expected events. In the standings, there are also two outliers: Boston again, second fewest in victimizations with almost a third fewer

American League

New York	Boston	Cleveland	Los Angeles	Baltimore	Minnesota	Washington	Chicago	Kansas City	Detroit
15	19	27	30	31	31	32	33	34	34

New York	Detroit	Baltimore	Chicago	Cleveland	Boston	Los Angeles	Minnesota	Kansas City	Washington
15	34	31	33	27	19	30	31	32	34

National League

Cincinnati	Saint Louis	San Francisco	Milwaukee	Pittsburgh	Chicago	Philadelphia	Los Angeles
15	22	25	27	27	30	30	33

Cincinnati	Los Angeles	San Francisco	Milwaukee	St. Louis	Pittsburgh	Chicago	Philadelphia
15	33	25	27	22	27	30	30

than expected, despite being sixth in the standings, and Detroit, last in victimizations yet second in the league standings.

In the National League, there are also two anomalies, one in the number of losses compared to the team's finish and one with the team's finish compared to the losses: the Cardinals had almost 30 percent fewer victimizations than should have been expected given their fifth-place finish, and the Dodgers had 10 percent *more* losses than expected yet finished second in the league.

All of this goes to show that, pennant winners aside, the victimizations were indeed random. The disparity between the pennant winners and the league average was not unexpected, but the width of the gap came as a mild surprise to me. What was totally unexpected, however, was that the runners-up in both pennant chases led their leagues in victimization. I have no explanation for that, other than that their cases don't seem as random as they should have been.

Appendices

I. My Favorite '61 Cards

1. Wes Covington
2. Walt Dropo
3. Rocky Bridges
4. Rocky Nelson
5. Hal Bevan
6. Vic Wertz
7. Clint Courtney
8. George Witt
9. Stan Musial
10. Mickey Mantle
11. Wally Moon
12. Ryne Duren
13. Gene Baker
14. Jim Golden
15. Rocky Colavito
16. Don Blasingame
17. Walt Bond
18. Jim Baumer
19. Clay Dalrymple
20. Early Wynn & Yogi Berra

II. Things I Wish I Had Had the Foresight to Do*

1. Started getting cards signed in 1961, and if not then, then in 1962 (and so on and so forth).
2. Gotten all the coaches' signatures on my team cards before they passed away.
3. Gotten Tom Zachery to sign the Babe Ruth Baseball Thrills card.

---

* Taking into consideration of course the fact that the elderly and rapidly fading author dwells in a shadow world which consists almost entirely of regrets and wishful thinking and which bears little resemblance to the actual oblate spheroid he currently occupies in three-dimensional space (while the fourth dimension, Doppler Effect–like, rushes by him, the past slowly receding and the future rushing towards him at an ever-increasing velocity).

Appendices

    4. Gotten Babe Pinelli's signature on the Don Larsen Baseball Thrills card.

    5. Gotten Mrs. Babe Ruth to sign the Babe Ruth Baseball Thrills card.

    6. Gotten Babe Dahlgren to sign the Lou Gehrig Baseball Thrills card.

    7. Gotten the signatures of the umpires on the World Series cards.

    8. Gotten the players in the background to sign the cards on which they could be identified.

    9. Gotten El Tappe's signature on some more 1st Series Check List cards.

    10. Gotten cartoonist Jack Davis to sign some cards and gotten one of his original signed baseball cartoons.

III. Things I Wish I Had Done 15 Years Sooner Than I Did

1. Either:
   a. Find someone to fashion cards in the style of the 1961 Topps set to get non-carded players to sign

   or

   b. learn how to do that myself.

IV. Poses on the Cards

1. Headshot/head and shoulder(s) shot: 268
2. "Batting": 71
   a. Waiting for a "pitch": 46
   b. Follow-through on a "swing": 25
3. "Pitching": 66
   a. "Follow-through": 49
   b. "Winding up": 12
   c. Looking for a "sign": 4
   d. Other: 4 (Golden, Roberts, Gibbon, and Wilhelm)

Appendices

4. "Fielding": 24
5. "Catching": 9
6. Miscellaneous: 9
7. Live Action: 1 (Covington)

Chapter Notes

Introduction

1. From the song "Comin' Back to Me," on the 1967 Jefferson Airplane album *Surrealistic Pillow*, lyrics by Marty Balin.

Preface

1. But do we not all exist perpetually in various "pre" states? Are not all of us yet breathing merely in a predeceased state? Are we not all in the non-act of preboarding? Do not Madison Avenue marketers and Wall Street corporations just see all of us among the many billions who, hovering in breathless anticipation, are permanently suspended in the pre-ordering state vis-à-vis their offerings? Do not all television evangelists see us as pre-donors in their heaven-anointed quest to acquire a bigger private jet, perhaps one with a bowling alley and a three-lane, Olympic-sized pool? Is not this book even now being pre-read by literally (please refer to the snarky but heartfelt grammar police note below) millions of our fellow citizens?

2. (Oh, and while I'm riding this horse, something cannot by definition be "one of the most unique examples" of anything. Something is either unique or it is not, period, full stop. Rare, even exceedingly rare, items are not "unique" unless they are. Saying something is unique when there is more than one of whatever it is that is being spoken about is like saying "This one of a kind first edition of a *Shakespeare First Folio* is one of only three known copies." Another example: in the philatelic world, the 1856 British Guiana one-cent magenta stamp is unique (its last known sale was for $9,480,000 in 2014). While stamps with two known examples are vanishingly rare, a paltry handful are unique. Stamps with two or three known examples generally sell in the poor-side-of-town price of a mere two to three million bucks. If you are a devotee of QVC, you may be willing to spend $19.98 on "this unique genuine Naugahyde and faux rhinestone pendant, but hurry, because there's only 9,000 left!," but one doesn't have to be a member of the glittering illuminati to reject that preposterousness.)

3. Picture if you will little sweetly chirping birds, golden, russet, and sky blue, fluttering about me as I stroll through a field redolent with the aroma of lilac, lavender, and honeysuckle while the sun, in all its golden glory, slowly rises to greet the day in a lucent penumbra of orange to purple cumulous clouds amidst the hazy air which is filled with the susurration of a warm wind through the boughs of the nearby willows.

4. Picture if you will the skeletal figure of a sere and whitened long-dead tree, windlashed and rainstormed, framed against a lightning-lacerated sky, dolesome and glowering, while the plangent rumblings of distant thunder mix with the thuddering crashes of waves against the rocky, crumbling headland to form an orchestral dirge signifying the end of all hopes and the death of all dreams.

5. By this I mean "jonesing" both in the sense of wanting something really badly, as in "After a trying day of lying and avoiding answering simple, direct

Notes—Chapters 1 and 2

questions, Brett was jonesin' for a frosty brew" and in this specific (Sam) Jones sense.

Chapter 1

1. Yep, five cents a pack, just like a candy bar or a pack of gum (and comics were a dime). The last time I looked, a pack of baseball cards costs around four dollars, and the same for what passes now as "comics." In other words, what a single pack sells for today would have brought you 80 card packs or 40 comics back when I was a stripling. The prices of those one-time staples of American youth have gone up over times the "official" rate of inflation (and effectively shut the youth of America out of the once overwhelmingly prevalent habit of "collecting" both cards and comics).

2. Again, yes, number 110 and not #89. More on that later.

3. It just occurred to me that I must be one of the few Americans who was in Germany both when The Wall went up *and* when it came down. In 1961 my dad, as stated, was stationed in Germany, and in 1989, I was in the Army myself and stationed in Berlin.

4. As they are today.

5. An erratic is a large boulder left in a place where no such stones should be, far from mountains or rivers that could account for its presence. They are either leftovers from when ice sheets covered the northern portions of North America or, in the case of the Willamette Valley, evidence of the Great Missoula Floods which inundated the area many times during the last ice age.

6. Not a dream or a wish. I saw this one morning when we arrived at a unit in the Cascades before sunrise (as usual) and we serendipitously parked in the one pull-off on the entire logging road where we could possibly have seen this wonder occur.

7. This surprised even me when I counted them up preparatory to embarking on this journey.

8. Although I found a Twins specialist in 2016 who had seven items signed by Mr. Henry, including two signed OYW cards, not only would he not sell me anything from his collection, but he also never even bothered to respond to the four emails I sent him over the years. Behavior like that escapes me.

9. By the way (and completely off topic, as is my wont), I am a full-on Tolkien fan (with more than a hundred books by or about Tolkien's life and works in my library) and have watched the *Lord of the Rings* trilogy at least 10 times, but . . . the scene inside Mount Doom? The one where the ring is destroyed? Nope, sorry. Great writing, dramatic in the extreme, but no way. Inside the magma chamber, it would have been hot enough to preclude Frodo, Sam, and Smeagol from entering, for they would've been broiled alive long before they walked out onto the ledge. (Or, alternatively, perhaps rock melts at 40c [313K] in Middle Earth.)

10. I was tempted here to say "into the mouth of madness," but figured that perhaps a Lovecraftian stylism was a bit much even for me, who (almost) never fails to avail myself of a reference to something within my sphere of interest.

11. Oh, how we waited for each year's *Street and Smith* edition to appear on the magazine racks of our local drug and candy stores, by which I mean combination news stand and soda fountain that could be found on the corner every few blocks on commercial avenues in the cities and in every small town in the region. Ahhh, the eggcreams...

12. The movie was *Judgement at Nuremberg*, and I must here implore the reader not to think that I am trying to minimize the events being talked about in the film, which in no conceivable way or to any extent at all compares to the mere collecting of autographed baseball cards.

Chapter 2

1. If by "fire" one means in this specific case getting Signatures on Baseball Cards.

Notes—Chapter 2

2. Here's an odd bit of trivia for you: When Mr. Groat left college, he was the all-time NCAA points leader. The fellow whose record he broke was a Pirates teammate, Johnny O'Brien (5'9" Johnny once scored 43 points against the Harlem Globetrotters (the most ever by an opponent) when they were still one of the best teams in the world). Figure the odds.

3. There were no vambraces in evidence anywhere in this set, as they had been lying unused in museums and stately manors since the days of chivalry, and greaves had not yet been developed for baseball usage.

4. Just a note about coaches: With one single exception, every coach I asked to sign a team card did just that. The only one who didn't, Otis Douglas of the Reds, did reply and told me that he was just a conditioning coach and didn't think that he should sign the team card. I should've let him know that that was okay with me and tried again.

5. Chuck had worn uniform #13 as a Brave before he was traded to Detroit. Coincidence?

6. The small black-and-white photo which appears on the back of the card was also taken in Wrigley Field in a game against the Pirates or the Reds, but the image is far too blurry to determine which players are depicted. My best guess for the sliding runner is Bob Skinner. The same photo appeared on the bottom of all seven check lists (except the coming attractions of Series 5 and 6).

7. His name, of course, was Zoilo, but just as with virtually every Latino player who was stuck with the insulting nickname "Chico" (which means Little Boy), he had to please his bosses, and since the popular TV show *Zorro* (1957–1959) was still fresh in everybody's mind, Zorro he became.

8. An essential part of my Carl Everett Scott Arnold Early Wynn Hawkins return address alter-ego.

9. Does the jingle "Wow!/I saw color TV/RCA Victor color TV/I know what I been missin' now/Wow! I saw Color TV" ring a bell with anyone besides me?

10. Look him up. One season in the minors, he struck out 262 hitters in 170 innings. He also walked 262 batters. He once threw 32 consecutive balls in a game. He frequently threw more than 200 pitches in a game and is reputed to have once thrown more than 280 before being relieved. So really—look him up.

11. I saw that same look on Neil DeGrasse Tyson's (This generation's Carl Sagan). face when the late Mr. Stephen Hawking was trying to explain to him one of the concepts that he (Mr. Hawking) was seeing clearly in his mind.

12. In fact, it looks more like Ebbets Field than any other park, but of course it isn't. My second choice, because of the absence of light poles, would be Wrigley Field, but the rowhouse profiles are wrong, so . . . I'm hopeful that some reader will recognize the field of his youth and let me know.

13. There's a really good article about Arthur Lee and the Crowns at *Marv Goldberg's R&B Notebook* site if you'd care to check it out.

14. Roughly $387,000 in today's world, it seems like an awful lot to me (and 99.8 percent of us) but is less than a hundredth of the top bonuses today and is equivalent to only 65 percent of today's MLB minimum salary.

15. See Chapter 4 to read what defines the various checklist varieties.

16. He was former Houston pitcher Brian Meyer's uncle.

17. In our family, we called them "Monaco Brows" for all the super-model types we saw when we visited that microstate when we were stationed in Berlin.

18. Two long flies that had home run distance but were just foul, and then a whiff.

19. By the way, one of my signed Triandos cards may be the last one he ever signed, as he passed away in between the time I sent it and the time I received it.

20. This card gives us some idea of when the photos were taken and the cards readied for printing vis-à-vis when they actually appeared in the store, since Ed was traded to the A's on March 30.

21. Believe it or not, I learned about the writ of replevin from a Hopalong

Notes—Chapter 2

Cassidy movie. I believe it was in the 1943 flick *Hoppy Serves a Writ*, but I am sure was in one of the later of his 66 films.

22. Apparently, he and, oddly enough, another bespectacled player, Clint Courtney, are widely regarded as the most fight-prone players in the majors, even ahead of Billy Martin (and they were both regarded as head-on battlers and not sucker-punchers). From what I've been able to discover, Torgy was more likely to emerge victorious from a scuffle than was Clint, but that fact didn't stop Scrap Iron from mixing it up.

23. Information from the *Pittsburgh Post-Gazette* of October 15, 2019.

24. Might I recommend his excellent mini-biography written by Terry Bohn which can be seen on the SABR web site.

25. It was an even poorer 12–35 (.355), 5.18 before returning to the NL at age 36 to pitch for the Phillies, for whom he went 24–17 with an ERA of 3.68 after he was 36 years old.

26. Whatever it was that Mr. Fisher had, I'll take some.

27. I recommend that any interested reader check out Alan Cohen's bio of him at the SABR web site. Apparently, he only played baseball his senior year of high school, but he managed to scratch, claw, dribble, bloop, surprise bunt, Baltimore Chop, Texas Leaguer and seeing-eye-hit his way to a .607 BA.

28. Paraphrased, on the odd chance that it might have gotten by the reader, from *It's a Wonderful Life*, the scene where Mr. Potter (Lionel Barrymore) is trying to talk George Bailey (James Stewart) into dumping the building and loan and coming to work for him.

29. His full name is Fred Allen Green. The name "Fred Allen" is probably not familiar to any reader under 60, but he was a really big cheese during the Golden Age of Radio. Anyhow, I asked him and no, he was not named after *the* Fred Allen. Oh, and by the way, his son, Gary, played in the majors and looks a lot like his dad.

30. Even though he actually *was* a four-decade player, at least according to many experts on things chronological, including the redoubtable baseball fan Stephen Jay Gould.

31. With *many* game stats (other than points scored) missing, Gene had at least six 20-rebound games in the NBA (and one more in the playoffs) as well as many more in the old Eastern Basketball League. A bruiser, he also averaged 13.8 boards (three more than Kareem Abdul-Jabbar and two more than Shaquille O'Neal) and seven fouls per 36 minutes for his career (16.8 and 8.9 in the playoffs).

32. In 1959 alone, there were 30 Western series on the three nationwide networks (NBC, ABC and CBS).

33. Lumpy was played by Frank Bank on *Leave It to Beaver*.

34. Source: Creighton Athletics Hall of Fame.

35. I haven't done a complete work-up on this, but I believe that Cincinnati's Archbishop Moeller High ranks second only to Oakland's McClymonds High in the number of hits (11,533—9,164) and home runs (1,284–1,204) their graduates have garnered in the Major Leagues. (I have since done a bit of further research and found that both schools trail Fremont High, which has totals of 14,822 and 1,584).

36. It seemed that if either Drott (#213), Dave Sisler (#239, son of George and brother of Dick, whose home run crushed the Dodgers in 1950) or Al Cicotte (#241, great grand-nephew of Eddie) was in a pack, the other two were also. I must've opened 20 packs with those three fellows in it, and I've often wondered if anyone else had the same experience.

37. Info about Yale from *Baseball-Reference.com*.

38. Actually, I found out that he had a sore elbow which required surgery, which hobbled him for much of the 1961 season. However, he did spend three seasons in Richmond followed by four in Rochester. Altogether, he won 120 games in the minors, and in 10 seasons in AAA, he won 95 games with a 3.14 ERA.

39. He was flamboyant, outgoing and, worst of all, he was "seen in the company

Notes—Chapter 2

of white women." Oh my, I do believe that I feel a case of the vapors coming on. Somebody catch me, please!

40. By the way, in 1,259 games in the minors, Johnny hit .296.

41. For the few readers who may not know, Don had a fearsome rep as a "head-hunter," leading the league five times and still ranked 19th all-time.

42. I know that $50,000 doesn't sound like a lot to some of us (although it sure does to me), but it was 12½ times the average blue-collar wage at the time. You also have to remember that the average price of a new car in 1960 was $2,600 (today it is $38,000), and the average price of a new home was $12,000 (in Missouri today, it's $191,000). Note that while a new car costs 14.6 times more than one did in 1960 and a three-bedroom house costs 16 times more, the minimum wage has only gone from $1 in 1960 to a princely $7.25 today. Overall, what cost you $5 in 1960 now costs more than $50. Even more telling in relation to baseball, the average price of a Cardinals ticket in 1960 was $1.85, and now it's $43, almost 24 times as much. And I can't tell you how glad I am that the average salary in MLB is $4,380,000. Clayton Kershaw got paid more to pitch an inning in 2019 than my father earned as a soldier from 1938 to 1962. In fact, Kershaw was paid almost as much per out as my dad made that entire time.

43. On April 26, 1962, Harry was sold by the Indians to the Mets for a player to be named later. On June 15, that player turned out to be Harry Chiti, so I guess that this one of those rare baseball deals where both sides got an equal value.

44. Strange fact about Gary: In the three years that he made the All-Star team, his combined record was 34–36.

45. "Winding up" is something pitchers used to do before throwing a pitch if there was no one on base. A "wind-up" consisted of leaning toward the plate while swinging one's arms behind the back, then leaning back, bending the push-off leg, and kicking one's front leg high in the air while lunging forward. Frequently, the front leg went above the pitcher's head before the forward motion began. You youngsters should go to YouTube and check it out (Warren Spahn and Juan Marichal would be a good place to start).

46. Played by Henry Travers.

47. On the off chance that those lines are unfamiliar to you, that is what Bruce Banner (played by Bill Bixby) used to utter just before transmogrifying into the Hulk (Lou Ferrigno) on the old *The Incredible Hulk* TV show.

48. An interesting (to me) sidenote: On the December 15, 1960, Frank and Gene Conley (see above) were traded for each other, at the time (and perhaps still?) by far the tallest trade in baseball history, with three-time All-Star Conley going to Boston for two-time All-Star Sullivan. In the event, Boston got far the better of the deal, with Gene going 29–32 for the mediocre Bosox and Frank going 3–18 for the futile Phillies.

49. You know the one, where Mr. Somerset Frisby (played by the inimitable Andy Devine) saves himself from alien abduction by playing his harmonica, which to the foreigners from outer space, are, and I quote, "death sounds."

50. Played by Dabs Greer, Clem Bevans, and Howard McNear.

51. Yes, you read right. Right up through the 1950s and even into the 1960s in some areas, every local burg, hamlet, and crossroads agglomeration of feedstore/garage/general merchandise/barbershop that had its own team that would compete against local teams of similar ilk, and all the rural areas from the Canadian border to the Gulf of Mexico and from the Appalachians to the Rockies would stage tournaments for either the county championship or the championship of the tri-county area. Many states even went so far as to have state championships for these teams.

52. For some reason, whenever I look at the Baumer card, I think of Hal Bevan (#456), and vice versa. I think it's because they both played very small parts on the Reds' pennant winners that year and because both had long and productive minor league careers, sparsely

Notes—Chapter 2

interspersed with short cups of coffee in the Bigs.

53. Almost, but in actuality not that close.

54. His 1960 card is an oddball in that his image is on two cards, one of which is J.C. Martin's. Let me explain: the 1960s had two photos of the carded player, one a small, full-body B&W photo on a solid background over the team's emblem. Well, the card labeled Gary Peters (#407) does have his B&W picture correct, but the color headshot is J.C. Martin. Conversely, card #348, labeled J.C. Martin, has the correct small B&W image, but the color headshot is of Peters.

55. I know it looks wrong (I thought so also), but I looked it up, and, pukingly, it is. Or rather, pukingly, it isn't.

56. Here's a bit of trivia for you: Bobby Gene was the last professional baseball player to have back-to-back 20-plus triple seasons, hitting 21 in 1953 (season split between St. Joseph and Fresno) and 22 in 1954 for Fresno.

57. His name was Selva *Lewis* Burdette, so his card should have said Lew Burdette. Oddly, up until the 1959 set, he *was* referred to as Lew, but then Topps shifted to the incorrect Lou for some reason. He signed his name Lou. I wonder why. Easier to write?

58. Although it doesn't show in this case, Sammy was definitely a member of the Chew Crew. However, due to the regulations set forth by the Writer's Committee (moi), he cannot be officially included in its brown-stained ranks.

59. Williamsport is where the Little League World Series takes place.

60. Walks and Hits per Innings Pitched. *Many* years before this became an "official" sabermetric stat, I was figuring BR/9 (Base Runners per Nine innings) numbers for pitchers, which seems to me to make more sense than WHIP. After all, hits, walks and strikeouts are figured per *nine* innings, why are baserunners not figured the same?

61. On August 9, 1960, Julio came in for the Senators with his team behind 7–3 and gave up a home run to Dick Williams in his inning of relief. In 1961, he once again came in in the seventh inning, this time with his team behind, 6–1, with and two men on base and gave up four straight hits. He did hold the A's scoreless in the eighth.

62. Younger readers might find this hard to believe, but yes, in 1961 you could buy a six-year-old car for under $500, sometimes a lot less. I had a friend who bought a '57 Ford for $150 cash in 1967, and our first car was a 10-year-old VW we got for $50 in 1973. Most middle-class families back in the 1950s and 1960s bought a new car every other year.

63. In his first year in pro ball, the 18-year-old Garver won 21 games with an ERA of 1.21 and hit .407 for Newark in the old Class D Ohio State League. To paraphrase Charlotte, the spelling spider, "Some season."

64. Bond and Brickell hold the unfortunate and never to be broken record for shortest life span of consecutive carded players.

65. Just as with Drott-Cicotte-Sisler, this is another player whose card I cannot look at without immediately linking it with another player or two, in this case Billy Harrell (#354) and Howie Bedell (#353). With these three fellows, it is not because they were always in the same pack of cards, but rather because of a feeling they evoked in me.

That happens to me a lot. For example, I cannot think of Martin Balsam, Nehemiah Persoff, or Eli Wallach without getting a picture of the other two in my mind. Ditto with the threesomes of Whit Bissell, Richard Carlson, and Hugh Marlowe and Scott Glenn, James Woods, and Willem Defoe.

66. Without, of course, "The Quota." For those who may not be familiar with that, it was the same one which held sway in the majors until the mid–1960s: preferably two and no more than three men of color on a team at a time.

67. For two seasons (1961–1962), Phil Wrigley decided to have the team led, rather than by a manager, a rotating number of coaches, using four in 1961 and three in 1962, with no set pattern as to which coach would manage in any

Notes—Chapter 2

particular game. It went about as well as could be expected.

68. Remember, this was back in the days when 25 home runs (and sometimes fewer) would get you into a league's top ten.

69. By the way, his 1962 card was taken from the same roll of film, either right before or right after the 1961 image.

70. Joanne, Patty Ann, Maryanne, Sharon, Frank, Peter, Paul, and Mark.

71. Well, it *should* be Yankee Stadium—it's not the Yankees' Spring Training park, and Duke is wearing the home-field pinstripes, so it *isn't* any other AL park, so . . . If you're interested in Duke, Andrew Sharp's SABR bio is a must.

72. Information from Ralph's autobiography, *Right Down the Middle* (Mullerhaus, 2016).

73. Any reader who played football in high school knows to what I am referring.

74. That was the name of the park the first year the Angels held Spring Training. The name was soon changed to Angels Stadium.

75. There have been only two pairs since: Bobby and Wilmer Shantz, 1960 Yankees, and Norm and Larry Sherry in 1960–1962 for the Dodgers.

76. This information is from Bill Nowlin's excellent biography of him at the SABRBio site.

77. From the Tom Petty song "Into the Great Wide Open."

78. 11B = grunt = infantryman. CIB = Combat Infantryman's Badge.

79. Basically, a landing craft set up with rows of rocket launchers, like the German *Nebelwerfer* or the Russian *Katyusha*, only with more launchers and on a naval vessel.

80. Hitting .336 and slugging .671 when he got hurt (his career high was .546), after his return his line was .286/.548, and he only added 16 more home runs to his total. He was on pace for a 50 home run, 150 RBI season. One would like to think that, had he played that full year, he might have reached 3,000 hits in time to keep a .300 career BA.

81. With thanks to Bill Griffith's classic non-sequiturial comic strip, *Zippy the Pinhead*.

82. Following Herb Score in 1955–1956 and Sandy Koufax from 1959 to 1962.

83. Where I also learned that he hit .500 playing mostly at shortstop.

84. Not "less" for crying out loud!

85. Yes, I know that he pitched a no-hitter, a 10-inning no-hitter, and took another no-hitter into the 11th (thus becoming the sole pitcher to hurl ten consecutive no hit innings in more than one game), that arm troubles took him out of two other games after six innings of no-hit ball, and that he also threw six one-hitters and nine two-hitters. He was quite an impressive pitcher, one who, in today's 100-pitch limit, bazillion-strikeout game, would be fanning batters at a Josh Hader rate and be mentioned in the same breath as Clayton Kershaw.

86. Plus, if it is a play at third base (which I *am* sure of), what is the home plate umpire doing out at third base?

87. Incidentally, he looks enough like actor Gordon Jones (in his later appearances) to be his brother.

88. It's called "sarcasm."

89. Oddly, despite his fearsome reputation, he is tied for 278th in hit batsmen (while ranking 22nd in innings pitched).

90. Early walked once every 11.8 PA. Taken at random, Salvador Perez walks once every 29 PA, Miguel Olivo walked once every 25.3 PA, Tony Armas walked once every 21.2 PA, Steve Garvey walked once every 19.8 PA, and then there's Shawon Dunston, the anti–Eddie Yost, who walked once every 30.9 PA.

91. Including five years over .300 in AAA-level ball.

92. Laborers in Willy Wonka's chocolate factory from Roald Dahl's book *Charlie and the Chocolate Factory.*

93. Among his contemporaries or near-contemporaries are Frank Robinson, Curt Flood, and Vada Pinson.

94. Although Ryne Duren came very, very close in 1958–1959 with ERAs of 2.02 and 1.88.

Notes—Chapter 2

95. Considering the Topps habit (at the time) of giving cards that ended with 0 or 5 to stars (and remembering that they passed on Al Kaline, Bill Skowron, and Duke Snider), it is hard to figure why they gave that honor to Gil in 1961, as he was coming off a year in which he hit nine home runs, had only 30 RBI, and hit a puny .198.

96. Remembering that coolness is in the eye of the beholder.

97. *Ozymandias* was a poem by Percy Bysshe Shelley in which he says, "Look upon my works, ye Mighty, and Despair."

98. The non-baseball info on Walt Dropo is from the UCONN website.

99. Trenton.

100. Or then again, probably not. I'm pretty sure he was a Dodgers fan.

101. Not what you think. It's *Little Golden Book*. Tibor, Gustaf Tenggren (28 titles), Corinne Malvern (32 titles), and Eloise Wilkin (47 titles) were my favorite *LGB* artists. My all-time favorite Gergely-illustrated *LGB* is *Seven Little Postmen*.

102. Yclept on all his other cards as Choo Choo.

103. Thanks to Joanne Hulbert, whose SABRBio article informed me that his dad owned a 12-chair (!) shop and that Billy worked in it during the off-season.

104. The actual title of an excellent 1969 movie starring Robert Redford and Robert Blake, and most positively and absolutely *not* a racial insult. Willie Boy was a Piaute-Chemehuevi who killed his girlfriend's father and then led lawmen on a hairy chase for almost two weeks through the deserts and mountains of Southern California.

105. Before The Flaming Carrot and Reid Fleming, World's Toughest Milkman, there was Herbie Popnecker.

106. I chose Boris Karloff's mummy instead of later and probably better-known Kharis-named mummies (played by Lon Chaney, Jr., three times) and Christopher Lee's 1959 portrayal because Boris was the first and most frightening mummy of them all.

107. For the non-cognoscenti, young Mr. Muntz is a chubby bully on *The Simpsons*.

108. Clostridial myositis, for the future veterinarians in the audience.

109. If the reader would like to see a photo of polar opposites in personality and appearance, check the photo of Oakland Oaks teammates Jackie "Golden Boy" Jensen and Billy "Pop Rocket" Martin.

110. As a "celebrity couple," the only more famous twosome at the time was, of course, Joe and Marilyn.

111. But pitching for the Mets was not the only time fortune turned its back on Roger. In 1959, Sam Jones (grrr) won the ERA title with a 2.83 mark. Roger, who fell a measly one and a third innings shy of the 154 innings needed to qualify for the title, had an ERA of 2.06. He would have had to give up *13 runs* in that one and a third inning in order *not* to win the league ERA crown. The chances of that happening are roughly the same as you getting hit by a meteorite while being chased down the street by a shark in Tulsa, Oklahoma, on a February 29 while riding a unicycle and juggling flaming chainsaws blindfolded.

112. Kinda the opposite of Bartolo Colón, who waited 19 years to hit his first and only home run. Even though they both hit .088 in the Bigs (that in itself is quite a coincidence), Hoyt was a far better hitter. They also both struck out 166 times (Ah ha! Two coincidences!), but Bartolo did it in 326 at-bats (51 percent of the time) while it took Hoyt 432 at-bats to get there (only 38 percent of the time, the same as Chris Carter). Plus, Bartolo only walked an amazing once (!) in 327 PAs (.003), while Hoyt strolled to first no fewer than 26 times in his 493 PAs (.05).

113. Line from the Lovin' Spoonful's song "Summer in the City."

114. I was a lowly E-5 making $942 a month, and we already had four kids.

115. From Herman Melville's *Moby Dick*.

116. Novel by hard-boiled detective fiction writer Raymond Chandler.

117. The post–1900 leader of course was Henry Schmidt, who won 22 games

for the Dodgers in 1903, his only season in the Majors.

118. He also set a major league record with six grand slams in 1961, but here's a bonus for the triviots out there: all six were hit in games in which Chuck Estrada was pitching. Figure the odds.

119. Even though his baseball cards said "Charley," he always signed with "Charlie."

120. Despite the surname, he was only one quarter French Canuck.

121. Catch phrase from the TV show *Hawaii Five-0*, spoken by Steve McGarrett (Jack Lord) to Dan Williams (James McArthur).

122. Lake Charles was in the Class C Evangeline League, where the racism was so bad that both Lake Charles and Lafayette were expelled from the league for having black players. He was sent to the (probably just as bad personally but not to the point of kicking out integrated teams) Cocoa Indians in the Florida State League. Felipe hit .333 and slugged .524 before joining the Giants in 1958.

123. Information from Mark Armour.

124. Mr. Sanders' suicide note famously read, "I'm bored."

Chapter 3

1. Here paying homage to Bob Dylan and his ground-breaking, game-changing 1965 album.

2. Well, most of us. Apparently around 35 percent of us lack the ability to "joy" and dwell in a dark world of conspiracy theories and an eternally festering slough of resentment and fear.

3. Everybody read comics in those days. Everybody. At 10 cents a comic, we could afford to.

4. Some comics lived on both sides of the wall, including the Archie comic family (*Archie, Betty and Veronica, Jughead*, etc.), DC's *Sgt. Rock* and the *Superman* comic family (*Superman, Superboy, Superman's Girlfriend Louis Lane, Jimmy Olson Cub Reporter*, etc.) ,and the Dell comics (*Walt Disney's Comics and Stories, Donald Duck*, and my all-time favorite comic book, *Uncle Scrooge*).

5. Note to parents or perspective parents out there: If you wait until your child reaches puberty before you start playing catch or H-O-R-S-E with them, it is way too late for them to develop basic skills. Start before they're four with nerf balls and four-foot hoops.

Chapter 4

1. Here referring to certain essential facts and/or minutiae of the '61 set, with a wink and a nod to Sergeant Joe Friday (as portrayed by the stone-faced and emotionless Jack Webb).

2. That's 128 kilos, for our Namibian readers and 3.58 talents (or 215 minahs) for any biblical scholars in the reading audience.

3. Should the reader wish to go deeper into the weeds re: the '61 SP issue, I would point you to the scholarly-almost-to the-point-of pedantic 1961 Topps SC Research portal on the Net54baseball.com Forums site.

4. Although, technically speaking, Tom Dotterer (see above) never played in a major League game either.

5. Players 6'6" or taller depicted on a card in 1961: 6'8" Gene Conley, 6'7" Frank Howard and Walt Bond, 6'6½" Dick Hall, 6'6" Don Drysdale, Don Gile, and Frank Sullivan. There were some 36 players shorter than 5'10".

Index

Numbers in ***bold italics*** indicate pages with illustrations

Aaron, Hank 15, 127, 128, 144, 167, 173, 174, 177
Abbott, Glenn 103
Acevieo, José 128
Adair, Jerry 40
Adair, Jimmy 61
Adams, Ace 50
Adcock, Joe 46, 83, 119, 126
Agganis, Harry 21
Aguirre, Hank 104
Ahab (captain of the *Pequod* in Moby Dick) 162
Ainderby Quernhow (village in North Yorkshire, England) 99
Al Lopez Field (Reds spring training site in Tampa, Florida) 39, 61, 89, 119, 132, 147, 167
Allen, Bob 452
Allen, Fred (radio star) 190n29
Allen, Lee (baseball historian and writer) 19
Allen, Rich 121
Allison, Bob 335
Alou, Felipe 166
Alou, Jesus 166
Alou, Matty 104, 166
Alou, Moises 166
Alston, Walt 54
Altman, George 161
Altobelli, Joe 159
Amalfitano, Joey 43, 176
Amaro, Ruben 47
American Campaign Medal 165
Anderson, Bob 91
Anderson, Craig 111
Anderson, Harry 41
Angelyne (Hollywood pop culture phenomenon) 71
Ankiel, Rick 16
Antonelli, John 50
Aparicio, Luis 134, 167, 176
Appling, Luke 142
Archbishop Moeller High School 190n35

Archer, Jim 162
Area 51, 154
Armas, Tony 193n90
Armour, Mark (author) 2, 195n123
Armstrong, Jack, All-American Boy 86
Arroyo, Luis 55
Arthur Lee and the Crowns (soul group) 43, 189n13
Ashburn, Richie 44, 89
Ashley, John (actor) 80
Aspromonte, Bob 65, 124
Aspromonte, Charles 124
Aspromonte, Ken 65, 124
Atlanta Federal Penitentiary 116
Atomic Balm 124
Averill, Earl (Hall of Famer) 114
Averill, Earl (son of a Hall of Famer) 124
Avery, Tol (actor) 131

Bacall, Lauren 59
Baggins, Frodo (hobbit) 188n9
Bahamas 67, 87
Bailey, Ed 128
Bailey, George (character) 190n28
Bailey, Jim 128, 157
Baker, Gene 108
Baldschun, Jack 148
Balin, Marty (musician) 187, 5n1
Balsam, Martin (actor) 192n65
Bank, Frank (television actor) 190n33
Banks, Ernie 36, 46, 61, 89, 112, 115, 144, 167, 174
Banner, Bruce (the Hulk's alter-ego) 191n47
Barber, Steve 53
Barker, Ray 131, 177
Barrymore, Lionel (actor) 190n28
Baseball Digest (monthly baseball publication) 6, 21
Baseball 1961 21
Baseball Photo Album of Major League Stars 22
Baseball Stars of 1961 21

197

Index

Baseball-Reference.com 142, 190n37
Baseball Thrills 21
Bass, Norm 97
Battey, Earl 102, 167
Battle of the Bulge 130, 160
Bauer, Hank 51, 55, 125
Bauer, Herman 125
Baumann, Frank 36, 161
Baumer, Jim 95, 183, 191
Be-Bop-A-Lu-La (1956 Gene Vincent hit record) 80
Becker, Art 43
Becquer, Julio 102, 164
Bedell, Howie 112, 113, 192
Bedford Avenue (street bordering Ebbets Field) 135
Bell, Buddy 77
Bell, David
Bell, Gary
Bell, Gus 31, 49, 215
Bell, Mike 77
Benjamin, Stan 146
Benson, Vern 111
Berenyi, Bruce 106
Beringer, Carol 43
Berra, Yogi 28, 101, 113, 130, 143, 173, 183
Berres, Ray 27
Bertell, Dick 134, 177
Bertoia, Reno 123
Best Sports Stories of 1961 21
Bevan, Hal 7, 138, *139*, 191n52
Bevans, Clem (actor) 191n50
Bevens, Bill 79
Biasatti, Hank 123
Big Duke's Blue Flame (Chicago blues club) 64
The Big Sleep (hard-boiled crime novel) 163
Bilko, Steve 4, 5, 23, 67, **68**, 69
Bissell, Whit (actor) 192n65
Blake, Robert (actor) 194n104
Blanchard, John 27, 47
Blasingame, Don 95, 183
The Blob (1958 sci-fi movie) 137
Blue, Vida 103
Boak, Chet 10, 19
Bohn, Terry (baseball biographer) 190n24
Bolin, Bob 137
Bolling, Frank 107
Bolling, Jack 107
Bolling, Milt 107
Bond, Walt 107, 178, 192n64, 195ch4n5
Borland, Tom 129, 131
Boros, Steve 111
Bouchee, Ed 72, 172
Boudreau, Lou 89
Bowie, David (singer) 121
Bowsfield, Ted 77
Boyd, Bob 73, 130

Boyer, Clete 30, 118
Boyer, Cloyd 118
Boyer, Ken 30, 36, 118, 167
Boyer, Lynn 118
Boyer, Ron 118
Boyer, Wayne 118
Branded (TV Western) 80
Brandon, Henry (actor) 137
Brandt, Jackie 152
Brecheen, Harry 61
Breeding, Marv 103
Bressoud, Eddie 74
Brewer, Jim 102
Brewer, Tom 132
Brice, Alan 27
Brickell, Fritz 107, 192n64
Bridges, Rocky 150, **150**, 183
Briggs Stadium 29, 34, 40, 43, 64, 65, 75, 82, 88
Bright, Harry 136
British Guiana 1 cent Magenta stamp 187n2
Brock, Lou 149
Broglio, Ernie 36, 129, 137
Bronze Star 54, 73, 125, 130, 140, 160
Brosnan, Jim 151
Brown, Dick 71
Brown, Hal 36, 78
Brown, Larry 71
Brown, Winston 7, 123, 177
Browne, Pidge 10
Bruce, Bob 40, 43
Brunet, George 19
Bruton, Billy 151
Bryant, Clay 43
Buddin, Don 46
Buhl, Bob 56, 157
Bunning, Jim 36, 64, 109, 122, 146
Bunny, Bugs 150
Burdette, Lew 36, 103, 192n57
Burgess, Smokey 101, 102, 140
Burma Shave (shaving cream famous for roadside signs) 86
Burnett, Carol (comedienne) 139
Burnside, Pete 507
Burwell, Bill 162
Burwell, Dick 52
Buzhardt, Johnny 25

Cabrara, Daniel 110
Cadore, Leon 126
Callison, Johnny 80, 142
Camilli, Doug 43
Campanella, Roy 144
Candlestick Park 29, 32, 41, 50, 72, 100, 112, 121, 351, 383, 162, 166
Cannizzaro, Chris 51
Cannizzaro, Chris, Jr. 51
Cardenas, Leonardo "Chico" 71, 82

198

Index

Cardwell, Don 124
Carey, Andy 152
Carlson, Richard (actor) 192n65
Carreon, Camilo 150, 173
Carreon, Mark 152
Carter, Chris 194n112
Casale, Jerry 195
Cash, Norm 45
Cassidy, Hopalong (Western movie star) 189n21
Causey, Wayne 97
Cavaretta, Phil 36
USS *Caxton* (destroyer) 165
Centene Stadium (home of the Dodgers minor league team in Great Falls, MT) 103
Cepeda, Orlando 132
Cerv, Bob 7, 165
Chamberlain, Wilt (basketball player) 71, 175
Chandler, Raymond (hard-boiled detective writer) 94n116
Chaney, Lon Jr. (actor) 194n106
Charlie and the Chocolate Factory (book by Roald Dahl; later a movie) 183
Checkerboard Lounge (Chicago blues club) 84
Cheney, Dick 161
Cheney, Tom 147
Chesbro, Jack 126, 177
Chew Crew 32, 52, 55, 57, 72, 75, 99, 107, 110, 146, 148, 149, 150, 155, 157, 192n58
Chief Wahoo 28
Chiti, Harry 88, 191
Chrisley, Neil 130
Christopher, Joe 42
Chrysler Imperial Crown Southampton 62, 81
Cibola (legendary "lost city of Gold") 163
Cicotte, Al 82, 190n36, 192n65
Cimoli, Gino 63, 101, 130
Cincinnati College of Mortuary Science 111
Cisco, Galen 99, 118
Clark, Glenn 10
Cleaver, June (character in *Leave It to Beaver*) 161
Cleaver, Theodore "Beaver" (character in *Leave It to Beaver*) 152
Clemente, "Bob" 7, 10, 15, 36, 122, **123**, 149, 174
Clevenger, Tex 94
Cline, Ty 129
Clinton, Lou 118
Cloninger, Tony 130
Coates, Jim 156
Cobb, Ty 118
Cohen, Alan (baseball biographer) 190n27
Cohen, Andy 56

Cohiba cigar 81
Coker, Jim 56
Colavito, Rocky 36, 71, 105, **106**, 174, 183
Coleman, Clarence 148
Coleman, Gordy 71
Coleman Barracks (military housing in Mannheim, Germany) 6
Colón, Bartolo 194n112
Combat Action Ribbon 165
Combat Infantryman's Badge (CIB) 91, 130, 193n78
"Comin' Back to Me" (Jefferson Airplane song) 187, Intron1
Comiskey Park 37, 39, 42, 64, 65, 69, 72, 75, 81, 92, 108, 114, 116, 120, 127, 131, 164, 165
Complete Baseball 21
Conley, Gene 71, 107, 191n48, 195ch4n5
Connie Mack Field (Athletics spring training site in West Palm Beach, Florida) 35
Connie Mack Stadium 25, 30, 42, 45, 47, 49, 50, 51, 53, 57, 58
Connors, Chuck 80, 178
Consolo, Billy 149
Cook, Cliff 125, 177
Cooney, Johnny 27
Cooper, D.B. (airplane hijacker) 111
Corcoran, Bill (autograph dealer) 7
Corrales, Pat 130
Costello, Rory (baseball biographer) 163
Cottier, Chuck 28, 152, 176
County Stadium 28, 41, 48, 63, 75, 84, 86, 87, 111, 127, 141, 153
Courtney, Clint 110, 183, 190n22
Covaleski, Stan 10
Covington, Wes 96, **96**, 183
Cox, Wally (Marlon Brando's best friend) 33, **35**, 111
Craft, Harry 52
Craig, Roger 159
Cramer (card company) 6, 7
Crandall, Del 48, 122
The Creature Walks Among Us (1956 sci-fi flick) 80
Creighton College 76, 190n34
Crewcut Company 31, 36, 50, 51, 52, 54, 56, 58, 60, 63, 65, 70, 71, 77, 80, 85, 89, 90, 114, 116, 124, 148
Crosetti, Frank 79, 133
Crosley Field 41, 44, 46, 49, 53, 62, 77, 82, 105, 115, 128, 151
The Crowd Seems Happy (book by Nicholas Dawidoff) viii
Crowe, George 36, 176
Cuccinello, Tony 27
Cunningham, Joe 153
Curry, Tony 67, 87
Curtis, Jack 140, 156, 173

199

Index

D-Day 130
Dahl, Roald (author) 193n92
Dahlgren, Babe 126, 184
Daley, Bud 36, 129
Daley, Pete 61
Dalkowski, Steve 18, 37, 54
Dalrymple, Clay 183
Daniels, Bennie 116
Dark, Al 78, 176
Davenport, Jim 37
Davis, Bob 15, 83, 177
Davis, Jack (Topps artist) 14, 184
Davis, Tommy 48, 64, 128
Davis, Willie 149
Dawidoff, Nicholas viii
Deal, Cot 249
Defoe, Willem (actor) 192n65
Degerick, Mike 27
de la Hoz, Mike 71
Del Greco, Bobby 58
Deliverence, movie 75
Dell Sports 21
Delock, Ike 88
DeMaestri, Joe 50
DeMerit, John 148
Demeter, Don 31, 156
Demeter, Steve 156
Devine, Andy (actor) 191n49
Diamond Classics (card set) 10
Dick Van Dyke Show (television program) 58
Dillard, Don 65
Dimaggio, Joe 6, 13, 174
Ditmar, Art 36, 151
Dobbek, Dan 48, 149
Donohue, Jim 57
Donovan, Dick 68, 127
Dotterer, Dutch 106
Dotterer, Tommy 106, 195
Douglas, Otis 189ch4n4
Downing, Al 79
Drabowsky, Moe 28, 115
Drake, Sammy 19
Dressen, Chuck 55
Dropo, Walt 15, 145, **145**, 178, 183, 194n98
Drott, Dick 80, 190n36, 192n65
Drysdale, Don 36, 86, 115, 174, 195ch4n5
Dunston, Shawon 193n90
Duren, Ryne 113, 183, 193n94
Durocher, Leo 43
Dykes, Jimmie 78
Dylan, Bob, Icon 74, 195ch3n1

Early, Arnold 118, 189n8
Ebbets Field 13, 111, 189n12
Ellsworth, Dick 130, 133
Elston, Don 64
Enatsu, Yatuka (pitcher) viii
Espino, Hector (Mexican League legend) 18

Esposito, Sammy 104
Essegian, Chuck 121
Estrada, Chuck 36, 124, 165, 195n118
European-African-Middle Eastern Medal 165

Face, Roy 84, 100, 101, 117, 172
Fair, Jodie (actress) 80
Fairly, Ron 146
Farley, Bob 63
Farrell, Dick 153, 172
Fawlty, Basil (*Fawlty Towers* character) 129
Fawlty Towers (British comedy) 129
Fenway Park 33, 63, 84, 65, 419
Fernandez, "Chico" (Humberto) 49
Ferrarese, Don 164
Ferrick, Tom 36
Ferrigno, Lou (body builder) 191n47
Fingers, Rollie 103
Finn, Huck (literary character) 64
Fischer, Bill 162
Fisher, Eddie 46, 62, 116, 173
Fisher, Eddie (singer) 62, 190
Fisher, Jack 130, 141
The Flaming Carrot (dimwitted superhero created by Bob Burden) 194n105
Fleer (baseball card company) 4, 6, 7, 49
Flood, Curt 1, 133, 193n93
Foiles, Hank 90
Fonda, Peter (actor) **83**
Forbes Field 24, 28, 40, 67, 73, 79, 88, 90, 92, 99, 100, 101, 117, 122, 131, 140, 147, 166
Ford, Whitey 48, 62, 101, 168, 174
Fornieles, Mike 49
Foss, Larry 162
Fox, Nellie 7, 32, 143, 163, 167
Fox, Terry 140, 174
Foxx, Jimmy 51
Foytack, Paul 84
Francis, Earl 37
Francona, Terry 149
Francona, Tito 149
Franks, Herman 142
Freehan, Bill 36
Freese, Gene 65, 71, 133, 178
Freese, George 52
Fremont high school 190n35
Friend, Bob 36, 88, 101, 167
Fritsch, Larry (baseball card dealer) 10, 178
Funk, Frank 115
Furillo, Carl 44

Gaines, Joe 84
Gardner, Billy 52
Garver, Ned 106, 192
Garvey, Steve 193
Gehrig, Lou 126, 177, 184
Gentile, Jim 164

200

Index

Gergely, Tibor (artist, *Little Golden Books*) 148, 194*n*101
Gernert, Dick 92
Gibbon, Joe 154, *154*, 172, 184
Gibson, Bob 76, 134
Gieger, Gary 33
Giel, Paul 118
Gile, Don 81, 195*n*4*n*5
Gilliam, Jim 81
Ginsburg, Joe 42
Glenn, Scott (actor) 192*n*65
Godzilla (*Kaiju* monster) 44
Golden, Jim 97, *97*, 183
Gomez, Ruben 119
Gondor, Jesse 79
Gonzalez, Tony 45
Goodman, Billy 84
Goofy (cartoon character) 91
Goonies (1985 movie) 49
Gordon, Joe 78
Gould, Stephen Jay (paleontologist, evolutionary biologist, writer) 190*n*30
Grammas, Alex 39, 176
Grand Master Flash and the Furious Five (hip hop group) 76
Grant, Jim 29
Grba, Eli 52
Great Missoula Floods 188*n*5
Great Moments in Sports 21
Green, Dallas 114
Green, Fred 67
Green, Gary 190*n*29
Green, Gene 75
Green, Lenny 4
Green, Pumpsie 454
Green, Green Grass of Home (song)
Greer, Dabs (actor) 191*n*50
Greiner, Greyson 16, 34, 39, 42, 56, 86, 93, 113, 123, 124
Griffith, Bill (creator of *Zippy the Pinhead*) 193*n*81
Grimes, Burleigh 107
Groat, Dick 24, *25*, 36, 144, 172, 173, 189*n*2
Groening, Matt (creator of *The Simpsons*) 157
Grzenda, Joe 36
Guteridge, Don 27

Hacker, Warren 27
Haddix, Harvey 46, 101, 126
Hader, Josh 193*n*85
Halas, George (football coach) 145
Hale, Bob 156
Hall, Dick 72
Haller, Bill 63
Hamlin, Ken 87
Handley, Gene 52
Hankins, Jay 97
Hansen, Ron 81

Harder, Mel 142
Hardy, Carroll 86
Harlem Globetrotters 189*n*2
Harrell, Billy 113, 192*n*65
Hartunian, Richard (actor) 80
Hatfield-McCoy Feud 129, 131
Have Gun—Will Travel (1957–1963 television western) 34
Hawking, Stephen (astrophysicist) 38, 189*n*11
Hawkins, Carl Everett Scott Arnold Early Wynn 189*n*8
Hawkins, Wynn 33
Haywood, Dan (movie character) *n* 23
Heffner, Don 36
Hegan, Jim 79
Heiser, Roy 10, 19
Heist, Al 99
Held, Woodie 38
Hemus, Solly 55
Hendley, Bob 117, 177
Henley Field (Tigers spring training site, Lakeland, Florida) 67, 111, 119, 146, 159
Henry, Bill 39
Henry, Ron 10, 19, 188*n*8
Herbert, Ray 147
Herman, Billy 118
Hernandez, Rudy 15, 51, 79, 177
Herrera, Frank 146, 166
Hershberger, Mike 27
Herzog, Whitey 48
Hi Corbett Field (Indians spring training site, Tucson, Arizona) 26, 33, 71, 151, 156
Hickok, Wild Bill 47
Hicks, Joe 121
Higgins, Mike 78
Hill, Herman 21
Hiller, Chuck 158
Hillerich & Bradsby Famous Slugger Yearbook 21
Hillman, Dave 104
Himsl, Vedi 52
Hoak, Don 79
Hobaugh, Ed 54
Hobbie, Glen 87, 89, 124
"Hocus Pocus and Frisbee" (1962 episode of *The Twilight Zone*) 92
Hodges, Gil 140, 173
Hoeft, Billy 85
Holman Stadium (Dodgers training site, Vero Beach, Florida) 27, 35, 54, 56, 110, 124, 146, 149, 159
Holt, Goldie 52
Holtzman, Jerome (baseball writer) 21
Hook, Jay 62, 71
Hopkins, Paul 126
Horace Clarke Era (1965–1976) 131
Horlen, Joel 27

Index

Hornsby, Rogers 126
Hot Rod Gang (1958 movie) 80
Hot Rod Girl (1956 movie) 80
Hot Rod Rumble (1957 movie) 80
Houk, Ralph 54
House, Frank 36
Housekeeper and the Professor (book) viii
Howard, Bruce ("The Head") 42
Howard, Elston 28, 147
Howard, Frank 91, 176, 195n
Howland, Olin (actor) 137
Howser, Dick 128
Hubbs, Ken 19
Hudlin, Willis 126
Hulbert, Joanne (baseball biographer) 194n103
Hunt, Ken (L.) 60, 85, 150, 173
Hunt, Ken R. 7, 77, 163
Hunter, Tab (actor) 153
Hutchinson, Fred 54
Hyde, Dick 62

Imhotep (chancellor for Pharoah Djoser ca. 2686–2648 BC; famed movie mummy) 156
In Pursuit of Pennants (Mark Armour book) 2
The Incredible Hulk (1977–1982 television show) 191n47
Indianapolis Clowns 148
Inside Baseball 21
Into the Great Wide Open (Tom Petty song) 193
It's a Wonderful Life (movie) 190n28

Jabbar, Kareem Abdul (basketball player) 190n31
Jack Russell Memorial Stadium (Phillies spring training site, Clearwater, Florida) 38, 74, 97, 102, 132, 148, 153, 156
Jackowski, Bill (umpire) 100, 101
Jackson, Al 162
Jackson, Larry 41, 157
Jackson, Ron 161
James, Bill (Sabrmetrics legend) vi
James, Charley 165
James, Johnny 139
Jankowski, Travis 16
Janning, Ernst (movie character) 22
Jansen, Kenley 40
Jansen, Larry 65
Javier, Julian 57
Javier, Stan 57
Jay, Joey 80
Jefferson Airplane (band) 187Intron1
Jensen, Jackie 65, 143, 158, 194n109
Johnson, Darrell 84, 111, 146
Johnson, Deron 40
Johnson, Ken 31
Johnson, Stan 97
Johnson, Walter 146
Jones, Gordon (actor) 193n87
Jones, Gordon (ball player) 134
Jones, Sam 4, 7, 17, 36, 162, 163, 194n111
Jones, Sherman 62, 116
Jones, Tom (singer) 42
Jones, Willie 7, 147
Jorgensen, "Spider" 43
Judgment at Nuremberg (movie) 188n12
Justified (television show) 52

Kaat, Jim 39
Kahlo, Frieda (artist) 104
Kaline, Al 15, 113, 131, 167, 174, 194n95
Karloff, Boris (actor) 194n106
Kasko, Eddie 157
Keegan, Ed 84
Kemmerer, Russ 37
Kenders, Al 19
Keough, Marty 56
Kershaw, Clayton 191n42, 193n85
Kharis (movie mummy) 194n106
Killebrew, Harmon 42
Kindall, Jerry 32
King, Jim 112
Kirk, Bill 97
Kirk Douglas Chin (medical condition) 54
Kirkland, Willie 29
Kissell, George 111
Klaus, Billy 69, **70**
Klimchok, Lou 141
Kline, Ron 53
Klippstein, Johnny 158
Kluzewski, Ted 39, 68
Konstanty, Jim 50, 143
Koplitz, Howie 36
Koufax, Sandy 31, 36, 37, 75, 84, 110, 111, 115, 193n82
Kralick, Jack 34
Kravitz, Danny 63, 177
Kubek, Tony 87, 101
Kubiszyn, Jack 142
Kucks, Johnny 45, 177
Kuenn, Harvey 148, 173
Kuenster, John (*Baseball Digest* editor) 21
Kunkel, Bill 103
Kunkel, Jeff 104
Kutyna, Marty 161

Labine, Clem 30
Lancaster, Burt (actor) 23
Landis, Jim 88
Landrith, Hobie 50
Laramie (television Western) 80
Larker, Norm 35, 54
Larsen, Don 65, 126, 177, 184
Lary, Al 82

Index

Lary, Frank 36, 82
Lary, Gene 82
Latman, Barry 164
Lau, Charlie 86
Lavagetto, Harry 78
Law, Vernon 36, 84, 100, 125, 173, 177
Layne, Hillis 97
Leave It to Beaver (television show) 190n33
Leavitt, Norman (actor) 137
Lee, Christopher (actor) 194n106
Lee, Don 58
Lee, Thornton 58
Leek, Gene 155
Lehew, Jim 62
LeMay, Dick 63
Lemon, Bob 146
Lemon, Jim 36, 137
Lenhardt, Don 118
Lepcio, Ted 80, 115, 159
Liddi, Alex 123
Lieb, Fred (baseball historian and writer) 19
Lillis, Bob 35
Lin, Betty (boutique owner; one of Eddie Fisher's wives) 62
Lindblad, Paul 103
Linsalata, Joe (umpire) 20
Littleton, Larry 72
Locke, Bobby 157
Lockman, "Whitey" 63
Lodigiani, Dario 97
Loes, Billy 81
Logan, Johnny 152, 153
Lollar, Sherm 92, 173
Long, Dale 51
The Long Season (1960 book by Jim Brosnan) 152
Look, Dean 27
Lopat, Ed 159
Lopez, Al 37, 107
Lopez, Hector 32, 176
Lord, Jack (actor) 195n121
Lord of the Rings (fantasy book trilogy) 188n9
Lost City of Z (legendary city of gold in the Amazon rain forest) 161
The Lovin' Spoonful (folk rock band from the sixties) 194n113
Lown, Craig 130
Lown, Turk 130
Lumenti, Ralph 142, 177
Lumpe, Jerry 51, 116, 153
Luplow, Al 141
Lynch, Jerry 46
Lyons, Eddie 111

Maas, Duke 122
MacKenzie, Ken 496
Macko, Joe 52
Mad (satire magazine) 14
Maglie, Sal 118, 126
Malkmus, Bobby 66, 156
Maloney, Jim 130, 133, 177
Malvern, Connie (artist, children's book illustrator) 194n101
Malzone, Frank 65, 136
Mantilla, Felix 63
Mantle, Maxie 98
Mantle, Mickey 13, 15, 18, 36, 51, 87, 95, 98, *98*, 100, 113, 114, 126, 127, 132, 143, 167, 174, 177, 183
Mantle, Ray 98
Mantle, Roy 98
Marichal, Juan 15, 128, 177, 191
Maris, Roger 13, 25, 36, 42, 61, 143, 173
Marlowe, Hugh (actor) 192n65
Marshall, Jim 41, 70
Martin, Billy 44, 102, 110, 172, 194n109
Martin, J.C. 52, 192n54
Marv Goldberg's R&B Notebook 189n13
Mathews, Eddie 36, 51, 109, 174
Mathews, Larry (played Richie on *The Dick Van Dyke Show*) 58
Mathewson, Christy 126, 177
Mauch, Gene 78
Maud Miller (poem by J.G. Whittier) 68
Maxwell, Charlie 34, 88
Maye, Lee 43
Mays, Willie 1, 14, 15, 18, 36, 57, 78, 144, 149, 167, 174
Mazeroski, Bill 7, 100, 101, 131, 167, 177
McAnanay, Jim 52
McArthur, James (actor) 195n121
McBride, Ken 75
McCarver, Tim 35, 111
McClain, Joe 144
McClymonds High School 190n35
McCormick, Mike 36, 100, 383
McCovey, Willie 152, 174
McCullough, Sam 159
McDaniel, Lindy 41, 87, 101
McDevitt, Danny 111, 159
McDougald, Gil 68, 101, 126
McDowell, Sam 142
McGaha, Mel 142
McGarrett, Steve (character on *Hawaii 5-0*) 195n121
McGwire, Mark 47
McIlwain, Stover 7, 10
McKechnie Field (Braves spring training site, Bradenton, Florida) 37, 38, 42, 63, 112, 123, 147, 148
McLish, Calvin Coolidge Julius Caesar Tuskahoma 61
McMahon, Don 90, 173
McMillan, Roy 141
McNear, Howard (actor) 191n50
Mejias, Roman 162

Index

Mele, Sam 159
Melville, Herman (author of *Moby Dick*) 194*n*115
Memorial Coliseum 71, 86
The Message (early hip hop song) 76
Meyer, Bryan 189*n*16
Meyer, Jack 49
Miami Stadium (Orioles spring training site) 43, 121, 131, 135
Miller, Bob 101
Miller, Stu 41
Mincher, Don 107
Minoso, Minnie 36, 120, 174
Mr. Potter (movie character) 190*n*28
Mize, John 97
Mizell, Vinegar Bend 162
Moby Dick (classic American novel) 194*n*16
Moeller, Ron 141
Monbouquette, Bill 165
Monroe, Marylin (actor; one of Eddie Fisher's wives) 62
Moon, Wally 48, 104, 183
Moore, Ray
Moosup, CN 15, 145
Morehead, Seth 48
Morgan, Joe 151
Morgan, Tom 89
Morhardt, Moe 52
Morland, Nate 108
Morton College 147
Moryn, Walt 44, 178
Mossi, Don 29, 176
Mount Doom (fictional volcano) 20, 188*n*9
Muffett, Billy 29
Municipal Stadium 38, 40, 46, 51, 81, 93, 110, 121, 141, 158, 164
Munster, Eddie (television character, *The Munsters*) 61
The Munsters (1964–1966 television program) 61
Muntz, Nelson (character in *The Simpsons*) 156, 194*n*107
Murphy, Danny 77, 94, 176
Murtaugh, Danny 7, 55, 101, 102, 166
Musial, Stan 16, 18, 93, **94**, 165, 174, 183
Myatt, George 130

Nagashima, Shigeo (Japanese ballplayer) 18
Naragon, Hal 45
Narron, Sam 162
Navy Occupation Service Medal 165
NBC Baseball 21
Neal, Charlie 110, 130, 177
Neeman, Cal 146
Neiger, Al 74, 176, 177
Nelson, Lori (actress) 79
Nelson, Rocky 99, **100**, 140, 183

Neumann, Dorothy (actress) 82
Newcombe, Don 144
Nichols, Chet 98
Nichols, Chet, Sr. 99
Nicholson, Dave 67, 177
Nieman, Bob 66
Nixon, Roy 37
Nixon, Russ 36
Nottebart, Don 32
Nowlin, Bill (baseball biographer) 193*n*76
Nunn, Howie 111
Nuxhall, Joe 135

O'Brien, Johnny 25
O'Connell, Danny 102
Oddbody, Clarence 90
O'Dell, Billy 46, 121
Oeschger, Joe 126
Ogawa, Yoko (author), viii
Oh, Sadahiro (Japanese baseball player) 18
Ohtana, Shohei 16
Okinawa (last and longest battle in the Pacific) 125, 140, 143
Okrie, Len 118
Old Timer's Baseball Photo Album 22
Oldis, Bob 57
Olivares, Ed 111
Oliver, Gene 144
Olivo, Freddy 19
Olivo, Miguel 193*n*90
Olsen, Zoe Ann (Olympic diver) 158
One Year Wonders (card set) 10, 178
O'Neal, Shaquille (basketball player) 190*n*31
O'Neil, Buck 108
Oompa-Loompa (laborers for Willie Wonka) 139
Orsino, Johnny 63
Osborne, Larry 75
Osmium (heaviest naturally occurring substance on earth) 153
Osmotherley (village in the North Riding of North Yorkshire, England) 98
Osteen, Claude 84
Otero, Reggie 84
O'Toole, Denny 105
O'Toole, Jim 105
Owens, Jim 109
Ozark, Danny 43
Ozymandias (poem by Percy Bysshe Shelley) 144, 194*n*97

Pafko, Andy 130
Pagan, Jose 90
Pagliaroni, Jim 153
Paige, Satchell 18
Palm Springs Stadium (Angels spring training site) 150, 155
Palmquist, Ed 43, 159

Index

Papa, John 61
Pappas, Milt 36, 96
Parker, "Salty" 63
Pascual, Camilo 81, 151, 176
Paths to Glory (book by Mark Armour) 2
Patrick, Butch (child actor) 61
Payne Park (White Sox spring training site in Sarasota, Florida) 44, 58, 156
Pearson, Albie 93, 178
Pennant Race (1962 book by Jim Brosnan) 151
Pequod (literary *Moby Dick* whaling ship) 4
Perez, Salvador 193n90
Perranoski, Ron 154, 173
Perry, Jim 36, 121, 167
Persoff, Nehemiah (actor) 192n65
Pesky, Johnny 118
Peters, Gary 99, 192n54
Petrie, Rob (television character) 58
Petty, Tom (singer/songwriter) 193n77
Pfister, Dan 97
Philley, Dave 117
Philley, Noel 117
Phillipine Republic Liberation Medal 165
Phillipine Republic Presidential Unit Citation Ribbon 165
Phillips, Bubba 46
Phillips, Emo (comic) 24
Piche, Ron 38
Pierce, Billy 74
Piersall, Jim 345
Pignatano, Joe 41
Pilarcik, Al 38
Pinelli, Babe 126, 183
Pinkston, Al (Mexican League superstar) 18
Pinson, Vada 31, 49, 82, 141, 172, 193n93
Pittsburgh Post Gazette 190n23
Pizarro, Juan 79
Podres, Johnny 48, 75, 84
Polo Grounds (Angels spring training site, Palm Springs, Arizona) 127, 136
Pompano Beach Municipal Park (Senators spring training site) 26, 53, 144, 150
Poopnecker, Herbie (comic book character) 194
Posada, Leo 35, 36
Post, Edward 119
Post, Wally 119
Povich, Shirley (baseball writer) 21
Powell, Boog 61
Power, Vic 85
Prescott, Bobby 19
Project Scoresheet vi, 2
Psammead (magical creature) 130
Purkey, Bob 27
Purple Heart 54, 73, 125, 130, 160
Putnam, Curly (singer) 42

Raines, Tim 146
Rakow, Ed 56
Ramirez, Manny 84
Ramos, Pedro 36, 155, 164
RCA Victor Color TV jingle 189n9
Redford, Robert (actor) 194n104
Reed, Jack 79
Regan, Phil 134
Reid Fleming, World's Toughest Milkman 194n105
Remagen Bridge 74
Rembrandt (painter) 160
Rendezvous Park (Cubs spring training site in Mesa, Arizona) 28, 44, 102, 130, 134
Renfroe, Marshall 7
Reniff, Hal 79
Repulski, Rip 53
Retrosheet vi
Reynolds, Debbie (actress; one of Eddie Fisher's wives) 62
Rice, Del 136
Richard, Terry (former Miss Louisiana; one of Eddie Fisher's wives) 62
Richards, Paul 54, 166
Richardson, Bobby 66, 101
The Rifleman (television Western) 80
Right Down the Middle (Ralph Terry biography) 193n72
Rigney, Bill 79
Rios, José 128
Rippelmeyer, Ray 90, 177
Rivera, Jim 104, 116
Rizzuto, Phil 143
Roach, Mel 77
Roarke, Mike 119
Roberts, Robin 30, 173
Robinson, Brooks 27, 167
Robinson, Earl 110
Robinson, Frank 115, 167
Robinson, Jackie 149
Rockwell, Roberta (actor) 137
Rodan (Kaiju monster) 44
Rodgers, Andre 67
Roebuck, Ed 27
Rojas, Mel 166
Romano, Johnny 26
Roof, Phil 130
Roseboro, John 115
Roselli, Bob 156
Rosen, Al 143
Roth, Allen (statastician) 19
Rubio, Jorge 10
Runnels, Pete 36, 75
Ruth, Babe 13. 18, 55, 125, 133, 183
Rutherford, Lumpy (television show character) 74, 190n33

Sad-Eyed Lady of the Lowlands (song) 74
Sadcecki, Ray 33, **34**

Index

Sadowski, Ed 63
Sadowski, Ted 85
Sagan, Carl (astronomer) 189n11
Sain, Johnny 79
Samples, Junior (*Heehaw* star) 31
Sanders, George (actor) 167, 195n124
The Sandlot (1993 movie) 49
Sanford, Jack 86, 121
Santo, Ron 33, 70, 89
Sauer, Hank 144
Sawatski, Carl 73
Schaffernoth, Joe 38
Schaive, John 86, 177
Scheffing, Bob 78
Scheib, Carl 119
Schilling, Chuck 148
Schmidt, Bob 32
Schmidt, Henry 194n117
Schmidt, Mike 127
Schoendienst, Elmer 505
Schoendienst, Joseph 505
Schoendienst, Julius 505
Schoendienst, Kevin 505
Schoendienst, Louis 505
Schoendienst, Paul 505
Schoendienst, Red 505
Schofield, Dick 101, 137
Schofield, Jack 137
Schofield, Richard 137
Schwall, Don 118
Schwarts, Harry (umpire) 20
Score, Herb 38, 68, 70, 108, 193n82
Scottsdale Stadium (Giants spring training site, Scottsdale, Arizona) 43, 46, 104, 132, 137, 152, 153, 161
Seerey, Pat 114
Seminick, Andy 146
Semproch, Ray 65, 132
Seven Little Postmen (*Little Golden Book*) 194n101
Shakespeare First Folio 187n2
Shantz, Bobby 101, 119, 141, 193
Shantz, Wilmer 193
Shaughnessey, "Shag" (executive) 19
Shaw, Bob 112
Sheldon, Roland 159
Sherry, Larry 127, 153, 177, 193
Sherry, Norm 153, 193
Shetrone, Barry 61
Shore, Ernie 99
Shore, Toots (famous N.Y.C. restaurateur) 66
Short, Bill 84, 177
Short, Chris 146
Siebern, Norm 88, 153
Siena College 113
Sievers, Roy 143
Silly Putty 60
Silver Star 54
Simmons, Curt 28
Sisler, Dave 81, **89**, 190n36, 192n65
Sisler, Dick 84, 190n36
Sisler, George 190n36
Skinner, Bob 71, 74, 89, 100, 101
Skowron, Moose 36, 101, 117, 166, 172, 177, 194n95
Smalling, Jack (autograph dealer) 5
Smith, Al 36, 64
Smith, Bobby Gene 102
Smith, Charlie 43, 146
Smith, David (founder of Retrosheet)
Smith, Hal R. 161
Smith, Hal W. 82, 101
Smith, John (actor) 80
Smith, Red (baseball writer) 69
Smith, Vinnie (umpire) 20
Snider, Duke 15, 44, 135, 173, 174, 194n95
Snowden, Leigh (actress) 80
Snyder, Russ 56
Sommers, Bobby (actor) 137
The Sopranos (television gangster show, 1999–2007) 99
Sosa, José 166
Spahn, Warren 18, 36, 72, 73, 74, 168, 173, 174, 191n45
Spangler, Al 41
Speier, Chris 1
Spencer, Daryl 114, 137
Spink, J.G. Taylor (editor) 18
Spock (vulcan) 58
Sport (monthly magazine) 21
Sporting News Baseball Register 21
Sporting News Dope Book 21
Sporting News Official Baseball Guide 21
Sporting News (weekly newspaper, 1886–2008) 21
Sports All Stars Baseball 21
Sports Illustrated 21
Sportsman's Park 36, 39, 41, 66, 76, 80, 87, 108, 119
SSPC card set 10, 11
Stafford, Bill 76, 90
Staley, Jerry 44
Stallard, Tracey 25, 42
Stars and Stripes (newspaper) 13
Steines, Rob (Topps customer service) vi
Stephens, Gene 47
Stevens, Connie (actress/singer; one of Eddie Fisher's wives) 62
Stevens, John 101
Stevens, R C 155
Stewart, James (actor) 190n28
Stigman, Dick 41
Stobbs, Chuck 126, 131
Street and Smith (annual baseball magazine) 20, 188n11
Strickland, George 142
Stuart, Dick 29, 53

Index

Sturdivant, Tom 95, 173
Sturgill, Andy (baseball biographer) 96
Sullivan, Dan (*Judgment at Nuremberg* character) 23
Sullivan, Frank 91, 173, 177, 191n48, 195ch4n5
Sullivan, Haywood 76
Summer in the City (1966 hit by the Lovin' Spoonful)194n113
Surrealistic Pillow (1967 album by the Jefferson Airplane) 187, 5n1
Sushi (raw fish) 3
Swarthmore College 73

Tappe, El 29, 52, 184
Tasby, Willie 139
Taylor, Benny 136
Taylor, Bob 136
Taylor, Sammy 85
Taylor, Tony 126
Tebbets, Birdie 130
Tell Them Willie Boy Is Here (1969 movie) 194n104
Temple, Johnny 58
Tenggren, Gustaf (artist; *Little Golden Book* illustrator) 193n101
Terry, Ralph 1ol, 122, 177
Thacker, Moe 28
Thomas, Frank 129
Thomas, George 159
Thomas, Gerald 159
Thomas, LeRoy 141
Thomas, Valmy 102
Throneberry, Faye 37, 91
Throneberry, Marv 37
Tinker Field (Twins spring training site in Orlando, Florida) 142, 149, 167
Tolkien, J.R.R. (author, linguist, scholar) 188n9
Torgeson, Earl 58, 79, 110
Touch of Evil (film noir classic) 3
Tracy, Spencer (actor) 23
Trautman, George (executive) 19
Travers, Henry, (actor) 191n46
A Treasury of Sports Stars in Action 22
Tresh, Tom 79
Triandos, Gus 55
Trout, Mike 16
True Baseball Yearbook 21
Tunis, John R. (author) 150
Turley, Bob 35, 101
Turner, Jim 84
Tuttle, Bill 157
The Twilight Zone (1959–1964 television program) 92
Tyson, Neil DeGrasse (astrophysicist) 189n11

Umbricht, Fred 19

Valdivieoso, Jose 164
Valo, Elmer 69
Van Dyke, Dick (actor) 58
van Hyning, Thomas (baseball biographer) 154
Veal, Coot 132
Velveeta 153
Verble, Gene 159
Verdi, Frank 159
Vernon, Mickey 54, 101
Versailles, "Zorro" 30, 189n7
Vincent, Al 80
Vincent, Gene (early rock and roll star) 80
Virdon, Bill 40, 100, 101
Virgil, Ozzie 40
Virgil, Ozzie, Jr. 40
Virgin Islands 102
Vogelsong, Kit (SVP of Topps Legal Affairs) vi

Wagner, Leon 7, 161
Walker, Harry 111
Wallach, Eli (actor) 192n65
Walls, Lee 42
Walsh, Frank (umpire) 20
Walters, Ken 124
War of the Worlds (classic 1953 sci-fi movie) 137
Warhol, Andy (artist) 1
Washington, Herb 149
Weiss, Bill, (minor league baseball researcher) 19
Werth, Jason 138
Wertz, Vic 65, 108, *109*, 183
West Side Story (1957 Broadway play) 79
Westrum, Wes 63
Whisenant, Pete 74
White, Bill 80, 87
White, Jo Jo 97
White, Sammy 130
White Whale (figurative nemesis from *Moby Dick*) 162
Whittier, John Greenleaf (poet) 68
Who's Best in Sports 22
Who's Who in Baseball 21
Wickersham, Dave 120
Widmark, Richard (actor; Sandy Koufax's father-in-law) 112
Wilhelm, Hoyt 140, 160, 174, 194n112
Wilkes, Ted 97
Wilkin, Eloise (artist; *Little Golden Books* illustrator) 93
Wilkins, Lenny (basketball player) 64
Will, Bob 151
Willamette Valley, Oregon 188n5
Willey, Carl 48
William Morris Agency 153
Williams, Billy 14, 55

Index

Williams, Dan (fictional detective) 195n121
Williams, Dick 27, (n)
Williams, George 146
Williams, Stan 36, 71
Williams, Ted 18, 86, 94, 114, 127, 153, 174
Willie Boy (Piaute-Chemehuevi murderer) 194n104
Wills, Maury 43, 134
Wills, Ted 161
Wilson, Earl 40
Wilson, Willie 149
Windhorn, Gordy 43
Winfield, Dave 145
Witt, George 92, **93**, 183
Wolf, Gregory (baseball biographer) 133
Wolf, Howlin' (blues singer Chester Burnett) 64
Wong, Robert (card designer) 18
Wonka, Willie (owner, make-believe chocolate factory) 193n92
Wood, Jake 152, 174
Wooden, John (UCLA basketball coach) 96, 146
Woodeshick, Hal 24
Woodling, Gene 89, 173
Woods, James (actor) 192n65
Woods, Jim 38
Woodstock 96
Wright, Stephen (comic) 24
Wrigley, Phil 192n67
Wrigley Field 29, 31, 32, 38, 46, 48, 55, 66, 70, 71, 72, 76, 77, 79, 80, 89, 90, 91, 92, 99, 115, 116, 120, 127, 134, 140, 146, 152, 161, 165, 189n6, 189n12
Wyatt, Whit 130
Wynn, Early 18, 36, 43, 108 138, 183

Yale 84, 147, 190n37
Yankee Stadium 25, 29, 30, 32, 34, 35, 37, 40, 41, 44, 45, 46, 48, 49, 55, 56, 58, 60, 62, 65, 66, 69, 71, 73, 74, 75, 76, 78, 81, 84, 85, 87, 88, 89, 91, 99, 101, 102, 104, 105, 106, 113, 117, 119, 121, 122, 130, 138, 143, 147, 149, 152, 156, 158, 162, 164, 165, 168, 193n71
Yastrzemski, Carl 92
Yost, Eddie 127, 177, 193n90

Zanni, Dom
Zimmer, Don 46, 89, 146
Zorro (1957–1959 television Western) 189n7
Zupo, Frank 61